PREGETHWR Y BOBL

JOHN JONES
TALSARN

THE PEOPLE'S PREACHER

AN ENGLISH TRIBUTE

BY
ALAN C. CLIFFORD

*To Godfrey with warm greetings in CHRIST, Alan
13 May '14*

CHARENTON REFORMED PUBLISHING

2013

Text © The Publisher 2013

Layout © Quinta Press 2013

First published in Great Britain 2013

by Charenton Reformed Publishing

www.christiancharenton.co.uk

ISBN 978–095551–658–0

Typeset in Bembo Standard 12 on 14 point

by Quinta Press, Weston Rhyn, Oswestry, Shropshire

Printed and bound in Great Britain by Lightning Source

British Library Cataloguing in Publication Data.

A catalogue record for this book is available from the British Library.

Cover concept: A. C. Clifford, formatting by Barkers Print & Design, Attleborough, Norfolk

Main picture:

Not far from his home, Tan-y-castell near Dolwyddelan, is the cataract at Nant-y-tylathau. Here young John Jones often retired to pray, meditate and practise preaching. *Photo:* the author

Inset: head detail of John Jones, ca. mid-1820s. Portrait by William Williams (Ap Caledfryn; 1837–1915) (By permission of Llyfrgell Genedlaethol Cymru/The National Library of Wales).

CONTENTS

In Memory
of
Pauline Edwards
Whose fragrant Christian life is recalled with gratitude and affection,
and whose translation of a key section of Dr Owen Thomas's
Cofiant John Jones, Talsarn *is greatly appreciated.*

ILLUSTRATIONS

The following coupled hymns (back-to-back) head each chapter as indicated:

PICTURE GALLERY

TITLE-PAGE SELECTION

PREFACE

While 'keeping up with the Joneses' has never been a life-style choice for me, there are certain Joneses— all of them Welsh—for whom I have great respect and deep affection. Had I tried to 'keep up' with them, I would have failed miserably, for they are Dr D. Martyn Lloyd-Jones, sometime minister of Westminster Chapel, London; Dr R. Tudur Jones, formerly Principal of Coleg Bala-Bangor and my doctoral tutor; and my mother-in-law Catherine Eluned Edwards, née Jones—whose virtues shine in my beloved wife Marian. To this distinguished list I now add the subject of this 'English tribute'—another Welshman—the Calvinistic Methodist preacher John Jones, Talsarn.

During my attendance at Westminster Chapel (1963–66), it was impossible not to enthuse about the numerous preachers of the past admired by Dr Lloyd-Jones. If the Englishman George Whitefield was one, the Welshman Daniel Rowland was another. These two probably headed Dr Lloyd-Jones's list of Gospel heroes. Going up to Bangor University in 1966, my interest in Daniel Rowland was further aroused on acquiring a second-hand book by yet another Jones! This was *Some of the Great Preachers of Wales* by Owen Jones (Newtown), published in 1885. This thrilling book covers Rowland, Robert Roberts (Clynnog), Christmas Evans, John Elias, William Williams (Wern), Henry Rees and, last of all, John Jones, Talsarn. During my early years in the ministry, this galaxy of preachers never failed to stir my soul to a remarkable degree. I would re-read the book during our annual Welsh holidays.

However, it is true to say that only recently has the last on the list—John Jones, Talsarn—made a personal impact on me not felt before. This is easy to understand, since my personal, pastoral and theological pilgrimage over the last thirty years alone makes sense of what I could never have appreciated earlier. I do in fact regret that I never grasped the wonder and significance of John Jones, Talsarn earlier. That said, I dare not sound ungrateful to God whose providence directs our course including our reading! Sadly, for several years, this book was mislaid. With interest being revived by the publication in 2002 of a translated chapter from Dr Owen Thomas's *Cofiant John Jones, Talsarn* (1874), the lost book was sought in vain. Then, a library transfer from my old study to a new one (a gift from my beloved Norwich congregation in 2009) led to its rediscovery. I confess to shouting 'Alleluia' when I spotted it! Besides other books, Owen Jones's book has now been re-read several times, with ever-increasing interest and excited appreciation of all it reveals.

My book will reveal the total impact of John Jones's towering testimony on the unworthy author. From every perspective— his personal faith and devotion to the Lord Jesus Christ, his grasp of biblical theology, his eloquent Gospel preaching, his nationwide labours for his Lord and Saviour, his compassion for people, his family life and, not least, his hymn-tune compositions—John Jones, Talsarn was an extraordinary man of God. While the preacher is the chief focus of this book, it must be said that his beloved wife Fanny was likewise an extraordinary woman of God. To demonstrate this, a separate appendix is devoted to her. If nothing else, this indicates that she was no mere appendage to his labours. I am especially grateful to my wife Marian for translating some hitherto-untranslated biographical material. Among other appendices intended to elucidate issues in John Jones's career, their youngest son David Lloyd Jones receives some detailed attention.

I trust any Welsh readers will pardon my deficiencies regarding 'the language of heaven'. The author of this 'English tribute' to a monoglot Welshman does not presume to attempt an exhaustive scholarly contribution. Indeed, I am not seeking to produce an original account of John Jones, Talsarn. Heavily indebted to Owen Jones and other mainly-English sources, I simply wish to re-tell his story. On the language level, and hoping that my enthusiasm for their fellow-countryman will provide some compensation, I ask for the kind indulgence of would-be critics.

I confess I have used mainly English translations, both published and informal (provided by Welsh-speaking friends). While I can read Welsh prose and poetry with a limited (yet hopefully-growing) understanding, I am particularly indebted to several friends and family members. Besides my wife Marian and her late sister-in-law Pauline Edwards (to whom this work is dedicated), I wish to thank my brother-in-law, Malcolm Edwards, the Revd Islwyn Davies, Dr Lynda Newcombe, the Revd & Mrs Noel Gibbard and the Revd & Mrs Evan J. George for their help and advice. Besides the kind help of the Revd Dr Eifion Evans and the Revd J. E. Wynne Davies, the staff of the National Library of Wales, Aberystwyth are thanked for their prompt and helpful responses to my enquiries. I am also grateful to the Editor of *The Treasury*, the Revd Iain B. Hodgins for kindly publishing articles of mine on John Jones, Talsarn. Last—and by no means least—I am grateful for the enthusiastic interest and encouraging comments of my good friends David Llewellyn Jenkins, Dr Hazlett Lynch, Stephen Quinton, David Fox, David Bond and Nigel Westhead.

If music may be said to transcend even the limits of language,

I feel I 'know' John Jones via the joyful spirituality of his heavenly hymn tunes. These have provided a window into his soul. The book's chapter breaks consist of twenty back-to-back scores of John Jones's music (to words by others). These are scanned from Emyln Evans, *Tònau Talysarn* (1908). Marian is also thanked for her piano renderings of the complete forty-two published hymn tunes of the preacher, several of which have been posted on YouTube. Our son Dr Hywel Clifford performed the 'gem' of a tune, *Tan-y-castell.*

For the type-setting, layout and production of this book I am grateful for the personal interest and professional expertise of Dr Digby James of Quinta Press. Barkers Print & Design are thanked for help with formatting the cover and the facilities provided by Lightning Source are much appreciated.

On a final personal note, I wish to testify to a change of perception regarding Snowdonia. Magnificent though the mountains are, as an English southerner brought up in the relatively-gentle undulations of Hampshire, I felt somewhat uncomfortable with the dramatic geographical changes involved in going up to Bangor University. I felt oppressed by the Nant Ffrancon Pass, especially when the weather was overcast. The distant mountains felt 'gloomy' indeed in such conditions. During my second year, the prospect from the flat window was the Menai Straights and gentle Anglesey, a much more congenial and familiar landscape. Now, however, all the phobias are gone. They have been banished by discovering the wonderful Christian influence of John Jones, Talsarn and his brethren. Because of their ministries in their rugged home territory and beyond, the once-threatening mountains seem to reverberate with Gospel joy. This book will explain why Moel Siabod is my favourite mountain. I trust it succeeds in transmitting something of what I have happily discovered ...

Dolwyddelen. M. S.

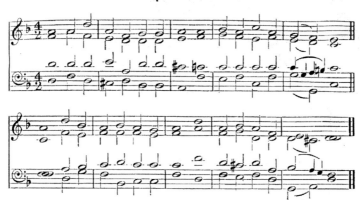

16

1 PAN hoeliwyd Iesu ar y pren,
   Yr haul uwch ben dywyllwyd ;
Ond wele ! yn y t'wyllwch mawr
Daeth gwawr o'r gair "Gorphenwyd !"

2 Pan y croeshoeliwyd Iesu cu,
   Pyrth uffern ddu a lonwyd ;
Ond trodd y pyrth i siomiant trist
Pan lefodd Crist " Gorphenwyd !"

3 Pan y dechreuodd Crist dristau,
   Telynau'r nef ostegwyd ;
Ond dyblodd cân y drydedd nef
Pan lefodd Ef, " Gorphenwyd !"

4 Holl lafur Crist trwy 'i boenus daith,
   A'i galed waith ddibenwyd,
Pan roes, â'i olaf anadl gref,
   Yr uchel lef, " Gorphenwyd !"

17

RHAN II.

MAE Duw yn maddeu a glanhau,
   Yn angeu'r Oen a laddwyd ;
A dyma waith efengyl gref
Adseinio'r gair " Gorphenwyd !"

2 I'r gwan gan Satan lawer gwaith
   Colliadau 'i daith edliwiwyd ;
Ond caed diangfa lawer tro
Wrth gofio'r gair, " Gorphenwyd !"

3 Troes cysgod angeu'n foreu ddydd,
   Ei 'stormydd a ostegwyd,
Wrth gofio, yn yr oriau blin,
   Am rin y gair, " Gorphenwyd !"

4 Daw gweiniaid Seion uwch law poen
   I ŵydd yr Oen a laddwyd ;
Ar ben eu taith cânt hwythau'n wir
Gydwaeddi'r gair, " Gorphenwyd !"

D. JONES, Treborth.

30   **Tan=y=castell.**   8.7. D.

57
1 DACW'R ardal, dacw'r hafan,
    Dacw'r nefol hyfryd wlad,
Dacw'r llwybr pur yn amlwg
    'R awrhon tua thŷ fy Nhad ;
Y mae hiraeth yn fy nghalon
    Am fod heddyw draw yn nhref,
Gyda myrdd sy'n canu'r anthem—
    Anthem cariad, "Iddo Ef."

2 Mae fy hwyliau heddyw'n chwareu
    'N llawen yn yr awel bur,
Ac 'rwy'n clywed swn caniadau
    Peraidd paradwysaidd dir ;

Ffarwel haul, a lloer, a thrysor,
    Ffarwel ddaear, ffarwel ddyn ;
Nid oes dim o dan yr wybren
    Ag sy'n fawr ond Duw Ei hun.
              W. WILLIAMS.

58
1 CADBEN mawr ein hiachawdwriaeth
    Welaf yn y frwydr hon ;
Holl elynion Ei ddyweddi
    'N gorfod plygu ger Ei fron ;
Plant afradlon sy'n dod adref,
    A fu 'mhell o dir eu gwlad ;
Rhai fu'n fudion sy'n clodfori
    Duw am iachawdwriaeth rad.
              MORGAN RHYS.

I
EARLY DAYS

'We are disposed to think that he, during those years (from 1821 to 1857), made for himself a deeper home in the affections of his fellow-countrymen than perhaps any of his mighty predecessors or contemporaries—so deep a home, indeed, that the longing that is still felt for him in the breasts of his hearers is as keen and strong as if he had died yesterday'.[1] So wrote Dr Owen Thomas of the subject of this tribute.

Born in the shadow of Dolwyddelan Castle, the traditional birth place of Llewellyn Fawr, Prince of Gwynedd, John Jones, Talsarn was an eloquent pulpit prince among the Calvinistic Methodists. In the royal service of Jesus Christ, the King of kings and Lord of lords, he was destined to make an astonishing impact on 19th century Wales. Like the prophets of old, says Owen Jones, 'His college was the rugged mountains, the wild scenery around his home, and the various trials through which he passed'.[2] He was born on 1 March 1796 at Tan-y-castell, near Dolwyddelen, Gwynedd. The farm— easily identified by the splendid Jones family monument—can be seen about half-a-mile beyond the village, on the left-hand side of the A470 road from Betws-y-Coed to Ffestiniog. The local scenery is magnificent, with the nearby mountain Moel Siabod (894 metres) dominating the view. On the edge of Snowdonia, the scenery compares well with the English Lake district and even the Cévennes region of France. The second allusion has, perhaps, a theological aspect. After all, just as the mountains of the Cévennes became the fastness of the French Huguenots, the mountains of Gwynedd had a significance for the Calvinistic Methodists—'the Huguenots of Wales'.

Born in this impressive region, John Jones was descended from a family that was distinguished for intelligence and godliness. Both of his parents were descended, through different branches, from William ap Richard and his wife Angharad who died in 1749. Angharad was remarkably talented and well educated. Besides a knowledge of Latin and English Law, she was an accomplished harpist and poet. John Jones, Talsarn undoubtedly inherited much from this remarkable woman. His father died at the age of 48 when John was only 10 years old. Before he passed away he told his weeping wife Elinor not to be troubled by any anxiety about his children, that God would give them grace, and that she would probably live to see it.

> The Lord will support you and I know He will care for you ... do not worry over the children. I have committed them to the Lord. They are now in His care. It has been hard on my soul for me to commit my children to the Lord ... but I have peace that He has heard me ... and that you will live to see these answers to prayer. The Lord will truly give grace to my children and [he emphasised with great assurance] you will see this. The Lord has told me that He will do this. I am now calm and peaceful in thinking of leaving you in the Lord's care and reassured on your behalf that He will care for you. 'Blessed be God, who does not turn my prayers away nor keep his mercies from me'.[3]

All this was wonderfully fulfilled. Recalling that there were nine children in all,[4] two of them—John Jones and David Jones—became eminent ministers in Wales, and another—

William Jones—was a faithful preacher of Christ in Cambria, Wisconsin, USA. Ministering there for forty seven years, he died 19 January 1885, universally lamented on both sides of the Atlantic. This information is recorded on a large slate tablet at Tan-y-castell. John Jones was the eldest of the sons. He was blessed with a strong constitution, and very good-looking. Not to ignore that his mother was beautiful, very intelligent and remarkable for her determination, he inherited much from his father, of whom Owen Thomas wrote: 'In his bodily frame he was tall and shapely, remarkably strong and energetic, and unusually handsome. His natural powers were far above the common …'[5] Thus John Jones, Talsarn had the ruddiness of the mountains upon his cheeks—like David, King of Israel—and his attractive facial features exhibited unusual intelligence. In the providence of God, he was endowed physically and mentally for the great work ahead of him.

John Jones possessed a deep and abiding sense of gratitude for his parents. In later years, when preaching at Penmachno near Dolwyddelen, and in the midst of a passage of great eloquence he said: "If I could call my dear father and mother up from their graves for another twenty years, I should be very glad to do so, in order that I might thank them for their fervent prayers in my behalf when I was a little boy. Still, they never died for me. But I have a Brother up yonder, who loved me and died for me."[6]

Owen Jones wrote: 'Even before he was ten years old he exhibited a very strong disposition to preach. He often preached to the boys and girls around him. If anything strange happened, if a funeral took place in the neighbourhood, or if there was a thunder-storm, it was made at once the subject of a new sermon'.[7] One of the impressive sermons of his childhood was upon the subject "Man, as consisting of body and soul":

Two heads I shall have in my sermon to-day: First, The Body. Second, The Soul. First, The Body. Out of what did God create the body of man? Out of the dust of the earth! Oh how wonderful! Do you not see it strange? A body made of dust! Dust seeing, dust hearing, dust talking, dust walking, dust standing on its head." (This was in reference to a feat common among boys, which he had not as yet acquired the skill to perform.) "Is not God great: to create a thing so noble out of dust, so beautiful out of dust, so powerful out of dust—a living thing out of dust? Second, The Soul. How did God create the soul of man? God breathed into his nostrils the breath of life, and the man became a living soul. But who can tell us what the soul is? What can it be? Who knows? This is the most wonderful; this is the most important; this is the most valuable. The body is but the shell around it. The soul is to last long; it is to last for ever. It will not go down to the grave; it will not be burnt by the fire of hell. It will last as long as God Himself.[8]

'At one time,' continued Owen Jones, 'when they were killing a cow at Tan-y-castell, for the use of the family, the boy watched the operation with great interest. He seemed deeply absorbed, and said not a word to any one. After all was over he retired, and commenced preaching on the subject'.[9] The death of the cow had affected him deeply:

It is a terrible thing to die. The death of a cow is awful enough. Did you see how she struggled. Did you hear how she groaned? She strove her utmost for life; but it was all in vain, die she must, when the time came. Man also must die; and for a man to die is awful indeed. For man has a soul; and this is what makes him great. The cow had no soul. I examined, I searched and watched her carefully—she had no soul. But there is a soul in man; and the soul does not die when the body does. The soul is to last for ever and ever.[10]

Such profundity in one so young was evidence that God's hand was upon him. In fact, he often roamed alone on the mountain-heath, at the foot of Moel Siabod, in order to meditate and preach. On returning home absorbed in his thoughts, this intense meditation continued after he went to bed.

The death of John Jones, senior naturally made a deep impression on young John. It made him pray more, as well as preach more; and his sermon subjects were always the awesome truths about eternity, the day of judgment and man's eternal destiny. This continued for about two years when the twelve year-old preacher suddenly stopped. Besides indicating a possible personal spiritual crisis, there was a good reason for this. After the death of his father, John felt that, as the eldest son, he ought to help his mother more about the farm. Becoming introspective and quiet, he ceased preaching to the boys and girls altogether. Around this time, he found immense solace in music, of which he was very fond, and for which he displayed remarkable aptitude. Shortly after, John became the leader of the choir in the Methodist chapel at Dolwyddelen.

While John continued to attend regularly all the chapel meetings, and with obvious spiritual commitment, he never engaged openly in public prayer meetings. Although he was 'head of the house', neither would he pray during family worship. Having become highly sensitive, and in need of pastoral encouragement, his behaviour aroused unwelcome criticism from the chapel deacons. They handled John harshly and unwisely. They told him that unless he took part in the prayer meetings, and unless he engaged in prayer at home, his Christian profession was worthless. He'd be better off in the world than in the church! Not surprisingly, this pharisaical attitude upset John and drove him away. He was then about nineteen years old when this appalling dismissal occurred. It commenced a three-year wilderness experience. Not surprisingly, John looked for companionship elsewhere. His mother became gravely concerned when he decided to attend the fair at Llanrwst with other young people. She protested in vain, for John was determined to enjoy himself. At the public house, he joined his friends with a half-pint of beer. But when high-spirited young women started flirting and sitting on the knees of the Dolwyddelen youths, the deteriorating situation rang alarm bells in John Jones's conscience. Suitably disgusted, he left the pub and made for home. On arriving back at Tan-y-castell, a relieved mother was told:

> Mother, you will never again need to try and prevent me going to the fair. I have never seen such a miserable place. What the young people call pleasure is the most mad thing I have ever seen. They are fools ... I will never again go near it.[11]

So John Jones distanced himself from the worldly youth of Dolwyddelen. Although he was then unaware of God's gracious workings, the prayers of his father, augmented by those of his mother, were being answered. Drawn back from the brink of depravity, he resumed regular attendance at chapel on Sundays and week-days, refusing still to attend the church meeting.

John's sister Mary lived on a farm at Llangernyw near Llanrwst and, in early winter 1818, he went there to visit her. During this stay, he started to experience the drawing power of the Holy Spirit. Initially he began to enjoy singing hymns again, gaining something of a local reputation as a singer. He also had a remarkable dream which made him think deeply about the Gospel and his relationship with Christ. The Revd Henry Rees who was then a young man just beginning his career, came to Llangernyw to preach. The sermon was impressively powerful. John Jones felt so deeply affected that he made up his mind to give himself altogether to Christ, and also to consecrate his life to His service in preaching the Gospel to his fellow countrymen.

He commenced reading the Bible with renewed diligence and he spent much time in meditation and prayer. Worshipping at the local chapel one evening, he was encouraged to sing a hymn. To a newly-composed tune of his own, he sang words by Morgan Rhys about Christ's pardoning mercy to sinners, a hymn he had first learned at Dolwyddelan. The words were 'Wel, dyma'r Cyfaill gorau gaed' (Well, here's the best Friend one could have), the tune very likely being the one later named 'Padarn'.[12] As he sang the last two lines, John, overwhelmed with emotion, stopped singing. Realising that the Spirit of God was at work, another man completed the singing, praying that God would bless the words to the young singer. Then, John suddenly fled the meeting into the night air. Others left with him but he rushed to find a lonely spot where he fell on his knees to seek God's mercy, throwing himself again into the arms of 'the best Friend one could have'.[13]

At this time, important and far-reaching events were affecting the Calvinistic Methodists. These events provide the context for John Jones's early years. In the wake of Daniel Rowland's death in 1790, the second-generation leaders were entering upon their eternal rest in the opening decades of the 19th century: Thomas Charles of Bala died in 1814, followed by Thomas Jones of Denbigh in 1820. However, during this period, the mighty preacher John Elias had reached the peak of his power and influence. In 1811, the year after the death of another leader, David Jones, Llangan, the Methodists asserted their separate ex-Anglican identity with the Connexion's first ordinations. Thomas Rees wrote in 1861 that 'The step taken by the Calvinistic Methodists in the memorable year 1811, which proved a mortal sin against a host of over-zealous

Episcopalians, was evidently well-pleasing to the King of
Zion; for the last fifty years have been incomparably the most
prosperous period in the history of the connexion'.[14]

Indeed, at the beginning of this period and only six years
after the separation, the King of Zion visited His people
with revival blessing! As the Beddgelert revival (1817–22)
was bringing Gospel blessing to thousands, John Jones and
his friends were also experiencing the Holy Spirit's power.
Indeed, in 1819, aroused by the wonderful news that a religious
revival had broken out in Dolwyddelen, John Jones returned
home from Llangernyw. On arriving, he attended a singing
meeting where a Christmas anthem was being sung. His
brother William was singing the bass part. On repeated singing
of the word 'Ceidwad' (Saviour), joyful shouting erupted.
Heavenly joy filled many hearts, the meeting continuing late
into the evening. Amusingly, John didn't feel entirely comfortable
with these proceedings. He did not lose control of himself
this time. However, on a later occasion, when his brother
David was leading family worship, John suddenly leapt to
his feet shouting:

> You thought, Satan that you would possess me, and actually
> that is what I also thought. But now I think you will be
> disappointed. You will never have me. Yes, for the Lord Jesus
> wants me. O praise be to Him! The dear Lord Jesus![15]

By now, there wasn't a dry eye in the house. John's mother
Elinor was loudly rejoicing at the Lord's gracious dealings
with her children.

Clearly, John Jones's long period of anguish and uncertainty
was over. He took a prominent part in the prayer meetings
that were held in the houses. He devoted every waking
opportunity to study the Bible and other available books. In
solitude he always prayed or muttered his thoughts on some

great Gospel truth. By now, he felt an ever-increasing desire to preach. However, family needs necessitated a regular income. So, for a year, he was employed on building Thomas Telford's new road (the future A5) from London to Holyhead. He worked on the section between Capel Curig and Llyn Ogwen.

Away for a week at a time, John Jones would return home over the mountain every Saturday afternoon, a solitary traveller on the lonely mountain heath. On Monday mornings he would start early for work with one overwhelming desire. He wished to enjoy the silence of the moors and to commune with God. As he walked, he punctuated his praying with preaching, his only hearers being the sheep—or so he thought! On one Monday morning, unknown to the preacher, an old man from Dolwyddelen was also crossing the mountain. After walking for a while, the old man could hear some sound and, seeing something like a man going before him, he walked faster in order to catch him up. In vain he hastened; the 'apparition' still continued to elude him. The following Monday, the same strange phenomenon recurred; but the puzzled pursuer failed to find and identify the mysterious sound. Owen Jones concludes that, 'The old man became convinced that it was an appearance from the other world; and he mentioned it to many. It was, however, only the young minister practising the art of which he afterwards became so consummate a master'.[16]

Arriving home on Saturday night from Capel Curig, John would enquire affectionately about the family at Tan-y-castell and attend to any needs. However, after his meal, he retraced his steps in the direction of Moel Siabod, seeking again the solitude of the mountain. At a distance of less than a mile there was a small river known as Nant-y-tylathau; and at a certain spot a fall of water. Here he found a convenient shelter beneath an over-hanging rock, and here he would remain till late in the night praying and preaching. The family noticed that whenever he came home from that spot, his facial appearance was unearthly, even angelic; and they could not talk much in his presence. Thoroughly absorbed in an ecstasy of meditation, he would sit down and close his eyes; and when any one talked loudly, he would open and roll his eyes, as if to request silence. Reading the Bible, and nothing but the Bible at this time, he would continue meditating, often starting out for this quiet spot at every opportunity, to utter his thoughts amid the sound of the falling water. Secretly, his brothers David and William went to hear him. The rain came down in torrents; but they stood in a spot not far from the preacher, listening to the sermon with rapt attention. David Jones said that he never heard his brother preach so powerfully as at that time.

John Jones had not yet declared to anyone his intention to preach. However, reports of the cateract performances were spreading. Several folk at Dolwyddelen began to feel that God was preparing John Jones for future ministry. Believing that he was in every respect adapted for that great work, the deacons of the church sent one of their number to converse with him about it. Somewhat diffidently, John then opened his heart on the subject. Shortly after, a prayer meeting at a place called Garnedd occasioned the young preacher's debut. As the meeting was about to commence, an old man got up and said, "John, come forward and preach a little to us; you have been doing it enough by that old cataract. Try it here to night."

Advancing, John Jones read his text: 'And if children, then heirs; heirs of God, and joint-heirs with Christ; if so be that we suffer with Him, that we may be also glorified together' (*Romans 8: 17*). Then, remarkably, he closed his eyes, and commenced preaching, continuing with astonishing eloquence and power. A man by the name of Owen Lloyd, who was quite uninhibited with his audible 'amens', had taken his place at the farthest end of the room. As the young man went on with increasing strength of utterance, he had a growing hold on the congregation. Owen Lloyd was unconsciously drawn from his seat, making his way ever closer to the speaker, whose eyes were still closed. Unaware of what was happening, the preacher asked loudly, "In whose hand, think you, the children of God are?" By now, Owen Lloyd, standing in front of the preacher, raised a clenched fist to the face of the preacher, saying, "In the hands of my Father, man!" At this point, John Jones opened his eyes. The rest of the congregation were gripped and enchanted by what they were hearing. Overcome with emotion, one woman actually failed to hold her baby. The little one dropped from her knees and, but for another woman close by, it would have fallen into the fire. After numerous exercises by the cataract at Nant-y-tylathau, this was the first sermon ever delivered in public by John Jones, Talsarn.

Notes

1 *Cofiant John Jones, Talsarn* (1874) cited in Owen Jones, *Some of the Great Preachers of Wales* (1885), 462; hereinafter *Great Preachers*.
2 *Great Preachers*, 527.
3 Owen Thomas, *Cofiant Y Parchedig John Jones, Talsarn* (Wrexham: Hugues and Son, 1874), 24, cited in Eryl Davies, *The Beddgelert Revival* (Bridgend: Bryntirion Press, 2004), 107.
4 The others were: Margaret (1788–1846), Catherine (1790–1859), Mary (1793–1865), Gwen (1794–1838), Richard (1799–1850) and Jane (1802–1875).
5 Cited in R. Hughes, (ed), *Memoir and Sermons of the Late Rev. David Lloyd Jones, MA, Llandinam* (Wrexham: Hughes and Son, 1912), 5.
6 *Great Preachers*, 525.
7 Ibid. 464.
8 Ibid.
9 Ibid.
10 Ibid. 465.
11 Owen Thomas, *Cofiant Y Parchedig John Jones, Talsarn* (Wrexham: Hugues and

Son, 1874), 55–6, cited in Eryl Davies, *The Beddgelert Revival* (Bridgend: Bryntirion Press, 2004), 120.

12 See Tune 38 in D. Emlyn Evans (ed), *Tonau Talysarn: Sef Casgliad o Donau y Parch. John Jones, Talysarn, Gydag Emynau* (Machynlleth a Gwrecsam: Hughes A'i Fab, 1908), 46.

13 Owen Thomas, *Cofiant Y Parchedig John Jones, Talsarn* (Wrexham: Hugues and Son, 1874), 59–60, cited in Eryl Davies, *The Beddgelert Revival* (Bridgend: Bryntirion Press, 2004), 122.

14 Thomas Rees, *History of Protestant Nonconformity in Wales* (London: John Snow, 1861), 459–60.

15 Owen Thomas, *Cofiant Y Parchedig John Jones, Talsarn* (Wrexham: Hugues and Son, 1874), 66, cited in Eryl Davies, *The Beddgelert Revival* (Bridgend: Bryntirion Press, 2004), 123. See also, Glanmor Williams, *The Welsh & their Religion* (Cardiff, 1991), 56.

16 *Great Preachers*, 467.

Brynteg. M. B.

42 Gwenffrwd. Hau.

Trefriw. M.H.

21

1 NEWYDDION braf a ddaeth i'n bro,
   Hwy haeddent gael eu dwyn ar go' :
Mae'r Iesu wedi cario'r dydd,
Caiff carcharorion fyn'd yn rhydd.

2 Mae Iesu Grist o'n hochr ni,
Fe gollodd Ef Ei waed yn lli,
Trwy rinwedd hwn fe'n dwg yn iach
I'r ochr draw 'mhen gronyn bach.

3 Wel, f'enaid, weithian côd dy ben,
Mae'r ffordd yn rhydd i'r nefoedd wen ;
Mae'n holl elynion ni yn awr,
Mewn cadwyn gan y Brenin mawr.
                    JOHN DAFYDD, Caio.

22

1 FFORDD newydd wnaed gan Iesu
   I basio heibio uffern drist, [Grist
Wedi ei phalmantu ganddo Ef,
O ganol byd i ganol nef.

2 Agorodd Ef yn lled y pen
Holl euraidd byrth y nefoedd wen,
'Roi rhyddid i'w gariadau Ef
I mewn i holl drigfanau'r nef.

3 Os tonau gawn a stormydd chwith,
Mae Duw o'n tu, ni foddwn byth ;
Credwn yn gryf, down, maes o law
Yn iach i'r lân yr ochr draw.

4 Myrddiynau o frodyr anwyl sy
O'u gofid oll yn gorphwys fry ;
Cha'dd neb o'r rhei'ny fyn'd yn rhydd
Heb brofi o bwys a gwres y dydd.

5 Pa'm y disgwyliwn fyn'd i'r nef
Heb gario'r groes a gariodd Ef ?
Mwy melus fydd y nefoedd pan
Yr elom iddi yn y man.
                    W. WILLIAMS.

2

THE GOSPEL PREACHER

The impact of John Jones's preaching was immediate. Owen Jones says, "He became famous from the very start."[1] While his educational advantages were slender, he possessed a heart burning with love towards God and his fellow men. In fact, he was 'possessed' by Christ to an unusual degree, driven by devotion to Him and the Holy Scriptures. Indeed, with an intense and perpetual reading of one book, the Bible, John Jones desired nothing more than to be a faithful and zealous spokesman for God. Like John Elias, he became popular from the very first, not only with ordinary folk but with educated and cultured people. Leaving Dolwyddelen, he went to Trefriw, and afterwards to Llanrhochwyn, near Betws-y-Coed and Llanrwst, where he was employed for some time.

At Llanrhochwyn, John Jones met the (later) Revd Evan Evans (Ieuan Glan Geirionydd) who, still living at home at the time (1820), was a member of the Calvinistic Methodist church at Trefriw. Well educated and concerned to encourage others, he led a weekly theological discussion class for young men. There were several intelligent youths in Trefriw at the time including John Jones's brother Richard. Aiding them in their discussions were avidly-read text-books such as Dr Edward Williams's *On the Equity of Divine Government and the Sovereignty of Divine Grace* and his *Defence of Modern Calvinism*. Accordingly, Dr Owen Thomas stated:

These meetings, as can be easily thought, and as he himself acknowledged with gratitude to the end of his life, were of immense advantage to Revd John Jones, not only because he didn't understand the English himself, but also, at that time, he only had very few Welsh books. A new field opened wide in the forefront of his mind at this time, and after that he meditated diligently on it for many years.[2]

This period of thought and reflection was vital, for John Jones was about to swim in waters made turbulent by decades of theological controversy. Occasioned by the appearance of Wesleyan Methodism in North Wales during the late years of the eighteenth century, fierce debates raged over the basic character of the gospel of Christ. Hitherto, Welsh Methodism had been broadly Calvinistic or 'Reformational'. Put simply, the preachers had proclaimed the gospel of 'free grace', by which they meant a salvation rooted in the sovereignty of God rather than human free will. That said, from Daniel Rowland onwards, down to the time of Thomas Jones of Denbigh, they had offered Christ freely, urging their hearers indiscriminately to trust in the all-sufficient sacrifice of Calvary. Believers, having come to Christ, were then encouraged to trace their salvation to the electing love of God rather than to their own power.

However, the Wesleyans preached a 'free will' version of the 'free grace' gospel. Teaching that Christ died for all mankind and not just a few, they challenged the Calvinistic doctrine of election. In Flintshire especially, the advent of John Wesley's Arminian teaching produced an over-reaction among the Calvinistic Methodists who resorted to a distorted and unbalanced emphasis on 'free grace' known as hypercalvinism. This was a gross caricature of John Calvin's very different teaching. Rejecting the universal gospel offer along with man's duty to repent and believe, they became fixated on the doctrines of limited atonement and the sinner's total inability to respond to God's grace. If the Wesleyans were 'free will' activists, the Calvinists had become 'free grace' fatalists.

So, the big questions had become: 'what is the gospel all need to hear' and 'how should the gospel be preached'? During the lively classes at Trefriw, John Jones—his benchmark being his Bible—became persuaded that the writings of Dr Edward Williams of Rotherham provided the best, biblically-balanced answers to the intricate and vexing questions of the day. Despite small points of difference, Dr Williams's perspective was similar to that of Daniel Rowland and Thomas Jones of Denbigh. This became John Jones's standpoint. He thus sought to avoid the extreme positions which had created such painful and often-acrimonious divisions among preachers and people. For a thorough and more detailed discussion of these matters, please see Appendix 3.

Suffice to say, many of the Calvinistic 'word warriors' considered Edward Williams's views to be unsatisfactory, even though he actually claimed support from 'authentic' John Calvin! However, they were blinkered by an 'idolatrous veneration'[3] of a scholastic theological system. They insisted on hypercalvinism's precursor—ultra-orthodox 'High Calvinism'—the like of which would certainly disqualify Calvin. John Jones had the insight to see through all this. Humbly bowing before the God who graciously elects from the mass of rebellious and hardened humanity a people to be His own, yet who makes a universally-sufficient provision through the Saviour's sacrifice for all mankind if only they believe, eternal loss being attributed to the sinner's wilful rejection of offered mercy, John Jones knew what message was to be preached. As Dr Owen Thomas made clear, John Jones knew where he stood and why:

He couldn't bear anyone say anything derogatory about Doctor Williams's work. He would be particularly surprised to hear men of Calvinistic ideas doing that; and always judged that they had not read the writings themselves, or had done so prejudicially or else inappropriately by virtue of their mental disability to place fair judgement on such writings.[4]

Looking ahead a little, when the Calvinistic Methodists agreed on their definitive *Confession of Faith* in 1823, 'High Calvinism' held sway, chiefly through the influence of the over-orthodox John Elias. While it was too early for John Jones to be involved in debates about the 'limited atonement' Article 18 of the *Chyffes Ffydd*, he eventually shared[5] the objections voiced in 1823 by Robert Roberts, Rhosllanerchrugog, that the article was 'wise above what is written'.[6] In short, in view of plain scriptural statements indicating universality in the atonement (Jn. 1: 29; 3: 16; 1 Tim. 2: 6; 1 Jn. 2: 2, etc), it was simply unbiblical to insist on *particularity* without *generality*. Hence, as Dr Owen Thomas wrote later, the *Confession* 'did not ... contain a clear, unambiguous statement of the infinite sufficiency of the Lord Jesus for sinners generally and indiscriminately, according to that understanding which had been fully regained in the ministry of the Methodists in the last years of Thomas Jones, Denbigh'.[7] This defect was not finally remedied *confessionally* until 1874. Thus it chiefly continued to exert a baleful influence within Welsh Methodism until 1841, the year John Elias died. Turning from the 'Battle of the Dogmas',[8] which John Jones did his practical best to shun, we now resume our narrative of the orator from Talysarn.

His theological foundations well laid, John Jones began his astonishing career in 1821. He commenced regular Lord's Day preaching. Very often he had to travel far and minister three times. But he generally returned early on Monday

morning. In a Monthly meeting (Presbytery), held at Bala
in 1821, he was accepted as a member, and authorised to
preach within the limits of the Presbytery. John Elias was
holding a service at Beddgelert, and John Jones, with others,
went over the mountain to hear him. The veteran Elias was
aware of the young preacher's growing reputation. Learning
that he had come to Beddgelert, he urged the friends there
to put him to preach with him. With some trepidation, John
Jones finally agreed to the arrangement. After the service
was over, John Elias said that he never realised he was a man
of such power: "I saw, the moment I heard him praying, that
he was no ordinary man; but when he commenced his sermon,
I felt at once that he was a man of God."9

In the summer of 1822, about a year after he commenced
his career, he went for a Sunday to Bangor, where he preached
most effectively. A Captain John Nanney, who happened to
be in Bangor on that day, cried out from the intensity of his
feelings; and the whole congregation was deeply moved.
Then there was a seaman who also felt the power of God
under John Jones's preaching. After the Sunday was over, he
returned to his home in the country, and said to his son, "I
heard a preacher at Bangor yesterday you never heard the
like before. He was most handsome in his person, and yet
most simple in his dress; but you never listened to such a
preacher in your life. I never saw any one like him but John
Elias. I went to Capel Curig [15 miles away] for the afternoon
service, and it was the same there again ; and I returned with
him to Bangor for the night service, and it was better in the
evening than in the morning."10

In the beginning of 1823, John Jones was urged by friends
to make his home at Talysarn where work was to be had. He
complied with the idea. Mr Griffith Williams, steward of
Talysarn quarry, was a relative of John Jones who was welcomed

to lodge at his home. Made shortly after his arrival, the following remarks by William Owen, Llanllyfni give us a glimpse of the young preacher whose name was forever to be associated with Talysarn:

> I well remember the first view I obtained of him. He was with Mr Griffith Williams, overseer of the quarry. He came there a young man, tall, of ruddy, fine countenance, wearing a cloth coat of blue and white colour, black waistcoat, dark, red necktie of Indian silk, woollen-cord trousers, and grey hose—the finest young man I ever saw. I took him to be the son of a gentleman farmer. He spoke but little; only a word now and again, replying to Mr Williams. He seemed to be deeply meditative and grave, and as if wishful to be alone.[11]

John Jones hardly associated with anyone at first. Yet his rather withdrawn and reserved nature aroused considerable interest. He would often leave the other workmen suddenly, and 'without intimation of any kind', writes Owen Jones, 'go to the ruins of an old quarry, Pwll-y-Fanog, or to the riverside beneath the wood quarry, and remain there, walking to and fro, for hours together; and generally, he would not be seen again at his work that day'.[12] Of course, his mind was preoccupied with pulpit preparation. As to his sermons, when he first came to Talysarn, they were often on the eighth chapter of Paul's letter to the Romans. He preached several times from the third verse of that chapter. One of his fellow-workmen asked him why he preached so much upon that chapter. His answer was, "Oh, there is plenty of room for me there to the end of my life, even though that should be very long."[13]

While this tribute focuses chiefly on John Jones, I have no wish to ignore others of that time who laboured effectively in gospel ministry. Reference has already been made to young Henry Rees and John Elias. Indeed, there were several others worthy of mention. Furthermore, a sketch of their lives and ministries helps provide the context in which the unique eminence of John Jones, Talsarn may be appreciated. Owen Jones supplies us with the following biographical details:

Having gone to Talysarn, John Jones had entered a new field of labour and a new circle of acquaintances. In the Carnarvonshire Presbytery of that day there were several men of great fame. Robert Jones, Rhoslan, was there, the author of the interesting volume, *Drych yr Amseroedd* (*Mirror of the Times*), being a history of religion in Wales for a period of 200 years. He was now old, having attained the age of seventy-eight. Another eminent man who was an active member of the above Presbytery was the Revd Michael Roberts, Pwllheli, son of John Roberts, Llangwm, brother of the famous Robert Roberts, Clynnog. He commenced preaching when twenty-two years old. He was well educated, and kept a school for many years, and had the reputation of being a thorough student. He preached regularly at Pwllheli once every week, on Thursday evening. He was one of the most eminent preachers of Wales. Though without the imagination and dramatic power of his uncle, Robert Roberts, yet he seemed to have possessed the great solemnity of spirit and countenance, and the great depth of feeling of that orator, together with a wider culture and a richer mind. Some of the services under Michael Roberts are amongst the most triumphant of the Welsh or of any other pulpit. He had a sermon upon Psalm 1: 5, 'Therefore, the ungodly will not stand in the judgment, nor sinners in the congregation of the righteous'. He preached it at a place called Pennant, not far from Criccieth, with such effects that almost every person in the place was brought into the church of God. It was the same sermon he preached at Llanidloes the same year, on the occasion referred to in the introductory essay. Mr Roberts, however, was of a weak constitution; and was afflicted from his youth with asthma. When he was about fifty-two years old, the disease seems to have taken a new course, and he lost, for some time, the use of his reason, like Robert Hall, and was kept from the pulpit for about thirteen years, after which he was restored, again to preach with great power, though not with the effect of previous years. In the year 1848, he preached on the Green at Bala, at ten o'clock, before Mr John Jones. He died 29 January 1849, in full possession of his faculties.

Another interesting preacher was Daniel Jones, Llanllechid. He was born in the year 1781. He faithfully attended the meetings of the Presbytery in those days, and was a man highly esteemed, and a minister of the Gospel of very good repute. His presence in the pulpit and his delivery were exceedingly impressive. His manner was altogether his own; his countenance wore almost an unearthly solemnity; the tones of his voice were intensely sad, and his themes were mostly the law, the judgment, and eternity. It is probable that no other preacher of the day exerted such a check upon the headlong career of ungodly men. He died in the year 1852.

Another minister belonging to the Presbytery at the time was the Revd Mr Lloyd, Carnarvon. He had been educated at Oxford, and had been duly ordained by the Church of England. Being afterwards, like Daniel Rowlands, converted to God, and seeing the Gospel in altogether a new light, he preached with new power and new influence. Hearers flocked to the churches; and he also, impelled by the love of souls, preached in unconsecrated places. He was accused before the bishop and, in the year 1805, was expelled from the Church of England. He died in 1841, after a life of good service with the Calvinistic Methodists. These, together with many other eminent preachers and deacons, were the members of the Monthly Meeting or Presbytery, into which, now, the Revd John Jones had cast his lot.[14]

The first Presbytery attended by John Jones was at Nefyn in February, 1823. He preached at 10 am before the Revd John Jones, Tremadog. His sermon was predictably from Romans 8, the text being verse 3: 'For what the law could not do, in that it was weak through the flesh, God sending His own Son in the likeness of sinful flesh, and for sin, condemned sin in the flesh'. 'This sermon was the omen of future success', wrote Owen Jones.[15] That said, his astonishing effectiveness could have an intimidating effect. In fact, the elderly preacher who followed him decided that that should be the last time he would attempt to preach after John Jones, Talsarn! Such an impact is explained by Robert Jones, Rhoslan who, having opened the service by prayer, declared: "Well, indeed, here is a preacher like old Rowland, with a voice much more melodious, and, possibly, talents more bright."[16] Michael Roberts also remarked: "There was something intensely powerful in the preaching of John Jones this first time I ever heard him in the Monthly Meeting at Nefyn."[17]

Apart from translated verbatim reports of his preaching, the most accessible source for John Jones's sermons is Griffith Parry's collection of 1869.[18] However, these are more detailed sermon notes than fully written-out texts. Frustrating for the English reader, they are all in Welsh! As an example of the preacher's evangelistic fervour, there is a remarkable early specimen, now translated for the first time by Dr Lynda Newcombe and Dr Noel Gibbard. Griffith Parry's note in his Welsh edition explains why the orator from Talysarn may claim our attention: 'Without doubt this sermon will be read with special interest, as an example of Revd John Jones early sermons. It was composed in the year 1823, when he was about twenty-six years old'.[19] Allowing for the abbreviated format, we can imagine from the remarks made about his preaching how this sermon might have sounded. It undoubtedly repays a single-sitting reading!

THE WATERS OF SALVATION

Ho! Everyone who thirsts, come to the waters; and you
who have no money, come, buy and eat. Yes, come, buy
wine and milk without money and without price.
(*Isaiah* 55: 1)

In this verse the Lord, as the God of salvation invites poor
damned sinners to enjoy full and sufficient salvation through
Jesus Christ. Even though full and sufficient salvation has
been arranged by God for sinners, it does not belong to
anyone unless they come to receive it through faith in the
truth. Therefore, it is necessary to call and invite sinners to
receive it.

Of all the amazing things in the Bible, one of the most
amazing is God's call and invitation to sinners. The subject
is the complete call of the Gospel.

I The Call

1. The persistence of the call is seen here. "O! come."

Firstly, God is persistent. He does not call in an indifferent
manner—He does not merely show the feast on the
table; but invites persistently. Not because He needs you
but because of His grace. "As though God were pleading."

Secondly, The missionaries are persistent. The sight of the
needy in the world, the sight of the way of salvation,
and the love of Christ motivates them so that they cannot
be less than persistent. Even if our gifts are small our
endurance and our duty are persistent. "We beseech you,
be reconciled to God."

2. This is a call that requires obedience: "Come."

Here we see firstly, that man as a sinner is far from God's
plan; far from any real idea about it and not able to
receive it—remote from loving and receiving it.

Secondly, there is a need to come close before one is able

to enjoy the remedy. It must be supported in your mind before it becomes the remedy and the salvation for you.

Thirdly Man must be active and not passive only in coming to Christ. Man's work is to repent and believe the Gospel.

3. A call for a worthy purpose: "To the waters." Not to the water, but in them—to enjoy, to drink of them; not to the service only, but to the waters—to enjoy salvation.

4. It is an extensive call: "Everyone".

Firstly, every nation. Under the old order the Jewish nation only enjoyed; to them God's sayings were promised. But now the curtain has been torn and every nation is called to enjoy the salvation.

Secondly, every circumstance. There is the same welcome for the poor as for the rich.

Thirdly, every experience. The highest and lowest experience is called to the waters. The lowest experience can come to the waters. There is sufficient to restore them.

5. A call suited to the need: "To the waters" Thirst is feeling the need for water. We all need salvation and we must take it to stop us feeling thirst. What of those who say they are without thirst? Is it the law? "If the ungodly will not return He will sharpen His sword." We must frighten you in the light of Sinai's lightning before you come to flee properly to Calvary.

6. A free call: "Without money, without price;" that is without anything—poor.

7. It is a call to receive a benefit: "Come and eat;" 'Come, obtain'—'Come, enjoy'—'Come, partake.' It is a call for something valuable: "wine and milk." All the things of the Gospel are worth calling for; every grace is of exceptionally great value.

II Of the waters one is here invited to

What are they? The whole of salvation for a sinner;

justification, sanctification, yes, everything to bring eternal happiness. Why are they called 'waters?' It is the custom of the Holy Spirit to express spiritual things by comparisons with natural; this shows that man by nature is more intelligent about natural things than about the things of God.

We will look at the similarity that exists between salvation and waters.

1. They are similar in their vastness. It is not possible to measure waters; so, salvation is similar—"Oh the depth of the riches!" God's salvation is great in the following ways:

Firstly, its origin, that is God's great love that is the original source. How much is the love? "For God so loved the world that He gave His only begotten Son."

Secondly, its eternal providence. Through providence God's salvation is planned.

Thirdly, its authorship. The one who is God's Son—the one who is above all, God be blessed forever and ever.

Fourthly, in his revelation. He is equally a great revealer and a great author to us. There is a jet-black curtain across our hearts and minds by nature. "Eye have not seen nor ear heard the things that God has prepared for those who love Him.—God has revealed them to use through His Spirit. It is the Spirit of God who reveals the things of salvation."

Fifthly, in the work he does in us. There is a "great crowd". What is the size of this crowd. "A great crowd no one could count."

They rise because of His great mercy: "the possession of Satan"—"the curse of the law"—"lying in His blood" Yes. This is even where Abraham is found. They are raised up to happiness—"to glory".

2. They are similar in their non-resistance. Just as the waters of a river, if its source is from a high point, it cannot be stopped. "The billowing waters." You cannot stand in front of them. A king or a general would demand in vain for the waters to stop. So the salvation is certain of its objectives. "I will do it and who will hinder." "The counsel of the Lord, that will stand."

3. Similar in alacrity.

Firstly the waters are ready all the time, in every season. Crops are not available at all times; but the waters are at all times. So come now!

Secondly the waters are available and easily accessible. God ordered the waters as streams near everyone's habitation. So then, "His name has been placed amongst men."— they are quite expedient.

Thirdly they are ready as they are—without being changed; the water is to be used as God created it. So the salvation is perfectly suitable to meet your needs; and you do not need to do anything. Only accept it as it is offered to you!

4. Similar in geniality. The poorest may come forward to the waters. No one will ask for payment. So "without money and without price." If you come with your money you hinder the bargain.

Firstly, it must be free with an eye on the objectives: "nothing to pay."

Secondly with an eye to God's purpose in it—He will gain great praise in His grace from it.

Thirdly, with an eye on its certainty. It is of faith, according to grace. If there were conditions on the part of man, they would be for the fulfilment of this, of faith as it would be according to grace.

5. Similar in efficacy.

Firstly the waters are effective in putting out fire. When a house is on fire one pleads for water. So there is fiery material in your conscience. The waters of creation are unable to put it out, but these waters will do so.

Secondly the waters are effective for cleansing. The water will cleanse the filthiest rag. Take it to the water and it will be cleansed. So many rags are carried to the waters of salvation. No one goes away from there without cleansing. Things start to get better when they are in the water and soon they are without spot.

Thirdly the waters are effective to relieve thirst. Man as a sinner is dying of thirst. Come to the waters and drink. The waters will take away your thirst for the world. You will become like Paul, content in all circumstances.

Fourthly the water revives that which is stagnating. "There is hope for a tree even if it is cut down," that it will "sprout through the aroma of the waters." So these waters—they have taken much parched wood to become fruit for God. "For he is a like a tree planted by the rivers of water. He shall bring forth fruit in his season and his life shall not wither. I am only small but "I will not wither."

III Of the invitation to the waters: "O come to the waters!"

1. The necessity to come. Even though the waters are virtuous, you will wither rather than have them. But if you have obtained them they are certain to cleanse you completely with their medicines.

2. What is coming to the waters?

Firstly , coming to Christ through faith—that is the source of the waters. Believe in Him.

Secondly come to God continually for fellowship so that you receive the perpetual healing of the waters.

3. The way to come to the waters.

Firstly as completely poor.

Secondly thirsty, feeling the need.

Thirdly continually. Not once but daily.

4. The signs that a sinner has come to the waters.

Firstly the fire of the conscience has been put out.

Secondly one produces fruit to the glory of God in the world.

Thirdly one is full of desire (as prophesied) to bring others to them.

5. Encouragements to listen to the invitation. "O Come."

Firstly, because you need the waters. There is fiery material inside you. You are thirsty. You will wither and become like dried wood if you do not come. "O Come!"

Secondly, the waters need you. These are waters that are pleading for work. "O Come!"

Lessons

We see:

Firstly God's great grace in arranging the waters, instead of condemning us as we deserve.

Secondly man's enmity. We do not want to come to Him to be healed.

Thirdly there is a need for God's Spirit to convince man of his need.

Fourthly the salvation is all of God. It all arranged by the Father.

Fifthly do not think about heaven without coming to the waters.

> O, waters of God's salvation,
> Their virtue so peculiar,
> Hasten, come, and fully enjoy,
> Here for us is succour.
>
> Come, the fallen race of Adam,
> Great Jubilee of peace declared,
> And all are called who bear his name,

Enjoy the lasting feast prepared,
Table laid, and eat we may
From dawn to the end of the day.[20]

Soon after settling down at Talysarn, John Jones was encouraged to attend a Methodist Association at Lampeter in August 1823. On his way south, he preached at Penrhyn, Dyffryn, and Barmouth. Understanding that there was a sizable 'anti-Trinitarian' Socinian community in this locality, he had prepared a special sermon on the Deity of Christ, and the necessary connection between His Deity and the infinite atonement He made for the sins of men. Had he been living now, one cannot imagine John Jones doing differently in view of the Islamic presence in the current University of Wales at Lampeter. Returning to his day, we allow Owen Jones to complete this chapter for us:

He fully intended preaching this sermon there; but as it happened, they knew nothing about his ability, and they did not ask him to take any part in the services. The day following, at ten o'clock in the morning, however, he was to preach at Llangeitho, and a great number of preachers and others followed him there, having heard something of the strange power that accompanied him. The famous Ebenezer Morris was there, and the Revd Ebenezer Richard, father of Henry Richard, Esq, MP. He preached the sermon he intended for the Lampeter Association with great power. After the sermon was over, they inquired how it had happened that a preacher of such ability had not been engaged at the Association? The true explanation was that he was unknown to them, and general regret was felt because that sermon had not been preached at Lampeter. From Llangeitho he went to Tregaron by two o'clock; from there to Lledrod for the evening service. The following day (Saturday), Llangwyryfon in the morning; Rhydyfelin, afternoon; Aberystwyth, evening. The Sunday after, he was at Aberystwyth in the morning; Garn, afternoon; Machynlleth, evening. On Monday he hastened home through Dolgellau and Trawsfynydd. This was the first of a long series of visits to South Wales.[21]

Notes

1   *Great Preachers*, 469.
2   Owen Thomas, tr. Pauline Edwards, *Cofiant Y Parchedig John Jones, Talsarn* (Wrexham: Hugues and Son, 1874), 85. Hereafter *Cofiant*
3   Such was J. C. Ryle's valid verdict on High Calvinism in *Expository Thoughts on the Gospels*, St John, Vol. 1 (London: William Hunt and Company, 1865), 159.
4   *Cofiant*, 86.
5   Owen Thomas, tr. John Aaron, *The Atonement Controversy in Welsh Theological Literature and debate, 1707–1841* (Edinburgh: The Banner of Truth Trust, 2002), 350–54.
6   Ibid. 323.
7   Ibid. 326.
8   *Great Preachers*, 491.
9   Ibid. 470.
10 Ibid.
11 Ibid.
12 Ibid.
13 *Cofiant*, 101.
14 *Great Preachers*, 472–3.
15 Ibid. 474.
16 Ibid.
17 Ibid.
18 Griffith Parry, Llanrwst (ed), *Pregethau Y Diweddar Barch. John Jones, Tal-y-Sarn* (Dinbych: Thomas Gee, 1869).
19 Ibid. 631.
20 Ibid. 631–5 (Welsh edition).
21 *Great Preachers*, 474–5.

COFIANT

Y PARCHEDIG

JOHN JONES, TALSARN,

MEWN CYSYLLTIAD A

HANES DUWINYDDIAETH A PHREGETHU CYMRU.

GAN

OWEN THOMAS.

CYF. II.

WREXHAM:

CYHOEDDEDIG GAN HUGHES AND SON, 56, HOPE STREET.

Biography of John Jones, Talsarn

Talysarn. 8au., 8ll.

76

1 PWY welaf o Edom yn dod,
   Mil harddach na thoriad y wawr,
Yn sathru dan wadn Ei droed
   Elynion yn lluoedd i'r llawr :
Ei wisg wedi ei lliwio gan waed,
   Ei saethau a'i gleddyf yn llym ;
Ei harddwch yn llanw'r holl wlad,
   Yn ymdaith yn amlder Ei rym ?

2 Myfi, 'r hwn wyf Alpha cyn byd,
   Wyf gadarn i ladd ac iachau ;
Fy ngeiriau a safant i gyd
   Pan ballo ffyddlondeb pob rhai.
Ond pam mae Dy wisgoedd yn waed
   A'th gleddyf mor goched ei fin,
Fel un a fai'n sathru dan draed
   Y gwinwryf yn ngwinllan y gwin ?

IOAN AB GWILYM.

Taldrwst. 2.8.

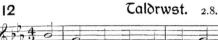

26

1 BRAINT, braint,
   Yw cael cymdeithas gyda'r saint,
Na welodd neb erioed ei maint;
   Ni ddaw un haint byth iddynt hwy;
Y mae'r gymdeithas yma'n gref,
   Ond yn y nef hi fydd yn fwy.

2 Fe gân,
   Y gwaredigion, fawr a mân,
Dragwyddol glôd i'w Prynwr glân;
   Pan ddelo'r tân i losgi'r tir,
Cânt godi eu penau a llawenhau,
   Eu poenus wae â heibio'n wir.

3 Daeth trwy
   Ein Iesu glân a'i farwol glwy,
Fendithion fyrdd, daw eto fwy;
   Mae ynddo faith ddiderfyn stor;
Ni gawsom rai defnynau i lawr;
   Beth am yr awr cawn fyn'd i'r môr?

4 Gwledd gwledd
   O fywyd a thragwyddol hedd,
Sydd yn y byd tu draw i'r bedd;
   Ond hardd fydd gwedd y dyrfa i gyd
Sy'n byw ar haeddiant gwaed yr Oen,
   O swn y boen sydd yn y byd.

27

1 BYDD, bydd,   [ddydd,
   Rhyw ganu peraidd iawn ryw
Pan ddelo'r cacthion oll yn rhydd;
   Fe droi'r eu ffydd yn olwg fry;
Cydunant byth, heb dewi a sôn,
   I foli'r Oen fu ar Galfari.

2 Ond gwledd
   Sydd eto'n bod tu draw i'r bedd,
Dros byth i'w chael i'r gwael eu gwedd;
   Lle bydd caniadau maith di-ri',
I bara beunydd yn ddiboen,
   Gan foli'r Oen fu ar Galfari.

John Roberts   John Hughes

3
MARRIAGE & ORDINATION

We cannot move on from the eventful year of 1823 without mentioning a happy event of immense personal importance to John Jones, Talsarn. For when, after his August preaching tour, he 'hastened home through Dolgellau and Trawsfynydd' to Talysarn, he was hastening back to Fanny, his bride of twelve weeks. Married on 14 May, their joyful union was truly a 'marriage made in heaven'. Never was it more true than in the case of John and Fanny Jones, that 'behind every great man there is a great woman'. It is no exaggeration to say that without Fanny's loving dedication and commitment, first to Christ and second to John, he would never have accomplished what he achieved in proclaiming Jesus, 'the lover of souls'.

T. C. Williams, one of three contributors to the Memoir of John and Fanny's youngest son, David Lloyd Jones (b. 1843), wrote in 1908:

> I know of no one else among us of whom it can be said that Memoirs have been written of both his parents. Dr [Owen] Thomas's biography of Mr Jones's father is one of our standard works in Welsh; and lately, an excellent [Welsh] Memoir of his mother was published, one of the few biographies of the note-worthy women of our country.[1]

Published in 1907 (initially a prize-winning piece at the Talysarn Eisteddfod of 1906), the biography referred to was

Cofiant Mrs Fanny Jones, Gweddw y Diweddar Barch. J. Jones, Talysarn by O. Llew. Owain of Talysarn.[2] Never perhaps was there a more beautiful depiction of true Christian womanhood than this book presents (see Appendix 1). The author derived much information from his mother who knew Fanny Jones. It contains numerous poems about her, including others depicting qualities reflected in her life. Born in 1805 at Cefn-faes, Ffestiniog, Frances (known as Fanny) was the daughter of Thomas and Ann Edwards. The family later moved from Ffestiniog to Llanllyfni, then to a nearby farm called Taldrwst. We are told that Fanny 'had a religious upbringing, and without realising it, her love for her Saviour grew intensely, and that love was rooted through every part of her life, until it flowered in beauty and fragrance. She used to say that she did not know of any time in her life that she did not love Jesus Christ'.[3]

After settling at Talysarn, John Jones began to serve the cause of Christ with intense dedication, preaching there on the second Lord's Day of 1823. He also established singing meetings in both Talysarn and Llanllyfni to which young people came in great numbers. Among them was Fanny Edwards, a bright and pleasant, lively and lovely young lady. While her beauty and cheerfulness tended to draw everyone's attention, John Jones was utterly smitten. It was love at first sight, even though he was slow in disclosing his feelings for Fanny. She also was drawn to John without showing her affection too obviously. However, the romance developed slowly but surely. Griffith Williams, Manager of Talysarn quarry (with whom John Jones lodged) realised that Fanny had won the young preacher's heart. "She'll make you a good wife, John Jones," he said.[4]

Fanny's biographer places the growing romance in the context of God's redemptive purposes for Wales:

We see through this that Providence was working in the background and working for her good in preparing the two hearts for each other. From the viewpoint of Heaven, Fanny Edwards was the 'perfect helpmeet', the most suitable from all aspects to help John Jones to prepare himself to be God's messenger, and to deliver with irresistible strength the great message entrusted to him from Heaven.[5]

The author further affirmed:

As Welsh people we are under a great debt to this woman, and we can never put a price on her service nor measure the work she did in being an instrument to give 'the People's Preacher' to the people ... In her self denial, Wales heard a message from Heaven—her efforts facilitated the way for Wales to be drenched by the irresistible eloquence of the 'hero from Talysarn'.[6]

John and Fanny commenced married life in a house built in the vicinity of Talysarn Chapel where they opened a shop. This was a major feature of Fanny's self-denying commitment to assist John in his ministry. At eighteen years of age, her maturity was extraordinary. She took all the care of the business upon herself, while her husband was still employed in the quarry as before. At the same time he laboured zealously in pastoral care at Talysarn and Llanllyfni. He preached frequently, conducted the church meetings and, utilising his musical talent, directed the singing.

Though he had the constitution of an ox, it was utterly impossible for any frame indefinitely to bear the strain John Jones placed himself under. Besides his daytime work, he had the regular responsibility of the week-day meetings at Talysarn and Llanllyfni. In addition, he often preached in other chapels during the week. On Saturdays, after working half the day in the quarry, he then started for the place he was due to preach at for the Sunday. Sometimes this would involve a journey of twenty or thirty miles. Then, after the morning service, he would have to go to a chapel six or eight miles distant for the afternoon, and return again in the evening to where he preached that morning. On Monday morning, he started early for home and, after dinner, went again to work to the quarry.

His wife felt that all this was too much for the strongest constitution, so she suggested an expansion of the business, in order to provide her husband freedom to devote all his time and energy to the ministry. Furthermore, he was not very competent in business matters; it was far better for the prosperity of the business to keep him up in his study! So Fanny undertook all the additional responsibility. Not to forget that the couple were blest with children in the passage of time, Fanny was aided by maids and assistants in the shop. 'The blessing of God was upon them', wrote Owen Jones, 'and the business prospered'.7

Before we resume the account of John Jones's ministry, we should note his grateful acknowledgement of Fanny's dedicated efforts. Her biographer says that 'often while on his journeys, he spoke of how much of a comfort Fanny was to him, and how she was such a blessing to him' in every respect. "Fanny" he said, "is a great help to me in going on through the journey of my life."8 There can be no doubt about the depth of John's love for Fanny. It is difficult not to feel that his beautiful hymn-tune 'Taldrwst' (for words by John Roberts, 'Braint, braint, Yw cael cymdeithas gyda'r saint') was a love song, expressing his devotion to Jesus *and* Fanny.

John was not yet a fully recognized minister among the Calvinistic Methodists. However, in 1824, in the Association held at Carnarvon, he was received as a member of the Association. He was now free to preach wherever he was invited. Decades before the railway age, he bought a horse to carry him on his distant journeys. It was routine to see the preacher starting from his home in North Wales towards the South, preaching on the way daily: in the morning at 10; afternoon at 2; and evening at 7. His journey would continue from Caernarfonshire, say, through Merionethshire, Montgomeryshire, Cardiganshire, down to the extreme ends of Carmarthenshire or Pembrokeshire. He would then return home by a different route, holding services on the way. Such a preaching tour would last for three or four months in those times.

Becoming increasingly popular, John Jones had constant calls to preach from all the counties of Wales. In the beginning of 1825 he travelled through parts of Anglesey. His hearers were enraptured wherever he went. It was during this journey that his famous biographer, Dr Owen Thomas, first heard him. In the month of May he went through Montgomeryshire, where his preaching proved a great blessing to the country. In September, he travelled through Denbigh and Flint. After this he remained at home in order to have plenty of time for meditation and study. He thus enriched his mind with biblical and other useful knowledge. The secret of his power lay in time alone with God. Not far from his house, there was a wooded area to which he resorted frequently. The local people recalled the time 'when "the People's Preacher" was walking back and forth in the woods, his two hands behind his back. He walked so much until he made a red path for himself, and that was known as "John Jones's path"'.9 This was time well spent, as events proved. In June 1826, he went to the Association at Llanerchymedd, in Anglesey, and preached with wonderful effect upon Christ's words, 'Verily, verily, I say unto you, except a corn of wheat fall into the ground and die, it abideth alone: but if it die, it bringeth forth much fruit' (*John 12: 24*). The enraptured congregation—overwhelmed by God's presence—lost its self-possession, quite overcome with feeling.

In May 1827, he started for another preaching tour to South Wales, going to the Association in Montgomeryshire on the way. He preached there with amazing power upon the prophetic words, 'He was wounded for our transgressions, He was bruised for our iniquities' (*Isaiah 53: 5*). The assembled crowd was blessed as Christ, the loving Saviour of sinners was lifted high! During this service, John Jones preached first, followed by a second preacher. The Revd William Jones, Rhuddlan, said to a friend on the occasion, "I never heard the like of him in my life! What will become of the man that rises to speak after him?"[10]

During this journey the 'People's Preacher' came to Swansea. At that time a three-day 'Vanity Fair' was held there. Alarmed at the decadence of such an event, local zealous Christian people were determined to bring the Gospel to the crowds. The fair being held in a field in the vicinity of the chapel, the faithful hired an area of ground nearby, in order to hold open-air services. The first service at 2 pm produced no noticeable effect. The next service was at six. By the evening the wild clamour of the fair had reached its peak. The Revd William Williams, Cardigan, preached first with good effect, followed by John Jones, Talsarn. Standing in the chapel window for all to hear, outside and within, he preached upon the words, 'And he shewed me a pure river of water of life, clear as crystal, proceeding out of the throne of God and of the Lamb' (*Revelation 22: 1*). Heaven's power was present with the prayerful preacher! The impact was dramatic. The force of the his eloquence suddenly distracted the gamblers. Many left their tables with the money on them! By now, the congregation of around four or five thousand people was riveted to his words. Owen Jones describers what happened next:

> The preacher was still in the window, his soul stirred within him at the sight of the people so much given to vanity. The

glow of his spirit was seen in his eye and countenance, which beamed with seraphic brightness. After preaching for some time with his face towards the open field and the fair, he turned to the chapel, and said to those within: "The throne is triumphant outside, how is it within?" The effect was electric in the chapel also. This sermon of John Jones proved a death blow to the vanity fair at Swansea, as that of John Elias proved before to the harvest fair at Rhuddlan.[11]

He returned from South Wales to the Bala Association in June 1827. Preaching for the first time in those great gatherings at 6 am, his comforting sermon was based on David's words, 'For this cause everyone who is godly shall pray to You in a time when You may be found; surely in a flood of great waters they shall not come near him' (*Ps. 32: 6*). In this Association, his young friend the Revd Henry Rees was ordained. After this, he returned home for a short time, and then started off again to Anglesey. Owen Jones continues the narrative:

He preached with great power in the Association at Amlwch, and again at Llanerchymedd, and returned home. On Sunday, 29 July 1827, he preached in much assurance at Bangor. We may infer what kind of meetings they were from the fact that an old preacher of the name of Henry Roberts, and several of the deacons of the chapel, were quite overcome with feeling. Before the close of this year, he went to Liverpool for two Sundays, and held services in the intervening week. From there he went to Runcorn, then to Manchester, and remained for two Sundays, preaching again during the intervening week. Returning, he went through Chester and Denbigh, preaching in both places, and then to a Presbytery at his native place, Dolwyddelen. After remaining at home for a short time, he started off again; and we find him in October at Beaumaris, Anglesey, preaching in the Association. Before the end of the same month we find him at a similar gathering in Dolgellau. From there he went on a preaching mission through parts of Merioneth, Denbigh, and Flint. And wherever he went, his preaching attracted great multitudes, and was followed with saving effects.[12]

Throughout 1828 John Jones laboured tirelessly in Gospel endeavour. His popularity knew no bounds, not least in his home county. Congregations invited him to every anniversary meeting, even in the vicinity of Talysarn. In the Associations held in Caernarfonshire, folk would be greatly disappointed not to see him there. Preaching in the Bangor Association of June 1828, his sacred oratory had a strong effect upon men of all denominations, and it was the means of adding a great number to the Church of Christ there. A few days later, he went to the Bala Association and officiated there. He heard the mighty John Elias whose sermon made a solemn impression on his mind. Indeed, says Owen Jones, 'he longed and prayed for ability to preach as he did, with such clear simplicity and force of conviction. He returned home with the words of the sermon continually ringing in his ear, and with the determination to serve God with a more thorough consecration than ever'.[13]

Invited by the Welsh church, John Jones visited London for the first time in October of this year. Before the Chester & Holyhead Railway (later worked by the London & North Western Railway)[14] forged a link between North Wales and the capital in 1846, such a journey was a demanding if not hazardous undertaking in the early 19th century. Before setting out, he preached at Beaumaris the previous Sunday. Folk from Bangor and elsewhere, hearing that he would be away for a lengthy period, attended the service in great numbers. Arriving safely after several days travelling, John Jones ministered in London for nine Lord's Days. Jewin Crescent Chapel regularly overflowed with eager worshippers hungry and thirsty for the Word of Life. Doubtless numerous souls were saved and strengthened by the faithful and anointed labours of Christ's servant. Returning through Shrewsbury, he preached there on Wednesday night, 10 December. Arriving home by Sunday 14 December, he rejoiced to find Fanny and the children safe and well. As he reported the sights, sounds and spiritual encouragements during his time away, the family were surely glad that he planned to confine his efforts for a while to his native Caernarfonshire.

Although John Jones had been preaching for several years, and had become famous throughout Wales and beyond, he had not received full ordination at this time. However, this occurred in the Bala Association in June 1829, when five others were ordained with him. At the close of the ordination service, John Elias delivered the charge. In the same Association, in the evening of the last day, John Jones preached on the words, 'The Lord reigneth; let the earth rejoice; let the multitude of isles be glad thereof. Clouds and darkness are round about Him; righteousness and judgment are the habitation of His throne' (*Psalm 97: 1–2*). He was aware of the deep and solemn importance of ordination to the full calling of the Christian ministry. 'His own sensitive spirit was deeply moved', wrote Owen Jones, 'and his sermon that night was delivered with great power. The Revd John Hughes, Wrexham, preached after him. In speaking of the event, Mr Hughes said, "It would have been disheartening even for John Elias to rise up after him"'.[15]

Ever since the first ordinations of 1811, the Calvinistic Methodists were aware of the high privileges and responsibilities of an ordained ministry. Freed at last from the shackles of Anglicanism, they were able to develop, establish and express a truly Reformed view of the Church. John Jones played his part in this, delivering an address on church polity at the Bala Summer Association in 1835.[16] From a Continental perspective, the Welsh Calvinistic Methodists were truly 'The Reformed Churches of Wales', later known as the Presbyterians of Wales—without denying that other branches of Welsh Nonconformity share some characteristics of Reformed churchmanship. The *Confession* of 1823 outlined the ethos and duties of the people of God, which John Jones and his brethren promised solemnly to uphold, teach and maintain:

> Christ the head of the church, has instituted ordinances, means of grace, and an order of worship, to be used in the church by all his people,—in private, in the family, and in the congregation. Through these ordinances, God gives grace, and nourishes and increases the grace given. They are the ordinances of preaching, reading and hearing the word, prayer, praise, mutual instruction, conversation [*cydymddyddan*], the exercise of every part of church discipline, and the sacraments of Baptism and the Lord's Supper.[17]

Whatever biblical reservations John Jones entertained about the 'Owenite' features of Article 18 'Of Redemption', he was fully committed to Article 37. In his high views of the sacraments, he was neither Baptist nor Anglican. Furthermore, 'he was anxious to keep these high in the estimation of the people'.[18]

Regarding baptism, John Jones's own family experience— as a son of godly parents and now a father of a growing family—was a constant reminder of God's covenant mercies. Owen Jones creates a beautiful picture of John Jones's understanding of the ordinance of covenant baptism:

> And whenever the Sacrament of Baptism or of the Lord's Supper was administered by him, he always performed the duty with the solemnity that was due to the occasion. In the case of the Sacrament of Baptism, he would deliver an appropriate address upon the duties which parents owe to their children, upon the profession of Christ made through baptism, the importance of bringing up the young in the church; at other

times he would speak of the meaning of the Sacrament, and of the great change that was signified by it. Some of these addresses were very thrilling, and his prayers were always fervent for the blessing of God upon the parents and the children.[19]

Owen Jones's account of John Jones's celebration of the Lord's Supper is a narrative of exquisite rapture, and deserves to be quoted in full:

His administration of the Sacrament of the Lord's Supper was more impressive still. This is done in Wales generally at the close of the service. After prayer and consecration the minister goes round the members with the bread and wine; and while doing so he speaks words appropriate to the occasion. Mr John Jones always took some special point in connection with the death of Christ: His love, His humiliation, His self-denial and obedience to the will of God; the sufficiency of His sacrifice, the cleansing through His blood, &c.; and he dwelt upon it, and expressed his thoughts until gradually he became warmed by the subject; his ideas flowed as from a fountain; his mind was thrilled; those emotions passed from him to the congregation; the people became absorbed in the same great subject; and they forgot themselves at last, and seemed lost in a sea of gladness and Divine joy. We have heard it said that his addresses at the Communion table were at times so fervent, so glowing, so heavenly, that the people could hardly venture from a feeling of awe and reverence to take the elements from his hand.[20]

A uniquely-glorious experience of such heavenly joy was felt when John Jones was preaching at the Tabernacle, Bangor one Lord's Day evening in the early summer of 1835. Again, Owen Jones paints the wonderful picture:

The service commenced at six o'clock. The sermon was not over till half past eight. Nevertheless, the people were not tired; under the spell of his oratory time was forgotten. On this

occasion there was a Communion service to be at the close.
The sermon itself was impressive; and the congregation had
been worked up to a high pitch of emotion. It was felt at the
Communion table that the service went on with great ease.
The preacher was in a most elevated mood, and grace was
evidently being poured into his lips, and a live coal from the
altar of the sanctuary had touched them; so that they glowed
with peculiar eloquence that evening. The preacher had gone
round the large chapel with the bread, and was now returning
for the wine. He took the cups in his hands, and held them
up with the wine in them, and with his sweet voice he said,
"Do you see, my friends, how the wine begins to redden?"
These words, with those beautiful notes of his, ran electrically
through the multitude. The tears rushed to the eyes of many,
as if to see what was the cause of such a shock, and they gave
vent to their emotions in words; and probably there was not
a man who did not feel that moment something creeping
shudderingly over him. After a while there was perfect silence
again, and he went on speaking upon the "precious blood of
Christ." The time had gone; no one thought of looking upon
the clock. Their minds had been absorbed. It was after ten o'
clock when he commenced praying in order to close the
meeting. He said, "Indeed, Lord, we would have praised Thee
to-night, only that it has gone late. Blessed be God, because
we have hopes of going into a country where there will be
no record of time to disturb our worship; and because we can
hope for the day when we shall never become tired of the
house of God." Before he had gone any farther, the feelings
of the people became too warm again; and their voices drowned
the voice of the preacher; and there they remained till it was
eleven o'clock.[21]

Such were the amazing labours of the Revd John Jones,
Talsarn. For all the joys of heaven poured out in such abundance,
his Lord's day travels denied him any rest. He often had to
preach in three places, many miles apart, each service concluding
with the Lord's Supper and sometimes a baptism. Clearly his
ordination as a minister of the Gospel had a profound influence

upon him. His biographer appropriately describes this period in the preacher's career: 'He consecrated his energies, his talents, and his genius more than ever to the great cause of Christ. And though his toil was incessant and his labours excessive, yet he was employed with the work he delighted to be in; and he enjoyed times of most thorough refreshing and happiness. His ministry advanced in power, and his popularity became greater still'.[22]

Notes

1   R. Hughes (ed), *Memoir and Sermons of the Late Rev. David Lloyd Jones, MA, Llandinam* (Wrexham: Hughes and Son, 1912), 108. This is the English translation of E. Jones, J. Williams and T. C. Williams, *Cofiant a Phregethau Y Diweddar Barch. David Lloyd Jones, MA Llandinam* (Gwrecsam: Hughes A'i Fab, 1908).

2   O. Llew. Owain, *Cofiant Mrs. Fanny Jones, Gweddw y Diweddar Barch. J. Jones, Talysarn* (Machynlleth a Caernarfon, 1907). Hereinafter *Cofiant Fanny Jones*.

3   Ibid. 28–9, tr. Marian G. Clifford.

4   Ibid. 36.

5   Ibid. 39.

6   Ibid. 43.

7   *Great Preachers*, 472.

8   *Cofiant Fanny Jones*, 43; tr. Marian G. Clifford.

9   Ibid.

10 *Great Preachers*, 476.

11 Ibid. 477.

12 Ibid. 477–8.

13 Ibid. 478.

14 Patrick Whitehouse & David St John Thomas, *LMS 150: The London Midland & Scottish Railway—A century and a half of progress* (Newton Abbot: David & Charles, 1987, 32.

15 *Great Preachers*, 479.

16 Ibid. 253.

17 Article 37, *The History, Constitution, Rules of Discipline and Confession of Faith of the Calvinistic Methodists or the Presbyterians of Wales* ... Translated from the Welsh (Carnarvon: The General Assembly, 1900), 110.

18 *Great Preachers*, 479.

19 Ibid.

20 Ibid.

21 Ibid. 480.

22 Ibid. 481.

COFIANT
Mrs. FANNY JONES,

GWEDDW Y DIWEDDAR Barch. J. JONES,
TALYSARN,

GAN

Mr. O. LLEW. OWAIN, Talysarn.

GYDA

RHAG-DRAITH

GAN Y

Parch. O. G. OWEN (Alafon).

MACHYNLLETH:
Cyhoeddedig gan Mrs. Jones, Cambrian House.

CAERNARFON:
Argraphwyd gan Gwmni y Cyhoeddwyr Cymreig (Cyf.),
Swyddfa "Cymru."
—
1907.

Biography of Fanny Jones

Tanrallt. M. H.

23

1 CYSEGRWN flaenffrwyth ddydd-
    iau'n hoes
I garu'r Hwn fu ar y groes:
Mae mwy o bleser yn Ei waith
Na dim a fedd y ddaear faith.

2 Cael bod yn foreu dan yr iau
Sydd ganmil gwell na phleser gau,
Mae ffyrdd doethineb oll i gyd
Yn gysur ac yn hedd o hyd.

3 Y plant a wasanaethont Grist,
Cânt ddiangc byth rhag uffern drist;
Mae myrdd o ie'nctyd yn y nef
Yn berlau yn Ei goron Ef.

4 O! na threuliaswn yn ddi-goll
O dan iau Crist fy mebyd oll;
Mae'r Hwn a'm prynodd ar y groes
Yn deilwng o bob awr o'm hoes.

PEDR FARDD.

24

1 GWAITH hyfryd iawn a melus yw
    Molianu D'enw Di, O Dduw!
Son am Dy gariad foreu glas,
A'r nos am wironeddau'th ras.

2 Melus yw dydd y Sabbath llon,
Na flined gofal byd mo'm bron;
O! na bai 'nghalon i mewn hwyl,
Fel telyn Dafydd ar yr ŵyl.

3 Yn Nuw, fy nghalon lawenha;
Bendithio'i air a'i waith a wna;
Mor hardd yw gwaith Dy ras, O Dduw!
A'th gyngor, pa mor ddyfned yw!

D. JONES, Caio. (cyf.)

25

1 O ARGLWYDD Dduw! bywhâ Dy
    waith
Dros holl derfynau'r ddaear faith;
Dros dir a môr disgleiria i maes
Yn nerth Dy anorchfygol ras.

B. FRANCIS.

37   Salesbury. 8.8.8., 6ll.

69 1 NIS gall angylion nef y nef
　　　　　Fynegu maint Ei gariad Ef,
　　　　Mae angeu'r groes yn drech na'u dawn;
　　　Bydd canu uwch am Galfari
　　　Nas clywodd yr angylion fry,
　　　　Pan ddelo Salem bur yn llawn.

2 Nis teimlodd neb ond Ef ei hun
　Anfeidrol werth fy enaid cun—
　　Uwch da, uwch aur, uwch perlau drud:
　Ni thalai dim ond gwaed fy Nuw—
　Angeuol, farwol loes, a byw,
　　A'm prynai o dragwyddol lid.

3 Y penaf drysor heddyw yw,
　O fewn y nefoedd, gwaed fy Nuw,
　　Holl sylwedd y caniadau i gyd ;
　A dyna'r gwaed a roddo'd iawn
　I ddwyfol ddigder, perffaith lawn ;
　　Fy hedd a'm cysur yn y byd.

4 Am iddo farw ar y bryn,
　Cadd f'enaid bach ei brynu'n llyn,
　　A'i dynu o'i gadwynau'n rhydd :
　Wel bellach, dan Ei haeddiant Ef,
　Fel cysgod cedrwydden gref,
　　Gorphwysaf mwy yn ngwres y dydd.   W. WILLIAMS.

(44)

4
NOT IN WORD ONLY

The preaching of John Jones, Talsarn reveals a unique combination of unction and truth. One without the other was alien to his heraldic mission. For 'the People's Preacher', the preaching of Christ had to be the preaching of a 'felt Christ'. Doubtless all his brethren shared this concern but in John Jones it was evident to an extraordinary degree. By the 1830s there were several instances to indicate that his preaching—however thrilling and gripping, however powerful and persuasive before—was increasing in power. One of the most memorable instances at this period occurred at Llangefni on 12 and 13 March 1832 during a Monthly Presbytery in the town.

On Monday evening he preached on God's power and human inadequacy from Job 22: 3–4. The following morning his text was "Thy bow was made quite naked, according to the oaths of the tribes, even Thy word" (*Hab. 3: 9*). An eminent deacon named Williams was present on the occasion. He testified that the power felt was utterly overwhelming as the preacher declared, "God has two bows at His hand—the bow of the Gospel and the bow of judgment; if we do not submit to the bow of the Gospel, the bow of judgment will surely vanquish us." And, seeing the effect upon the congregation, John Jones interjected a prayer (as he often did), "O Lord, my God, it is not difficult to bring this people to Thy feet. Put the arrow on the string ... Down with your arms!" 'Then followed a chorus of 'amens'. Mr Williams described the effect as resembling a great fall in a quarry', wrote Owen Jones: 'At first a little earth comes down, then a few stones fall, then there is a great slip, with a dead, heavy thud, then another, greater still, and another crash, crash, until at last the whole overhanging rock falls with tremendous catastrophe'.[1]

Accordingly, Dr Owen Thomas observed:

> This was, perhaps, one of the most wonderful meetings he ever experienced in his life. We have heard from time to time a great number of those that were present speaking of the event; and the unanimous voice of all is, that they hardly ever were in such a meeting. The effect upon all the hearers was indescribable. There was hardly a man there but was completely overcome. Mr [John] Elias wept aloud, and Mr Cadwaladr Williams was quite subdued. No one had courage enough to preach in the remaining services of the day. Some, if not all, of those who had been appointed to officiate went home; it was from the immediate neighbourhood that they had preachers to remain with them to finish the services of the day.[2]

As a result of this sermon, many were brought to Christ and added to the churches. Sitting next to the above-mentioned Mr Williams, a man in a backslidden state who had turned his back on God and His people was wonderfully restored. Another man on this occasion (or a similar one in Anglesey) said to a minister he was sitting beside, "Well, did you ever hear such a thing?" The minister replied, "No, never; nor do I expect to hear anything like it from this to the Judgment day."[3]

In the same year John Jones preached at the Bala Association. John Elias was prevented from attending due to an accident. Since the veteran preacher often had an intimidating effect on the younger men, his absence possibly influenced John Jones. Certainly he preached happily with great liberty and power. The popular South Wales preacher, John Evans[4] was due to preach with him; 'but the beauty, the eloquence, the force of the first preacher was so overwhelming that he refused to do anything after him; and the people were dismissed'.[5]

As outlined by Owen Jones, the appalling cholera outbreak of the 1830s[6] was a significant factor during John Jones's ministry at that period:

> The year 1832 was remarkable in parts of Wales from a religious point of view. This was the case in Caernarfonshire. The cholera had broken out in some parts of England. At that time there were not many papers to carry news; people had to be satisfied with rumours, which, though having generally a basis of truth, were yet exceedingly vague. Rumours of cholera were thick in the land. This tended to impress men with the solemnity of life, and the overwhelming responsibilities which attached to every man in this world. There was an air of soberness and earnestness over the people; they did not seem to be so hard-hearted, and it was easier to preach to them than before. This terrible disease called them like a trumpet from their indolence and sins to the Gospel of Christ.[7]

Political action was immediate, so, with this dreadful nationwide threat, the Government appointed 21 March 1832, as a day of fasting and humiliation. In view of widespread public alarm, 'the People's Preacher' John Jones was himself deeply stirred by the situation; he preached with extraordinary power on the subject. During this year, conversions were numerous, more than two thousand members being added to the churches in Caernarfonshire, many of them through the ministry of John Jones.

Under the circumstances, it is not surprising that bogus conversions occurred. Undoubtedly, things happened in the ensuing religious revival which could not be justified; there were unwelcome extravagances. That said, there was an undeniable revival of religious life. Powerful gospel preaching changed the character of thousands, and made them better people.

There can be no doubt that the impact of John Jones's preaching stemmed from his walk with God. The incandescence of his ministry had the two components of light and heat. As with the sun, though these may be distinguished yet they cannot be separated. Thus John Jones was equally concerned faithfully to declare God's truth as well as transmit its power. As his career advanced, his understanding grew as did his power of utterance. In his youth on the slopes of Moel Siabod, his Bible in his hand, he had communed with God. Whatever else he read in later years, he remained essentially *homo unius libri*—a man of one book—to the end of his life. Of course, it was Bishop William Morgan's Welsh Bible (1588), and one of John Jones's hymn tunes was named *Salesbury* after William Morgan's precursor William Salesbury, the first Welsh translator of the New Testament (1567).[8]

Owen Jones shows that our preacher's lack of learning was in no way detrimental to his influence:

> It may be that in his youth he enjoyed but few advantages of education. Notwithstanding this, in after years, he worked hard to make up for the loss, and was admirably successful. It is true enough that others were better in their knowledge of the Greek and Latin languages, and in their acquaintance with history, the geography of the earth and the astronomy of the heavens. But in the pulpit, even at this early period of his life, when only about thirty-six years old, he stood on a par with the best preachers of the time, in the holy fervour of his spirit, and the Divine influence that followed him.[9]

Popular preachers are often considered superficial. Not so John Jones. He was a profound thinker. This was undoubtedly one of the chief elements of his success. His habits of thought may be traced back to hours of meditating and preaching on Moel Siabod and at the cataract in Nant-y-tylathau. His mental life involved incessant thought. Fed by his constant acquaintance with Holy Scripture, there was within him a the continuous whirl of ideas. In this respect, he was spiritual rather than sensual, as Owen Jones rightly observes: 'And thus in his youth, he accustomed himself to think; he trained his mind to do without the feelings that come continuously from the senses—sight, hearing, taste, &c., and to work graspingly and strongly upon the words of God'.[10]

Owen Jones perceptively reveals the source of true knowledge, a fount John Jones was so profoundly acquainted with:

> A man's success as a preacher will, in the end, depend upon the amount of strength he has for this—the intensity of inner thought, the energizing, the feeling for the infinite and holy, and the amount of silent research he makes into the deep caverns of his own soul. Ideas ever take the lead in human affairs; they are the fiery steeds that draw the world after them;—true of all the advancements of science and invention; but true in especial of religion and spiritual things. The nearest point of contact in this world with God and the other world is man's spirit. Here, first of all, he may expect to find the Spirit of God, which searches the deep things of God. It is here above all he may look for flashes of light from heaven. And it is to the extent a man enters into his own spirit with the Bible and the truths of the Gospel he will be able to make his mark upon the world.[11]

If John Jones had lacked education, he was obviously not defective in intelligence. Indeed, he was a thinker, and a deep one. His sanctified thinking has been described as 'philosophical' in character, a tendency for which some have criticised him.[12] However, it is chiefly the spurs to infidelity supplied by the likes of Descartes and Spinoza, Locke and Hume, Kant and

Hegel that have given philosophy a bad name among Bible-believing Christians. Unlike myself (the present author), John Jones did not study philosophy (as I did at the University College of North Wales, Bangor in the 1960s). His monoglot Welshness preserved him from the sceptical influences which have ruined many (myself excepted, by the grace of God). Of course, when the Apostle Paul warned against the dangers of philosophy (see 1 Corinthians 1: 20ff; Colossians 2: 8), his targets were doubtless the likes of Plato and Aristotle, Epicurus and Zeno. Yet, when we realise that 'philosophy' means 'love of wisdom', Paul was not opposed to loving the true wisdom found in Christ, the Light of the world (see 1 Corinthians 1: 30). Such is the ocean which mankind is called to traverse and explore. Such are the depths worthy of our thought and reflection. In this respect, John Jones was a true philosopher. As Owen Jones rightly concludes: 'He philosophized about the plan of salvation: the love of God to a lost world, the death of Christ and His resurrection, and the work of the Spirit—these were the great themes of his philosophy'.[13]

We have already seen John Jones's Bible-based, Christ-centred 'philosophising' at Trefriw in 1820. Aided by the writings of Dr Edward Williams, his 'carefully-balanced' inductive perception of biblical data led him to reject the 'logically-lazy' and equally-rationalistic extremes of 'left-leaning' Arminianism and 'right-leaning' High Calvinism alike (my explanation). By the next decade, he began to witness the practical impact of all this. Especially among the Calvinistic Methodists, his fears over a growing hypercalvinistic antinomianism were being justified. This involved an excessive stress on the sovereignty of God and a neglect of human responsibility. In short, a deadening hypercalvinist inertia was killing evangelism and the pursuit of holiness. Owen Jones describes the situation as John Jones saw it:

It struck him that the preaching of the time was not exactly what it ought to be. It pained him to see so little effect often following the sermons of the day; and it dawned upon him that there was something wanting. In the denomination to which he belonged, the chief Calvinistic doctrines were preached by some in their greatest bareness. The doctrines of election and reprobation, the total depravity of man, and his utter inability to do anything towards salvation, had great prominence at that time. God's side of the question of salvation was made most clear: the love of God, the death of the Saviour, and the work of the Spirit were painted with great vividness before the congregations. But the preachers were inclined to forget the human side of it. They did not remember that the plan of redemption was through men, and for men; and that the Gospel as presented to us in the Bible was the best and only means of arriving at the desired end—the salvation of men; and that it was specially adapted as an instrument for that purpose. In the preaching of many Calvinists there was, if there is not yet, a terrible gap between the Gospel and the sinner.[14]

The situation had clearly alarmed John Jones and those who shared his concerns. In fact, having sampled much of the preaching of the period, he wrestled with the issues for about two years, even losing sleep in the process. During many a long night he pondered and prayed on the best and most effective way of presenting the true Gospel to the people. Owen Jones describes the results of our preacher's soul-struggles:

He studied the Bible with redoubled care and diligence, and became fully convinced that the human side, so to speak, of the Gospel was far too much lost sight of in the preaching of the day. He determined to give greater prominence to this in future, and to cast the responsibility of damnation altogether upon the shoulders of the sinner himself. His discourses brought the love of God, the death of Christ, heaven with all its bliss and glory within the reach of every man, and made every individual man responsible for the loss of them.[15]

The first indication of John Jones's change of emphasis was heard in a sermon preached at Bala during the summer Association of 1834. His rousing text was, 'Behold, these three years I come seeking fruit on this fig-tree, and find none: cut it down; why cumbereth it the ground?' (*Luke 13: 7*). None of his hearers could doubt the urgent necessity of their personal response to the Gospel. There was even a change in the preacher's style. Instead of the old puritan-style sermons with their endless divisions and sub-divisions, it was a brilliant development of one great theme. Other sermons at this period reflect the same approach. He was greatly encouraged to see increasing fruit for his labours. Many were professing a living faith and joining the churches. Despite misgivings in some quarters, there were tangible results. 'Men felt under his sermons that to go to perdition was a terrible calamity', wrote Owen Jones, 'and that the responsibility of it rested upon their own shoulders. Every Sunday there were some fresh candidates for membership where he preached. His popularity with the multitude became greater than ever before'.[16]

It was in the year 1835, in the Association held at Bala, that he brought out these views prominently in the public hearing of his fellow-ministers. His text was: 'No man can come to Me except the Father which hath sent Me draw him: and I will raise him up at the last day' (*John 6: 44*). The following gripping and enlightening extract deserves to be read in its entirety:

> If the Government of England were to send an order to the British Admiral to bring the Fleet home from the Mediterranean Sea, you would not suppose that the Government intended

that the Admiral and his men should carry the ships home? Nothing of the kind. We all know full well that the meaning of the order would simply be that the Admiral should make the proper preparations; that they should employ the proper means in order to bring the ships home—weigh the anchors, turn their prows towards the deep, that they should put them in the way of the great forces of nature spread the sails, and steer the vessels home; let the winds play upon them, and the waves and the tides carry them. Meanwhile, the men on deck might take it easy; they could enjoy themselves, and sing their native songs, while the mighty elements co-operated to bring them home. In the same manner, God in the Gospel calls upon you to repent, to believe, and to lead a pious and godly life. But He does not mean that you should do all this of your own individual resources. No; He intends that you should put yourselves as you are under the operation of the mighty forces of the Gospel; that you should faithfully employ the means which He has commanded. Turn the prow of thy little vessel to the deep; let it sail upon the wide ocean of Christ's Atonement; spread the sails, and steer it on by the guidance of the Word of God. The winds will blow, the mighty forces of redemption will p]ay upon thy vessel; the tides will carry it, and thou shalt find thy little bark one day in the haven of eternal rest. You have, my friends, something yourselves to do, and it is of no use at all to expect the operations of the Spirit of God, while we ourselves neglect our duty. 'But what can I do?' Canst thou not read? Open thy Bible; look at it, read it; bring thy mind into contact with the great saving forces, and wait for help from above. 'But I cannot pray.' Canst thou not try? Canst thou not bend thy knee, and put it down on the ground? 'But I must pray from the heart, and this I cannot do.' Wouldst thou give Him thy heart? Give Him thy body, give Him thy tongue; and if thou canst not say a word, there is One up there who can open His lips to intercede for thee. Try fairly; do your best for your own salvation. Do not, at least, rush headlong into perdition. I, indeed, have made up my mind long ago that I shall not go there so. If I must go to hell at all, I shall not go there straight along. No; I shall loiter a good deal about the Garden of Gethsemane; I shall go many a round about the hill of Calvary; I shall bend my knees daily at the throne of grace. I shall be good enough for hell, if I have to go there, after all these efforts. But, blessed be the name *of* God, we have every reason to believe that this is the high road to heaven, and that no one ever went to hell in that way, and that no one ever will.[17]

Such a presentation of the Gospel would hardly be contested now among evangelical folk. Yet at the time, many with ultra-orthodox views objected to it even if they saw the dangers of full-blown hypercalvinism. So what impact did this astonishing fusion of truth and unction make? According to a report:

> The vast congregation lay in his hand, and thousands of 'Amens' rose in response to his prayers that the Lord would stir up the people to strive to enter the kingdom of heaven [Luke 13: 24]. Mr Ebenezer Richard[18] was listening, and was weeping like a child. Great shining drops ran down his cheeks and his warm 'Amen' was as loud as any'.[19]

Sadly, the eminent John Elias showed signs of disapproval. He did not relish such preaching. In a meeting later that evening with preachers and elders, the subject of the Holy Spirit's work in transforming a sinner was discussed. John Jones—defending the emphasis of his sermon—affirmed that when the mind is illuminated by the Spirit with the knowledge of Christ, anxiety is created to be rescued from sin, leading to repentance and faith. In a hasty and ill-tempered response, John Elias failed to see that the discrepancy between the two preacher's views was not what he feared. Ebenezer Richard stood up to warn the assembly that a wrong spirit in contending for truth can injure the cause of God and grieve the Holy Spirit. Everyone was humbled by the rebuke, including John Elias.[20]

In his endeavours to rescue preaching from the fatalistic grip of hypercalvinism, 'Great credit is due to Mr Jones', concluded Owen Jones, 'for this insight which he had into the genius of the Gospel, and for the originality and the courage with which he preached it'.[21] All sections of today's 'Reformed constituency' would benefit from John Jones's Bala sermon!

The practical emphasis of John Jones's ministry helped arouse a concern for vital godliness. Immorality and drunkenness were widespread, with too many professing Christians being adversely influenced by the prevailing decadence. Active steps were needed to impress on the people the urgency and necessity for sanctified daily living, so, the year 1836 saw the promotion of Temperance reformation in Caernarfonshire. Owen Jones describes the combined efforts of 'brethren' joining 'pleasantly together in unity' (*Psalm 133: 1*):

> Mr Jones took an active part in all the philanthropic efforts of those times. It is interesting to observe that in the first Temperance Association of North Wales, held at Caernarfon, August, 1837, three of the great orators of Wales met together on the same platform. William Williams, Wern, was the chairman of the Committees, John Elias the chairman of the public meetings. Christmas Evans dwelt in the town at the time, and he spoke enthusiastically in one of the assemblies. John Elias preached in the evening of the first day; Williams, of Wern, at two o'clock, the following day. Mr Jones was one of the first advocates of temperance in Caernarfonshire; his orations were masterpieces, and sparkling with the humour which he possessed in such abundance.[22]

For John Jones, gospel preaching must always promote holiness. While justification and sanctification are to be distinguished, they must never be separated in Christian experience. True saving faith is of necessity a loving and obedient faith. Such was the character of his ministry as he took his message around Wales and beyond. In 1837 he preached with great power at Mold, Flintshire. The following year found him preaching at the London Easter Association. At the close of 1840 he was again in South Wales. In a sermon at Tre-fin, Pembrokeshire he powerfully set forth the duties and joys of family worship. His text was, 'But as for me and my house, we will serve the Lord' (*Joshua 24: 15*). Our chapter closes with his beautiful and powerful picture of Christian fatherhood. Who can deny the relevance of his message for modern society where domestic disintegration is increasingly common?

One of the grandest sights in nature is to see the father at the head of the table, taking the loaf, and cutting the bread for his little children; they with innocent eyes looking up to him and waiting for their share. Art can never produce anything comparable to that. They have not in London anything that will equal it in beauty and sublimity. But, however grand that may be, the scene which follows in the godly man's family is far superior even to that. After the wants of all have been satisfied, and after those healthy children have each of them said that they want no more, behold the father!—the man whom the Lord hath blessed, accompanied by his wife, who is as a fruitful vine by the sides of his house, and his children like olive plants round about his table—behold the father taking the old family Bible in his hands! Hear him reading the Word of God, and giving unto his little ones of the bread of life. And after that is over, see how the father and the mother, and those little ones with their tiny limbs, bend their knees before their Father in Heaven; and pray together for God's mercy; and that hearth becomes another holy of holies, consecrated to God for ever in the minds of the family. Perhaps, before twenty-four hours have elapsed one of the verses that were read will yield strength and support to some member of that family in the valley of the shadow of death.[23]

Notes

1 *Great Preachers*, 482.
2 *Cofiant*, 218 cited in *Great Preachers*, 482.
3 Ibid.
4 See Owen Thomas, tr. John Aaron, *The Atonement Controversy in Welsh Theological Literature and debate, 1707–1841* (Edinburgh: The Banner of Truth Trust, 2002), 369.
5 *Great Preachers*, 483.
6 See *Cholera in Wales*, G. Penrhyn Jones, National Library of Wales Journal Vol X: 3 Summer 1958 (http://www.genuki.org.uk/big/wal/Cholera.html). Accurate statistics of the 1832 epidemic in Wales are not available since the Registrar-General's Department was not established until after that date, its first annual report being issued in the year 1839. Creighton 3 gave the following mortality figures for cholera in some Welsh towns during that epidemic:

	Deaths		Deaths
Newport	13	Denbigh	47
Abergavenny	2	Caernarvon	30
Merthyr Tydfil	160	Flint	18
Swansea	152	Newtown	17
Haverfordwest	16		

The disease had virtually burned itself out in Wales by the early months of 1833, although a recrudescence did occur in London and in a number of scattered localities in England. No further cholera epidemic of note occurred in Britain until the severe and widespread infection of 1848–9.

7 *Great Preachers*, 483.
8 See http://wbo.llgc.org.uk/en/s-SALE-WIL-1520.html
       William Salesbury (1520?–1584?) was a scholar and chief translator of the first Welsh New Testament. He was educated at Oxford and, in all probability, it was while he was there that he left the Roman Catholic Church and became a Protestant. His industry was actuated mainly by two motives: a desire to make the Holy Scriptures available to the Welsh, and a desire to impart knowledge and learning to them in their own language. He was the most learned Welshman of his day: he was proficient in Hebrew, Greek, Latin, and a number of modern languages, and was a master of many different subjects. But, above all, he was a Welsh scholar and man of letters, and was one of the most brilliant representatives of Renaissance humanism in Wales. It would be hard to find anybody who has rendered greater service to the Welsh nation than William Salesbury. His great contribution was his translation of the Scriptures into Welsh, thus laying the foundations of modern Welsh prose.
9 *Great Preachers*, 484.
10 Ibid. 485.
11 Ibid.
12 Dr Eifion Evans (e-mail, 29 Sept 2011): 'With regard to John Jones I have some misgivings … he seems to have preferred philosophy to theology'.
13 *Great Preachers*, 485.
14 Ibid. 486.

15 Ibid.
16 Ibid. 487.
17 Ibid. 487–9.
18 See Owen Thomas, tr. John Aaron, *The Atonement Controversy in Welsh Theological Literature and debate, 1707–1841* (Edinburgh: The Banner of Truth Trust, 2002), 379.
19 John Morgan Jones & William Morgan, tr. John Aaron, *The Calvinistic Methodist Fathers of Wales* (Edinburgh: The Banner of Truth Trust, 2008), ii. 745.
20 Ibid. 746.
21 *Great Preachers*, 489.
22 Ibid.
23 Ibid. 489–90.

Goleuad. 7.6. D.

41

1 MAE 'r ffynnon yn agored ;
   Dewch, edifeiriol rai ;
Dewch chwithau, yr un flunud,
Sy'n methu edifarhau :
Dewch, gafodd galon newydd,
Dewch chwithau, na chadd un ;
I olchi pob budreddi
Yn haeddiant Mab y dyn.

2 O ! Iachawdwriaeth gadarn,
   O ! Iachawdwriaeth glir,
Fu dyfais o'i chyffelyb
Erioed ar fôr na thir :
Fe rodd Ei fywyd drosom :
Beth all Ef ballu mwy ?
Mae myrdd o drugareddau
Difesur yn Ei glwy'.

3 O ! râs didrai, diderfyn,
   Tragwyddol ei barhâd !
Yn nglwyfau'r Oen fu farw
Yn unig mae iachâd !
Iachâd oddi wrth euogrwydd,
   Iachâd o ofnau'r bedd ;
A chariad wedi ei wreiddio
Ar sail tragwyddol hedd.

       W. WILLIAMS.

32 **Theophilus.** 8.7. D.

62 1 WYNEB siriol fy Anwylyd
    Yw fy mywyd yn y byd ;
Ffarwel bellach bob eilunod,
    Iesu, 'Mhriod, aeth â mryd ;
Brawd mewn myrdd o gyfyngderau,
    Ffrind mewn môr o ofid yw ;
Ni chais f'enaid archolledig
    Neb yn feddyg ond fy Nuw.

2 Mae fy enaid oll yn caru
    'R Oen ogwyddodd droswy'i ben ;
Dwedodd ar y groes, "Gorphenwyd!"
    Pan groeshoeliwyd ar y pren ;
Caru 'rwyf lyth'renau Enw
    'R Hwn fu farw yn fy lle ;
Dan y groes, ac yn y gofid,
    Cyfaill ffyddlon yw Efe.

                       MORGAN RHYS.

5
MERCY IN THE STORM

We have noted that, during the years (1830–40), John Jones, Talsarn turned his energies towards practical gospel preaching. Whether or not he ever read his works, he was one with the seraphic 17th-century English Puritan Richard Baxter[1] (ignorantly dismissed as an Arminian by William Williams, Pantycelyn[2]) who declared that 'Practical divinity … my soul doth live on, and is the happiest part of my learning'.[3] The reason for the Welshman's emphasis was what he considered the defective preaching of the times. In this he also shared the Puritan's dread of antinomianism. Thus he felt an urgent need to give greater prominence to practical piety. That said, the great truths about the everlasting love of God, the humiliation and death of Christ, &c.—were the subjects in which his soul delighted. For this 'Welsh Baxter', 'his noble intellect, his bold imagination, his pathetic spirit found in these abundant scope', wrote Owen Jones; 'Like a great ship on the high seas, far away from the rocks and the dangers of the coast, he could spread his sails to the wind, and steer right on'.[4]

Reflecting Dr Owen Thomas's exhaustive historical overview, Owen Jones usefully and profitably summarizes the stormy and unhappy history of theological disputes in Wales. While our 'dumbed-down' era shows little appetite for such information, it relates to matters of profound importance thus:

After some few years of trouble in matters of doctrine in the Connexion to which he belonged, and after undergoing himself not a little anxiety and pain of mind, about the year 1841 things became finally settled.[5] There is nothing that militates so strongly against the religion of the heart as contention about doctrines. When quarrels and disputes arise, true religion feels at once their benumbing influence; and it is very little aggressive work that is then done. In the times of the Reformation there was but little, if any, real missionary work done. The disputings of those times were nevertheless a great blessing to the world; and many a revival of religion followed. Still, this was after the din of battle was over. After the revival in Wales in the times of Rees Prichard, Henry Wroth, Walter Caradoc, Vavasor Powel, William Erbury, and others, there followed contentions about doctrines, about baptism, church government, &c. The inevitable effect was a great religious depression; corruption and darkness again spread over the land.[6]

Despite the wonderful impact of the Methodist awakening, it also produced doctrinal disputes with unhappy consequences, as Owen Jones explains:

Howell Harris and Daniel Rowland fell like thunderbolts upon the immorality of those times. Mighty effects followed their preaching. A new connexion, the Calvinistic Methodist, sprang up. The preaching of Howell Harris and Daniel Rowland, David Jones, Llangan, and others caused a great revival throughout Wales. But before the end of twenty years a dispute arose about the preaching of Howell Harris. It was maintained that he used expressions concerning the death of Christ which were wrong and heretical. This little matter caused great strife and angry feeling. And in an Association held at Llanidloes in the year 1751 a separation took place. Howell Harris retired altogether to Trefecca. The churches through the land became two parties one siding with Howell Harris, the other with Rowland. They were called "the people of Rowland" and the "people of Harris." So general did it become, that it threatened at the time to ruin the Connexion altogether; and such would inevitably have been the effect but for a new revival that broke out ten or fifteen years later.7

These things being so, Owen Jones sees some good in theological debate, even if, on balance they have a pronounced unwelcome, negative aspect. His confident 1880s perspective must not permit us to forget the disastrous impact of a later liberalism in twentieth-century Wales and elsewhere:

> But, like wars, these contentions are, perhaps, necessary now and again. But we ought always to avoid religious controversies just as we ought to avoid war. And the men that become involved in them, like David, the King of Israel, become, to a certain extent, unfit for the erection of the great spiritual temple of Christ. They can only contribute, like David, a portion of the gold and silver, the wood, the iron, and the stones for the building of the house of God. But they cannot build. They are men of war, and there are marks of blood upon their hands. So is it ever the case. Now, the Church of Christ in Wales is enjoying a time of comparative peace after many religious wars, so to speak.8

Being relevant to a proper view of the legacy of John Jones, Talsarn, Owen Jones then focuses on the conflict between Calvinists and Arminians in Wales:

> Before the beginning of the eighteenth century the religious bodies in Wales, the Church of England, the Presbyterians, the Independents, and the Baptists, were all of them Calvinistic. As far as is known, there was in that age only one man who cherished Arminian views; and he was Henry Gregory, a Baptist minister of marked piety in Radnorshire. After the opening of that century some Presbyterian churches imbibed the same ideas. The great Arminian controversy, commencing about 1729, raged for many years in Wales with blighting and withering effects. However, by the close of the eighteenth century there was considerable religious tranquillity; and the various churches

of the land assumed a bright and prosperous appearance. Differences seemed to have vanished, and the various bodies laboured harmoniously together against the common enemy.[9]

Owen Jones then outlines events in early nineteenth-century Wales. These created the contemporary context of John Jones's unique contribution:

> In the beginning of the nineteenth century Wesleyanism came to Wales. John Wesley had been in the Principality many years before the beginning of this century, and had, with his praiseworthy and indefatigable efforts, established several small societies in the English-speaking districts of Glamorganshire and Pembrokeshire. But in the first years of this century a successful effort was made to establish Wesleyan Methodism in the Welsh-speaking districts. After this, great, and probably undue, prominence was given to the preaching of Arminian views; and they also caricatured some of the Calvinistic views. The consequence was that a great controversy which lasted for years was now fairly started. It prevailed in the pulpit and in the Press for the next thirty years. In addition to this there arose several important differences between the Calvinists themselves, some of them embracing narrower, others broader views. There sprang up also certain differences amongst the Calvinistic Methodists, which differences were finally settled after the meeting at Mold referred to below. In a General Assembly of delegates from North and South Wales, held at Llanidloes, in the end of July, 1840, it was agreed that the best thing that could be done was to have a special meeting of inquiry into the various rumours that were afloat about departures from orthodox doctrines, and into some charges that were made against preachers in Flintshire.[10]

Ever since his Bala sermon of 1835, John Jones increasingly became a target of suspicion. With a series of ultra-orthodox essays appearing in the *Treasury* during 1838–40, he felt his views were under attack. From his standpoint, arguing for 'limited atonement' and denying the universal sufficiency of Calvary was 'to blaspheme the atonement of Christ'.[11] Accordingly, John Jones attacked such thinking in his preaching. Even Dr Owen Thomas criticized his hero for this, describing his sermons at this period as 'one-sided'.[12] Owen Jones adds that our preacher was 'to some extent affected by this spirit of contention. And it had some deteriorating influence upon his preaching for a time'.[13]

One has to ask if even this friendly criticism is justified. To clarify the problem, it needs to be correctly identified. Indeed, what was 'one-sided' about John Jones's sermons? We are not told in specific terms. Matters become clear when we scrutinize the standpoints of both John Jones and John Elias whose views represent the polarized positions among the Calvinistic Methodists of the period. While both preachers rejected Arminianism, John Jones may be called a 'biblical Calvinist' whereas John Elias was a 'confessional Calvinist'. Whereas for the former, 'The Bible was the chief book of his life',[14] the latter was governed by an undue attachment to the objectionable phrase (limiting Christ's atoning death to the elect) 'and those only' ('a hwy yn unig') in Article 18 of the 1823 *Confession of Faith*. His extreme reaction to Robert Roberts, Rhosllannerchrugog's objection was, "I would prefer to lose my right arm than to lose these words from our Confession of Faith."[15] Such a reaction to an unscriptural, man-made phrase is appalling for a Protestant. Calvin would never say such a thing, although Beza might.[16] Well might John Jones have said concerning the universal wording of John 1: 29, 3: 16, 1 Timothy 2:6 and 1 John 2: 2, etc, 'I would prefer to lose my right arm than to lose these words from the Holy Bible'. There is a precedent for such a thought, since Dr John Davenant, one of the English delegates at the Synod of Dordt said as much.[17] This is the point. The standard

'Owenite' exegesis (as per the Puritan Dr John Owen), *effectively* eliminates such biblical statements by 'explaining them away'. For John Jones, the issue at stake was as fundamental as the Gospel itself. In his view, despite his eminence as a preacher, despite his missionary-minded opposition to hypercalvinism, John Elias's ultra-orthodox thinking was flawed. If John Jones was 'one-sided' in preaching 'polemically' and 'argumentatively'[18] as he did, he was perfectly correct in doing so. He was 'contending earnestly for the Faith once delivered to the saints' (*Jude 3*). So much head- and heart-ache would have been avoided had the Welsh Confession been modelled on the Canons of Dordt rather than the over-orthodox Westminster Confession of Faith. Even Dr D. Martyn Lloyd-Jones considered the latter to be 'too Calvinistic'.[19] He probably thought the same of the 1823 Welsh Confession (see Appendix 8).

Besides the issue of the extent of the Atonement, there were heated debates over human inability. On this issue John Elias and John Jones, Talsarn had been united before the uneasiness of 1835 exposed differences. They continued to be united against the fatalism of hypercalvinism, agreeing on the distinction between moral and natural ability. In short, they agreed that a sinner's inability to respond to the grace of God is *moral* not *natural*. In short, as with our physical skills, our basic psychological faculties still function, despite the fall. Sin has not turned us into inanimate blocks of wood or lumps of stone. Sin has corrupted not deleted our faculties. Our moral inability arises from the wicked bias of our sinful hearts. It is a case of 'will not' come to Christ, not 'can not'. Thus sinners—duly responsible before God for their actions—are rightly exhorted to repent and believe, encouraged at the same time to seek the aid of divine grace to respond to the calls of the Gospel.[20]

While most of John Jones's material is locked away in Welsh, we are indebted to John Aaron for translating an important letter from Owen Thomas's biography,[21] written just before decades of damaging debate were happily ended at the Calvinistic Methodist conference in Mold, Flintshire in March 1841 to which Owen Jones refers. It was a lengthy plea to Thomas Richard of Fishguard to attend the conference, since John Jones believed his very presence would help restrain John Elias and his ilk from imposing their oppressive opinions on others:

> You know of our brother, the Reverend Mr Elias, that he is prone to impetuosity and to extremes in almost everything he takes up; and of ★★★ and ★★★ and ★★★ that they are so extremely narrow in judgement.[22]

Bearing on the issues of hypercalvinism, this letter reveals John Jones's deeply-felt, pastorally-driven theological concerns. After complaining about an ill-digested and excessive prominence given to predestination, and a preoccupation with an over-refined orthodoxy, he exposes the causes of widespread barren evangelism:

> In a word, for some years they have been preaching in a polemic, controversial way, and not in the most appropriate way for convincing a sinner of his danger and of exhorting him to flee from the wrath to come. If the wickedness and misery of man is under consideration, the sermon tends not to stress that the fault is completely due to man, but rather shows *how it is he became* a sinner and then refers to the covenant of works. If the atonement is the subject, the tendency will be to stress the particularity of its appointments rather than the fact that it is the only refuge for life for the sinner and he be urged to flee to it; if the work of the Spirit is preached, the emphasis will not be on the encouragement to seek him and the directions given as to how to find him in the means by

which he works, but rather that everything attempted or sought
is in vain until the Spirit come; etc., etc.

John Jones believed that many of the problems he identified
were due to an over-reactionary response to Wesleyan
Arminianism in North-eastern Wales in the early 19th century
resulting in something akin to Islamic fatalism:

> Our fathers made such an attack upon Arminianism here in
> north Wales that the common people were led to harmful
> extremes on the contrary side. They are full of Antinomian
> views which have as disastrous an effect upon them as
> Mahometanism has upon the Egyptians. What is most necessary
> therefore, in my view, before such an attitude of mind and
> judgement, is to drive them out of their false hiding places,
> to tear away their excuses, and to press them in the most
> importunate way to give themselves to the Saviour.

Assured of his theological foundations, John Jones felt
liberated to preach in a 'practical' rather than a polemical
and excessively-doctrinal manner:

> We do not choose to preach practically in order to oppose
> our brethren or from a contentious spirit, but, before my Judge,
> I can testify that it is from the demands of conscience and
> from seeing the good effects produced that I have so purposed.

John Jones also believed the content of preaching has a
vital bearing on fruitfulness, that a close biblical correlation
exists between style and success:

> Know, dear brother, and I mention it with tears, that many
> of our older brethren in the ministry preach many of their
> sermons with the purpose of persuading their listeners to
> believe in things that are not necessary to salvation. It is as
> clear to me as that the sun is in the sky that they are not
> producing any good effect. In contrast, I can declare with

confidence, and prove it by many evident facts from at large, that practical, convincing and exhortative preaching has been, under the blessing and unction of the Holy Spirit, the means of returning many hundreds in Caernarvonshire this last year. It is believed that between 1800 and 2000 have been added to our churches in the area during the year, and it is acknowledged that it is the change in the style of ministry, with less topical sermons and a more practical, persuasive emphasis, that was instrumental in this. But such is the jealousy of these for preaching their own narrow views that they cannot acknowledge these conversions as being the work of God's Spirit and they then declare boldly in the Associations that they suspect the genuineness of the work. How it grates upon my ear to hear such words and in such a place, more or less blaspheming the work of God's Spirit in the souls of sinners. At Rhosllannerchrugog there was the addition of some hundreds to the church last year. It is well known that the labours of our faithful friend, Mr Robert Roberts, were the means of bringing forward this revival—his warnings and encouragements to the church to pray for revival and to maintain frequent meetings for prayer amongst themselves, pleading for a visitation from the Lord. Gradually the church was brought to a state of deep longing for such a visitation, and they did not have to wait long after that.

This lengthy letter reveals our preacher's distress and anxiety for what might happen. Hence he pleads for Thomas Richard to be present at Mold:

Your presence, even if you did not utter a word, would surely provide such a degree of restraint upon Mr Elias as to keep him in order. I have great respect for our brother Mr Morris, but I know that he will follow the stream, and if the Conference were to favour the narrower party the results would certainly be significant, not only in Flintshire but also in the other counties.

On a lighter note, John Jones's famous imagination—sixty

years before the Wright brothers achieved the first powered flight—was not deadened by his anxiety:

> Remember me kindly to Mrs Richard. I would imagine that the friends from Flintshire would send a flying machine to collect you, rather than be without you. The Lord defend you and open up your path to us.

While Thomas Richard was unable to make the long journey from Pembrokeshire to Mold, in the providence of God, John Elias was also too ill to attend the conference. In fact, it proved to be his last illness. While John Jones and his brethren deeply lamented the loss of the mighty preacher, events proved propitious for a biblically-balanced view of the Gospel. In short, the complementary twin 'Amyraldian features' of the atonement's universality and particularity were widely embraced. As we noted earlier, such an understanding found eventual confessional expression in 1874, the very year Owen Thomas's biography of John Jones, Talsarn was published.

Owen Jones concludes his account of this unhappy period:

> That meeting was held in March, 1841. The inquiry was prosecuted with caution and care. The result was that all the accusations fell to the ground; those who made them failed to substantiate a single charge. John Jones and Henry Rees were members of this committee of inquiry. John Elias was unable to attend, owing to the illness, from which in a few months he died. The result was peace.[23]

It is difficult not to conclude that the passing of John Elias was the chief cause of peace. Had he been present at Mold, one can only guess what the outcome might have been. That said, despite these doctrinal differences, a fundamental bond of affection remained between the brethren. None can doubt their total unity at the throne of grace. All these men shared a common prayerfulness, a fact illustrated by a touching incident. Owen Jones paints the poignant picture for us:

> After [John Elias's] death, [John Jones's wife Fanny] went to visit Mrs Elias in her affliction. The study was locked, and no one had ventured into it since John Elias left it. Mrs Elias unlocked the door, and they went in together with great sadness and solemnity. Mrs Elias then said, pointing to the ground, where the carpet had been quite worn out: "This is the place where he bent his knees to pray; I often came to call him to breakfast and found him on his knees. And on this very spot I frequently wiped away a flood of tears. I saw him many a time with the tears flowing in streams down his face; and from mere awe and reverence I was not able to say a word."[24]

Believing that this controversial period had an adverse impact on John Jones's preaching, Owen Jones was happy to report the return of brighter days:

> After these matters were settled his mind became at ease, and his spirit was greatly refreshed. He started off with new impulses and new ideas of consecration to the work of God. And the storm that was threatening to arise, and had partly arisen, having now abated, his mind fell back upon the Divine side of the Gospel and the glorious themes with which his soul felt so much ravished and enchanted. His preaching gained additional strength, and became more majestic.[25]

Owen Jones then provides a most dramatic account of John Jones's preaching in the Methodist Association at Llanerchymedd, Anglesey held on 13–14 June 1844.[26] To edit it would spoil it, so here it is in full:

> Mr Jones preaches at two o'clock in the afternoon, Mr Rees Phillips, Llandovery, being before him. The latter's text is: 'Remember that Jesus Christ, of the seed of David, was raised

from the dead, according to my gospel' (*2 Tim ii. 8*). But he is
not able to make any impression upon the people. The preaching
takes place in an open field, and the congregation is a very
large one. But the day is exceedingly sultry, and a heavy fog
covers all the land; and there is not a breath of air stirring.
There is felt to be a great deadness over the service. He sits
down. John Jones comes to the front, square shouldered, strongly
built, with fine face and ruddy countenance. He also feels the
heavy pall of darkness that rests upon the field. Nevertheless,
after giving out a hymn, he takes his text, 'That by two immutable
things, in which it was impossible for God to lie, we might
have a strong consolation, who have fled for refuge to lay hold
upon the hope set before us: Which hope we have as an anchor
of the soul, both sure and stedfast, and which entereth into
that within the veil' (*Heb. 6: 18–19*). His voice is very deep and
low, and the people press closer together in order to hear him.
Though the preaching has hitherto been disappointing enough,
yet they have still a hope that it may turn out better with the
great orator of Talsarn. But as he goes on this hope soon
vanishes; for it is clear that he also is affected by the heaviness
of the weather.

What can a preacher do in such circumstances, with
thousands of souls before him? Doubtless John Jones had
cried to God in the Talysarn woods days before? Would the
Holy Spirit come in power, despite the weather?

He proceeds for a quarter of an hour without fixing the
attention of any. Another quarter of an hour goes, and there
is no change. The people are beginning to get tired. Most of
them are on foot in the middle of the field, and to stand there
as a question of duty, and with no attraction of any kind, on
such a day as this, is difficult indeed. Another quarter of an
hour passes just like the rest. During this quarter of an hour
one might see a friend here and there whispering to another,
"A heavy service!" "A dead sermon!" But—stop! Did you see
that sudden move quite through the body of the preacher?
And look—the face of the multitude begins to stir, as the

yellow corn under the light breeze. What is it? What was that?
Look at the eyes of the people, how they open with one glare
towards the desk. The eye of the preacher flashes with a new
fire. He lifts up his arm, and his voice sounds triumphantly
over the field; and it mounts like a rocket till it comes to the
end of the sentence—*We have the oath still behind*—it ascends
beautifully and melodiously, and falls most sweetly upon the
ears of the multitude: "We have the oath still behind. Why did
God add His oath to His promise? Did He ever promise without
fulfilling? Was there any need of the oath to strengthen the
promise? Could the promise not stand upon its own merits?
No, indeed, there was no need; only for those terrible doubts
that rise in thy stubborn heart; and that an oath for confirmation
is to thee an end of all strife. This is our comfort and consolation
in facing a large multitude on a sultry day like this—'I have
sworn by Myself,' saith the Lord. By whom? 'By Myself.' By
one of the angels? 'No; Gabriel would have been but a moth
to swear by in the redemption of man.' By one of the hills,
then? 'No; the hills shall be removed.' By one of the mighty
mountains, then? 'No; Snowdon and Siabod ere long shall be
seen skipping like rams, and tumbling into the midst of the
sea.' By whom, then? 'By Myself.' He could find no one greater,
and then He swore by Himself."

This astonishing, anointed oratory was clearly making a
powerful impact. The Holy Spirit did come in power:

Thus he went on with rushing eloquence, till the people,
some of them, swooned before him, and many shouted till
he could not get on for the interruption. When a pause
came, he went on again, and said, "I have sworn by My
holiness. His holiness is pledged. I have sworn by My great
name. His glorious name is pledged. 'The Lord hath sworn
by His right hand.' His almighty power is pledged. Enough,
then, for ever:

"The   Lord   our   God,   with   his   right   hand
Who heaven and earth created."[27]

In repeating these two lines, his voice rends the air. In glowing colours after this he paints before the people the strength of the refuge they have [in Jesus Christ] to flee to. The effect is like the rushing of a storm. People fall down, many weep, many sob aloud, many shout, many sing. The victory is complete. The deadness of the congregation, the sultriness of the weather, and all other hindrances, have been completely overcome. And all as sudden as the fall of an avalanche, or the crash of a thunderbolt.

Notes

1   Baxter's name nowhere appears in the index of Dr Owen Thomas's *Cofiant John Jones, Talsarn*. However, several of Baxter's works were translated into Welsh, including the famous *Call to the Unconverted;* see Eifion Evans, 'Richard Baxter's Influence in Wales' in *The National Library of Wales Journal*, XXXIII. 2, Winter 2003, 149ff.

2   Ibid. 150. This might well explain why Owen Thomas did not present Baxter's views in his historical survey. His whole case would have been reinforced had he known Baxter's agreement with Amyraut whom he did cite. Of a kind Dr Thomas would have approved, Baxter's views on the atonement are clearly evident in the *Call to the Unconverted*.

3   Cited in N. H. Keeble, *Richard Baxter: Puritan Man of letters* (Oxford: Clarendon Press, 1982), 69.

4   *Great Preachers*, 491.

5   Owen Jones's note is: 'For a full account of these times, see Dr Owen Thomas's "Dadleuon Duwinyddol Cyrnru," in his *Cofiant John Jones, Talsarn*, 262–609 more especially 538–609'. This is, of course, the huge Chapter XI of Dr Thomas's *Cofiant*, translated as Owen Thomas, tr. John Aaron, *The Atonement Controversy in Welsh Theological Literature and debate, 1707–1841* (Edinburgh: The Banner of Truth Trust, 2002). Hereinafter, *Atonement Controversy*.

6   *Great Preachers*, 491–2.

7   Ibid. 492.

8   Ibid. 492–3. Owen Jones's note is: 'It is only during the last 80 years that the Church of God has become truly missionary and during this time there has been an *increase* of 200 millions over the globe'.

9   Ibid. 493.

10 Ibid. 493–4.

11 *Atonement Controversy*, 348.

12 Ibid.

13 *Great Preachers*, 494.

14 Ibid. 528.

15 *Atonement Controversy*, 324.

16 Ibid. 123.

17 With regard to the Dordt Canons' affirmation of the universal sufficiency of the

death of Christ, Davenant declared he 'would sooner cut off his hand than rescind any word of it' (see my Introduction to John Davenant, *Dissertation on the Death of Christ* (Weston Rhyn: Quinta Press, 2006), p. xiii); also Dr Owen Thomas's accurate depiction of Davenant's contribution at Dordt in *Atonement Controversy*, 124–5.

18 *Atonement Controversy*, 334.

19 See Alan C. Clifford, *My Debt to the Doctor* (Norwich: Charenton Reformed Publishing, 2009), 29.

20 *Atonement Controversy*, 338. See Appendix 3.

21 Ibid. 350–54.

22 Ibid. 350. John Aaron's note is: 'According to D. E. Jenkins, the references suppressed are to Henry Rees, John Hughes, Pontrobert, and John Jones, Tremadog. *A Review and Revision of the Biography of John Jones, Talsarn by Owen Thomas* (MA Thesis, Liverpool University, 1924), 178'.

23 *Great Preachers*, 494.

24 Ibid. 286.

25 Ibid.

26 Ibid. 494–6.

27 "Yr Arglwydd a'i ddeheulaw gref,
Hwn a wnaeth nef a daear."

PREGETHAU

Y DIWEDDAR

BARCH. JOHN JONES,

TAL-Y-SARN:

GYDA

RHAGDRAETH GAN Y GOLYGYDD.

DAN OLYGIAD

Y PARCH. GRIFFITH PARRY,

LLANRWST.

DINBYCH:

ARGRAPHWYD A CHYHOEDDWYD GAN THOMAS GEE,

MDCCCLXIX.

John Jones's Sermons

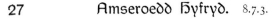

27 Amseroedd Hyfryd. 8.7.3.

52

1 TYRED, Arglwydd, â'r amseroedd
   Mae fy enaid am fwynhau—
Pur dangnefedd heb dymhestloedd,
   Cariad hyfryd a di-drai ;
Gwledd o hedd tu yma i'r bedd,
Nid oes ond Dy blant a'i medd.

2 Rho i mi arwydd cryf, disigl,
   Heb amheuaeth ynddo ddim,
Gan nad beth fo arnaf eisieu,
   Dy fod Di yn Briod im' :
Gwel'd fy rhan, ddeil i'r lan,
Yn mhob brwydr, f'enaid gwan.

3 Nid all dim o'r storom danbaid
   Nid all dim o'r gwyntoedd cry',
Guro i lawr yr enaid egwan
   Welo 'i drysor ynot Ti :
Teimlo'th hedd, gwel'd Dy wedd,
Gonera angeu tu yma i'r bedd.

4 Af ar hyd fy ffordd yn ddiddig,
   Af ar hyd fy ffordd yn hy',
Teithia'r anial mewn gorfoledd
   O hyd golwg atat Ti :
D'eiriau Di, melus cu,
Sydd yn ddigon i myfi.

5 Pan y collwyf wel'd Dy wyneb,
   Pan annghofiwyf waed Dy groes,
Dyna'n dyfod, fel y diluw,
   Dywyll, anial, ddyrys, nos :
Gradd o ffydd wed'yn sydd,
Dawel, dêg, yn dod â dydd.   W. Williams.

Beddgelert. 6.4.

29

1 DAETH ffrydiau melus iawn
    Yn llawn fel lli',
O ffrwyth yr arfaeth fawr,
    Yn awr i ni ;
Hen iachawdwriaeth glir
Aeth dros y crindir cras ;
Bendithion amod hedd—
    O ! ryfedd ras.

2 Fe gymerth Iesu pur
    Ein natur ni ;
Enillodd Ef i'w saint
    Bob braint a bri.
Gadawai'r nef o'i fodd,
    Fe gym'rodd agwedd gwas ;
Ffrwyth y cyfamod hedd—
    O ! ryfedd ras.

3 Llonyddodd Iesu'r dig,
    Do, ddig Ei Dad ;
I'r gyfraith ar y groes,
    Y rhoes fawrhâd ;
Cyhoedder drwy bob man
    O'r lydan ddaear las,
Fod Duw yn awr mewn hedd—
    O ! ryfedd ras.

4 Fe gymerth Iesu blaid
    Trueiniaid trist ;
Ysigodd ben y ddraig ;
    Ein craig yw Crist :
Cawn ninau fod yn bur,
    Uwch cur a phechod câs,
Yn berffaith ar Ei wedd—
    O ! ryfedd ras.

PEDR FARDD.

6

MESSENGER OF MERCY

Pursuing our preacher's amazing Christ-exalting, God-honoured career thus far, we have discovered—in Owen Jones's words—that 'His discourses brought the love of God, the death of Christ [and] heaven with all Its bliss and glory within the reach of every man.[1] The decade of deadening debates now passed, he was free to focus on 'the glorious themes with which his soul felt so much ravished and enchanted. His preaching gained additional strength, and became more majestic'.[2] Like a great ship on the high seas, far away from the rocks and the dangers of the coast, he could spread his sails to the wind, and steer right on'.[3] Accordingly, the 'Preacher of the People' was God's messenger of mercy to the people. Owen Jones continues the narrative for us:

> In October 1844, there was an Association held at Ffestiniog. Preaching services held in the evening of Wednesday, 2 October, and at six o'clock in the morning of the following day. The weather was not very favourable, and the services the previous evening, and the morning of this day, were held in the chapel. But it was intended, if the weather permitted, to hold the ten o'clock service out in the open field. Heavy showers put an end to these plans, so it was announced that the services would be held in the three chapels at the same time—the Independent, the Wesleyan, and the Methodist. The Revd Daniel Jones, Llanllechid, and the Revd John Jones were published to preach in the Methodist Chapel. The text of Mr Jones was: "How

excellent is Thy loving kindness, O God! therefore the children
of men put their trust under the shadow of Thy wings" (*Psalm
36: 7*). In the Welsh Bible *loving-kindness* is *trugaredd,* the English
equivalent of which is 'mercy'. The subject of the sermon was
The immeasureable value of the Mercy of God." 4

'The preacher seemed to be most self-possessed', wrote
Owen Jones, 'as if he felt within himself that morning a
flowing fountain, perennial and lasting, of ideas and thoughts,
arranging themselves readily in the most appropriate illustrations,
and the most suitable words and sentences for the occasion.
He moved on coolly, deliberately, in the first part of his
sermon, preparing the way skilfully for the thoughts which
were to follow'.5 Thus he declared:

> The Mercy of God is exceedingly happy here, inasmuch as
> she has the boundless riches of God at her command: all the
> Divine attributes, omniscience, almighty power, and all God's
> unsearchable and inexhaustible treasures. You often come in
> this world to the limits of human pity. That is strong indeed;
> yet, it soon comes to nought for want of power. What would
> the mother not have done for her child in the pains and pangs
> of death? If she could extinguish the sun to save the life of
> her child, I would not guarantee its light a moment more for
> the world. Alas, poor thing, she can do nothing but look through
> her tears at the pains and struggles of her dear child in the
> hands of death. But, as to the Mercy of God, she goeth forth
> triumphantly equipped with all the power of omnipotence to
> help her dear ones.
>   And, again, Mercy has all the watchfulness of omniscience
> to see that no wrong is ever done to the objects of her care.
> When I look at some things in my Bible, I am almost inclined
> to think that she felt jealous at times of the Justice of God,
> and that she keenly watched His movements, for fear He might
> injure some of her children. I fancy that when He started
> anywhere in the direction of this little world, she would always
> be somewhere at His heels. And often, I fancy, would she slip

before Him, and hide her dear ones from the arrows of His vengeance. One day, I see Justice preparing himself for the destruction of the old world, by bringing a deluge of desolation upon its inhabitants. But I see, at the same time, Mercy, in her beautiful robes, rushing quickly in advance, and hiding Noah and his family in the Ark. I see Justice, on another day, getting ready to start out, arming himself with fire, brimstone, and thunderbolts, in order to destroy Sodom and Gomorrah, and the cities of the plain, because of the cry of their sins and *the* iniquity of the people. 'Oh!' says Mercy, 'and I have also a few there;' and quickly she wings her flight, and saves Lot and his family. On another, greater day, Justice arrays Himself in more glory and majesty than usual. He prepares to appear on Mount Sinai. And Mercy sees Him going, and murmurs—'He is starting on a mighty errand to-day, and vengeance is in His heart.' Justice goes, but Mercy follows. 'It is my day to-day,' says Justice; 'thou must stay at home, Mercy.' 'No, no; I must come with thee,' she replies, 'for fear thou slay them all.' 'I am not going to destroy, but to proclaim my rights. Thou, Mercy, canst not say a word to-day.' Justice arrived on Sinai, and a dark cloud fell upon it; the lightning flashed, and the thunder rolled, the earth quaked, and the mountain burned with fire, and there was blackness and darkness and tempest. And the voice of the trumpet was heard exceeding loud; and Justice proclaimed the eternal law. The people were afraid, and so terrible was the sight, that Moses said, 'I exceedingly fear and quake.' Nevertheless, I see Mercy in the background; midst the blackness of the clouds, I see her fair form. She is in an expectant attitude, waiting for an opportunity to put in a single word. The eloquence of Divine Justice rushes on unbroken; she eagerly watches for a pause, that she may introduce a mere word. And while Justice at one point was just taking his breath on the mountain, the voice of Mercy was heard clear and far, saying, 'And showing mercy unto thousands of those that love Me.'

O heavenly cherub, guide me; O angel of God, lead me; Saviour of men, stand by me; O Gabriel, lend me thy genius to declare the Mercy of my God! Why? Because Mercy is my dear mother; on her care was I cast from the womb; her arms embraced me, her tender hands fondled me when I was a little babe; on her breasts I hung, and on her knees was I dandled, when I was a simple child. In the days of my youth her eyes watched over me; when the storms beat upon me, she delivered my life; through the dark and dreadful wilderness of this world, she has guided me, and taken me under the shadow of her wings. It is from her also that I expect everything in the future, from this to the end of life. And it is into her hands I wish to throw myself for eternity. Eternity! eternity! I know thee not; I understand nothing of thee as yet. A short while and I shall be one of thy inhabitants. But, whatever thou art, I shall venture into thy darkness in the arms of Mercy. And it is at her bounteous table I hope to feast for evermore. How excellent is Thy loving-kindness, O God! therefore, the children of men put their trust under the shadow of Thy wings.[6]

Often do we find in this world a rich man with a generous heart, who is ready to do everything for those he loves; ready to sacrifice the world and all its wealth and glory for the sake of his dear ones. But, so infinite and boundless is the mercy of God, that heaven itself had to part with the SON, in order that Mercy might be enabled to give peace and everlasting life to her subjects.[7]

The impact of John Jones's preaching was extraordinary, wrote Owen Jones: 'And when the preacher, with his rich volume of voice, sounded the word 'Son' in tones of most sublime pathos, the congregation responded with a sound of joy, till the preacher could not be heard for a while'.[8] Present on the occasion, the Revd Robert Parry, Ffestiniog, says, "I was on the pulpit steps, and could see everything distinctly; and in the whole of my life I never witnessed such a scene; nor do I hope to see such a sight again. When he said that heaven itself should be emptied of the only-begotten Son before anything should be wanting to ensure the salvation of the sinner, something fell that moment upon the whole congregation which is altogether indescribable. The whole multitude with the suddenness of a thunderclap gave one general cry. Their pent-up feelings burst forth—they shouted, they wept, they loudly rejoiced. And the effects of this sermon did not pass away in the chapel, but was seen for a long time afterwards. For years after many joined the churches, and they attributed the turning point in their lives to that sermon."9 Owen Jones continues with his vivid narrative:

> In the afternoon of that day Mr Jones was to preach again. And, as the weather was a little better, they were going to hold that service in the open field. Mr William Havard preached first; but before he finished the rain came again. After he sat down a man came to the front of the stage to announce that Mr John Jones would preach in the chapel, because of the rain. There were some thousands of people on the field. As soon as they heard that Mr Jones was to be in the chapel, they started off with one great rush. Eye-witnesses say they never saw anything of the kind before. One man that saw many a time the rush into the theatres, and into the great meetings held in London and other large cities, testifies that they were nothing compared with this: umbrellas thrown away, hats flying in the air, men falling down, others passing over them; in the chapel, a great hurly-burly, doors slamming, dresses rending, windows breaking, &c. Mr Jones preached here again with great unction; but, as might very naturally be expected, not with the tremendous power he had in the morning.[10]

We dare not forget that John Jones and his brethren were engaged in spiritual warfare. They did not believe that liberty in preaching was something automatic on account of their oratorical gifts. Owen Jones account provides a sobering account:

> In the year 1846 he made a journey of several weeks through Brecknock, Monmouth, Glamorgan, and Carmarthenshire. Though it appears that he did not preach with so much light and fervour as usual during this tour, yet, on more than one occasion, he had services of wonderful power; one was at

Tredegar, where the vast congregation of about 6,000 people were completely subdued by his tender pathos; another was at Merthyr Tydfil, where he preached the same sermon that he had on that great occasion at Ffestiniog. At Cardiff, it appears, the service all through was a hard one; after he sat down his friend, Revd Robert Hughes, Uwchlaw'r-ffynon, who had preached before him, said, "It was rather hard here to-night?" "Hard," was the reply, "there is a demon of hardness in this place that Mr Rees could make nothing of when he was here the beginning of summer; if any man could have overcome it he could. It is out of all reason to send a man to preach to such a place as this."[11]

While John Jones was not seemingly intimidated by 'men of learning', there's no denying that he thought his lack of formal education might prejudice some against him. Yet he handled such situations with humour. When he was preaching at Talgarth, near the Calvinistic Methodist College at Trefecca, the Principal and students came to hear him. As the great preacher from North Wales went on in his discourse, he playfully referred to his learned hearers:

If my friend and I are somewhat loose in our sermons to-night, you will pass it by, I have no doubt; if we do not keep to any rules of composition, and if we wander a little, you will know how to pardon it, I am sure. And it is my habit, sometimes, on a sudden, to pray to God in the middle of my discourse, when I feel so inclined. But my learned friends here will give me their indulgence, for I have not been trained as you are.[12]

An old man sitting near the pulpit really thought that John Jones was afraid of his learned audience, so he stood up to provide some moral support. Looking up at the preacher, he said with evident concern, "Go on," Mr. Jones, *bach;* go on; you are better than ten thousand of them, with all their learning."[13]

In the year 1847 John Jones made another preaching tour through South Wales, in the company of the Revd John Jones, Bryn'rodyn, Caernarfonshire.[14] As we've noted, travel was not convenient at that time, several years before the railway era. Our two preachers each had a horse to carry themselves and everything else they needed. Their journey started on Wednesday, 30 June 1847. The first service was held at Peniel, near Beddgelert, at two o'clock in the afternoon. Being so close to home, John Jones was disinclined to preach here. However, friends prevailed on him to do so. It was a most happy service, and was remembered by many for a long time afterward. His text was '… I know Whom I have believed and am persuaded that He is able to keep what I have committed to Him until that day' (*2 Timothy 1: 12*). At the close he said:

> We know not what is to meet us from this to the end of life's journey, but we know who is able to save. I know not what troubles and sorrows may come to my lot; I know not what their nature may be; I know not how long they may last, nor what my feelings may be when I suffer them; but I know who is able to save. I know not where I may die, whether on the lonely mountain when returning from some distant journey, or far away from home amongst strangers, or whether I shall be allowed to die in the bosom of my family, with my wife and children standing round my bed—I do not know. But I know who will abide with me when all men are leaving me, who is able 'to save them to the uttermost that come unto God by Him.[15]

There were at Peniel at that time several old men, who had turned to Christ in the revival which began at Beddgelert in 1817, and from thence spread all round. 'Their appearance in the seats just around the pulpit was very imposing', noted Owen Jones; 'They were all strong and stalwart'.[16] When

John Jones was preaching this afternoon their feelings were increasingly aroused. Before the end of the sermon they were gradually lifting up their hands until the preacher came to the end of his sentence, and then bursting out with the words, "Blessed be God !" "Amen!" "Amen!"

In the evening of this day he preached at Ffestiniog. Next day they continued through Trawsfynydd, Dolgellau, and Machynlleth to South Wales. Owen Jones continues the narrative:

> There was an Association at Carmarthen, 7–8 July this year. It was a great day in the town. Mr Jones had been preaching on the way there, and had been very successful. The people were following him from place to place in hundreds. At some chapels on the way he had spoken with overpowering effect, especially so at Cardigan. And, having heard him, or having heard of him, there were thousands of people in the Association. There were other ministers there, but no one was talked of but John Jones. Ministers from other denominations had come there in great numbers in order to hear him. Mr Jones's text was: 'For what is a man profited, if he shall gain the whole world, and lose his own soul? or what shall a man give in exchange for his soul?' (*Matt 16: 26*). His subject was—That for a man to lose his soul is the greatest loss possible. He described the worth of a human soul. In order to show this, he gave a vivid and beautiful description of the human body:[17]

The preacher then made this profound point:

> And if the dwelling in which it is to reside for a short time is so beautiful, what must the occupant be? But why do I try any more to show the worth and glory of the soul? Go to Calvary, and look at the atonement made for it by the Son of God. The loss of the soul is a great loss, because there will be only one to bear it. Very great losses happen in this world; but there is, often enough, a company of people to bear them. But oh, my soul! if thou art lost, that terrible calamity will fall

upon thine own shoulders. There will not be a single devil, or
a condemned spirit that will be ready to share the burden with
thee, for they also will be in the same woeful condition.[18]

Then he breathed a short prayer, "O Lord, show unto this
people the danger of losing their immortal souls." Going on,
he said:

> To lose the soul is a terrible loss, because it arises from neglect
> and carelessness. A woman sitting by the fire at night, with her
> little child on her knee, drops asleep; while she sleeps, the child
> falls into the fire, and receives mortal injuries. The woman
> raves and pulls her hair in her madness. Why? Because the
> child perished by her own neglect. Twenty years after she
> remembers it with a pang, and can never forgive herself. But
> what is that to this? Ow! Ow! my brethren, what a dire calamity
> to lose the soul from sheer neglect![19]

There was not a dry eye in the chapel. The entire
congregation seemed absorbed with solemn interest in one
great theme—the loss of the soul. They were all praying that
they would never meet such a terrible disaster. With a change
of tone and appearance, the solemn gloom passed from the
preacher. His face now gleamed with delight and hope. Lifting
up his voice, he declared melodiously, "There is a possibility
of saving the soul!" The people gladly responded, "Blessed
be God!" He lifted up his voice again to a higher pitch,
sounding the same sweet words, "There is a possibility of
saving the soul!" With all restraint gone, the congregation
then broke out in praise to God for His mercy and goodness.

John Jones preached the same sermon at Aberdyfi on his
return. Here he made use of another illustration:

> The mother is gone out of the house, leaving her little
> daughter there; while she is absent, the house takes fire, and
> the little girl is burnt to death. The mother returns and finds

the house on fire, and her daughter dead. She exclaims, "Oh, that I had taken her out with me! Oh, that I had left her under the care of my neighbours! Oh, that I had not neglected my dear child!" Then he said, "What is the loss of a house or a child to the loss of an immortal soul![20]

While he spoke in this manner, a woman who had lately met with an similar accident gave out a sudden cry of despair. The voice of the preacher and the wail of the woman together, had a strange effect upon the people. Many sobbed and wept.

On Sunday 18 July, the second after the Methodist Association, John Jones preached again at Carmarthen. His travelling companion records that he never in his life witnessed anything so overwhelming as the effects of his sermon on the parable of the ten virgins:

> And at midnight there was a cry made. Yes, the intellect of the man that day will utter a 'cry,' his consciousness of danger will utter a 'cry,' the coming of the Doctor into the house will utter a 'cry,' his awakened conscience will utter a 'cry.' The Judge Himself will utter a 'cry.'"

While Mr Jones made these remarks a solemnity and dread came over the people, till the chapel was full of sobbing, sighing, and weeping. But when the climax of dread had been reached, with great beauty of utterance he said:

> My friends, the hand that was pierced is here to-night, offering unto you the wedding-ring; Christ is willing to be yours in that day if you receive Him now.[21]

'After the sermon was over', continues Owen Jones, 'the two preachers went to stay for the night to the house of a certain Mr Harris. While they were at the table, they heard great sobbing and weeping in one of the rooms overhead. When they inquired what it was, Mrs Harris said that their servants, after coming from chapel, had forgotten everything, and had gone upstairs to weep'.[22]

John Jones made several preaching tours in the following year, 1848. He preached at the Bala Association. His text was the same as at Carmarthen: "For what is a man profited, if he shall gain the whole world, and lose his own soul? or what shall a man give in exchange for his soul?" (*Matt 16: 26*). He preached the same sermon with extraordinary power 'until the minds of all that were on the Green that morning were intent upon one thing—the loss of the soul, and the way of salvation through Christ'.[23]

Our 'messenger of mercy' consecrated all the powers of his soul for the Gospel of Christ. Preaching absorbed all the energies of his life. To perfect himself in this great work he spared no efforts. Monday he generally spent to review the work of the Sunday. He carefully went over the sermons he preached, and observed where they were deficient, or where his delivery was not what it ought to be. Thus he improved himself from time to time, until gradually he became the most efficient and most popular preacher of the age in Wales. The epithet is applied to him to this day, "The preacher of the people." And no one since his time has arrived at anything like his popularity. We can form an idea of what it may have been, when we consider that if he went on a journey to the populous mining districts of South Wales, as soon as they heard of his approach, the people would flock to the doors of their houses in hundreds; the workmen would for the time leave their work, and the women, with babies on their arms, and the little children, would stand on the sides of the streets to watch the great orator of Talsarn passing; just as they would have done if a king or a queen had gone that way.[24]

Notes

1   *Great Preachers*, 486.
2   Ibid. 494.
3   Ibid. 491.
4   Ibid. 498.
5   Ibid.
6   Owen Jones's note is: 'This part of the sermon was supplied by the Rev. James Jarrett, Plymouth, Pa., U.S. America; the rest is a free translation from "Biography of J. Jones" by Dr O. Thomas, Liverpool' (*Great Preachers*, 500).
7   *Great Preachers*, 501.
8   Ibid.
9   Ibid.
10 Ibid. 501–2.
11 Ibid. 502.
12 Ibid. 503.
13 Ibid.
14 Owen Jones's note is: 'Mr Jones has written some account of this tour through South Wales, from which we take the following facts. See Dr Thomas's Biography of John Jones," pp. 653–658', Ibid. 503.
15 *Great Preachers*, 503–4.
16 Ibid. 504.
17 Ibid.
18 Ibid. 505.
19 Ibid.
20 Ibid. 506.
21 Ibid.
22 Ibid.
23 Owen Jones's note is: 'This very sermon, the Saturday before, he had preached at Liverpool, but with no power at all' (ibid, 507).
24 *Great Preachers*, 532.

33   **Glasfryn.**   8.7. D.

64

1 DYMA babell y cyfarfod,
   Dyma gymod yn y gwaed ;
Dyma noddfa i lofruddion,
   Dyma i gleifion feddyg rhad ;
Dyma fan yn ymyl Duwdod
   I bechadur wneud ei nyth,
A chyfiawnder pur y nefoedd
   Yn siriol wenu arno byth.

2 Ffordd a drefnwyd cyn bod amser
   I gael diangfa o ddrygau'r ddraig :
Mewn addewid gynt yn Eden,
   Fe gyhoeddwyd Hâd y wraig ;

Ffordd i gyfiawnhau'r annuwiol,
   Ffordd i godi'r marw'n fyw ;
Ffordd gyfreithlawn i droseddwr
   I hedd a ffafr gyda Duw.

3 O ! ddyfnderoedd iachawdwriaeth !
   Dirgelwch mawr duwioldeb yw,
Duw y duwiau wedi ymddangos
   Yn nghnawd a natur dynolryw !
Dyma'r person a ddioddefodd
   Yn ein lle ddigofaint llawn,
Nes i gyfiawnder waeddi " Gollwng
   Ef yn rhydd, Mi gefais iawn."
                        ANNE GRIFFITHS.

2   Jiwbili.   M.B.

3

1 TOSTURI dwyfol fawr
   At lwch y llawr sy'n bod,
Pan gymerth Duw achubiaeth dyn,
   A'i glymu'n un â'i glod.

2 Pan ddaeth y Mab o'i fodd
   I farw yn ein lle,
Agorodd ffordd i'n dwyn at Dduw;
   Ein Ceidwad yw Efe.

3 Mae Iesu'n fawr ei fri,
   A'i glod yn llenwi'r nef;
A holl hyfrydwch pur y plant
   Yw ei ogoniant Ef.

                 EDMUND PRYS.

4

1 CYDUNED Seion lân,
   Mewn cân bereiddia'i blâs,
O fawl am drugareddau'r Iôn,
   Ei roddion Ef a'i ras.

2 P'le gwelir cariad fel
   Ei ryfedd gariad Ef?

P'le bu cyffelyb iddo erioed?
   Rhyfeddod nef y nef!

3 Fe'n carodd cyn ein bod,
   A'i briod Fab a roes,
Yn ol amodau hen y llw,
   I farw ar y groes.

4 Gwnaeth Iesu berffaith iawn
   Brydnawn ar Galfari;
Yn ei gyflawnder pur di-lyth
   Mae noddfa byth i ni.

5 Anfeidrol ydyw gwerth,
   A rhin ei aberth mawr,
I achub rhyw aneirif lu
   O deulu gwael y llawr.

6 Y rhai yn berffaith lân,
   A beraidd gân i gyd,
I'r bendigedig unig Oen,
   Yn iach o boen y byd.

         PARCH. JAMES HUGHES.

7
THE CONQUERING CHRIST

On New Year's day, 1849, John Jones began a preaching tour through parts of East Merionethshire and Montgomeryshire. Having been absent from the region for many years, the people looked forward to his coming with great enthusiasm and expectation. Hearing him several times during this tour, Dr Owen Thomas said he preached consistently with immense power. Many were converted, backsliders were restored and others were confirmed in their faith and obedience. Consistent with our preacher's desire to combat antinomianism, his aim was twofold: first, to magnify our Saviour's mercy, and second, to press upon believers His kingly claims. In short, Jesus was to be owned as Saviour *and* Lord. In no way was grace to be used as an excuse for disobedience (see Romans 6: 1).

There was a Monthly Presbytery Meeting planned at Caersws, 11–12 January and John Jones arrived there in time to preach on the first evening. His text then was 'For who hath despised the day of small things?' (*Zech. 4: 10*). The Holy Spirit's power being evident, the overwhelmed congregation was reduced to tears. At 2 pm the following day he preached again.[1] His text was 'Why stand ye here all the day idle?' (*Matt. 20: 6*). After explaining the meaning of the parable, and the connections of the text, he applied the words to his hearers in their relation to Christ. He spoke there as a servant pleading for his Master, who had sent him for the purpose of hiring labourers:

I have come here to-day for my great Master, in order to hire you for His service. Why stand ye here all the day idle? 1. Why? Have you anything against the Master?

Then with astonishing eloquence he exhibited the glory of his Master, and contrasted Him with the master of the ungodly, the devil:

2. Why stand ye here idle? Have you anything against the work required of you?

Then he showed how easy, how reasonable, and how glorious the service of Christ was, and on the other hand how wretched and miserable the service of sin:

3. Why stand ye here idle? Have you anything against the pay? On the one side you have life eternal, and on the other, the wages of sin is death, eternal death. Jesus Christ pays well in this world; if there were no world beyond, it would be worth while serving Him for the sake of the happiness to be enjoyed in this world.

4. Why stand ye here all the day idle? Have you any complaint against His other servants?

He then described the noble qualities of the old servants of Christ, from antediluvian times up to the present: how they were the salt of the earth, and the light of the world; how they were men of whom the world was not worthy; while, on the other hand, the servants of Satan were serpents, the generation of vipers, and full of the deceivableness of unrighteousness:

5. Why stand ye here all the day idle ? Have you anything against the table prepared for you in His service?

He then described the glorious repasts to be enjoyed in

the house of Christ: how sumptuously they fare upon the fat things, upon the wine well-refined; how the servants of Christ are satisfied with marrow and fatness; how upon the table in the house of Christ lie in abundance the hidden manna, the fruit of the Tree of Life, and the grapes of Canaan. He contrasted this sumptuous fare with the meagre table prepared by the devil for his servants; ashes, grapes of gall, and the apples of Sodom. After going on in this manner for a while, with sweet voice and beautiful expressions, and after bringing the congregation into a most happy state, the people hanging on every word, he continued:

Now, I have laid the claims of the two Masters before you in as fair a way as I possibly could. I am sure I have given the devil fair play; but I question very much whether I have done justice to Jesus Christ. Now, I am going to give you the question, Which will you have? We can do nothing better now than divide the house, that we may see who is on the one side, and who on the other. And in order that no one may have any reason to say that we did not give the devil every fair play, I shall be happy to put his case first before you; and now be you, his servants, ready to answer for him.

O Beelzebub, the prince of darkness, the Arch-enemy of God, the great leader of the troops of hell, we are happy here to-day to acknowledge thy power; thy service is dear unto us, and from our hearts we wish thee to live for aye, and to rule over us evermore, and to sway thy sceptre to the farthest bounds of creation! Now out with your 'Amen'.

But no one answered a word:

Where is your 'Amen'? How is it you are so silent? I give you another chance. 'O noblest Satan, Hell's Imperator, the mighty commander of the devils of Gehenna, who didst not shrink when the thunderbolts of God Almighty fell around thee fast, who didst defy the Omnipotent to arms, and succeed so far as to scatter misery and woe over some of the happiest parts of his realms! We love to follow thee, we delight in thy leadership, and we pledge ourselves to be ever faithful to thy banner. Live and rule over us for ever and ever.' Now, then, for your 'Amens'.

Not a lip was opened, not a word was uttered. In the silence, the preacher paused for a moment, and said:

Are there not any of the devil's servants present here to-day? If there are, you are not going to deny him, are you? Where are you who called upon him so lustily and bravely in the fair the other day? I am going to make you one other offer. Now then, or never. Stand up boldly for your master. 'Blessed be thy name Prince of Gehenna, the mighty king of the infernal regions, and the emperor over the abyss of hell; thou who foundest thy kingdom upon tyranny and oppression, who wieldest thy power in deception and darkness, and who writest thy laws with the blood of thy subjects. May the crown deck thy brow, and may thy mighty kingdom be established for ever. Let God be stripped of all His rights; let His power be for ever overwhelmed; and let all dominion and power and glory be thine for evermore. And hasten thou to draw us nearer and nearer unto thee, and to make us more faithful subjects of thy glorious kingdom'. Now, then, for your 'Amen' in his behalf.

Still there was nothing but silence. Then he went on again:

Well, my friends, I do not think the devil himself can complain of unfairness to-day. I have given his adherents every advantage; and if there had been any here, I fancy they would have stood up bravely for him ere now. A happy meeting this! Here we are, all of us present, the servants of Jesus Christ; at least, if there are any of the devil's subjects here they are ashamed to own him. But let us see, on the other hand, how many there are for Jesus Christ. Let us see if they are ashamed to own Him. Where are you his old servants in Montgomeryshire here? Some of you have been in His service for many years;

and you know full well by this what kind of Master He is. Let us hear, then, what you think of Him. Now is the time!

Then John Jones interjected a prayer, of the kind that often punctuated his impassioned preaching:

O blessed Jesus, who gayest Thyself for us, and who hast redeemed us with Thy precious blood; and who, of Thine infinite grace, hast delivered us from the thraldom of sin and the hard service of Satan; and who hast received us into Thine own easy and happy service, and to Thine own house. We bless Thy name for Thy loving-kindness towards us; and we are ready to serve Thee evermore; and we wish no better heaven than to be for ever in Thy presence, and to cast our crowns down at Thy feet.

With the last words from the lips of the preacher, the responding 'Amens' of the people filled the house. Continuing fervently, he said:

Yes, truly, I am glad to hear that 'Amen'. I recognize it as the old Amen, which I used to hear in Montgomeryshire twenty-four years ago. And it proves to me that the old servants of Jesus Christ here are still many, and that they are ready to praise Him and to own Him. Let us see again if there are any to-day that are for giving themselves afresh to His service.

Then another prayer:

O mighty Jesus, the Son of God, the Redeemer of mankind, who hast been anointed from eternity to be King over us; we are sorry from our hearts that we have, lived for so long a time without giving ourselves to Thee. But now, we come as we are. Receive us, dear Jesus, and deliver us through Thy blood, and take us to serve Thee and to live for Thy glory for evermore. Mayest Thou live for aye as our King, and may everlasting crowns be on Thy head. Amen!

The 'Amens' gladly responded again in all directions. "Yes," said the preacher, "there it is again. Let us make one other offer, that we may see how many of you are ready to give Him your whole heart." Having served and honoured his Master so gloriously, the preacher brought his hearers to a place of happy consecration:

> O dearest Jesus, who hast remembered us in our low estate, who, though Thou wert rich, becamest for our sakes poor, who didst bear our sins in Thine own body on the tree, take the rule over us; sit as everlasting King over our hearts. May Thy kingdom have no end, and may it reach the uttermost bounds of creation. Blessing and glory and wisdom and honour and power be for ever Thine, Amen!

The 'Amen' which followed this from the congregation was as full and sudden as a clap of thunder. It seemed that all took part in it.

The Caersws sermon is certainly one of the most dramatic examples of John Jones's sanctified pulpit power, if not the greatest. Tempered always with the compassion of Christ, our preacher was an absolute master of 'aggressive evangelism'. Indeed, says Owen Jones, 'His thoughts were arrayed in his mind like regiments of soldiers; and he had only to send them one after another to the attack'.[2] Furthermore, it was always clear that the preacher was not at the limit of his resources. One always felt an infinite possibility of more. There was no effort, and it seemed all so easy. Every man ought always to have plenty of reserve force whatever he is doing. It is an essential condition of success. When John Jones, Talsarn, was in the pulpit the distant tramp of the army of the reserve could ever be heard. There was a colossal presence and a permanent possibility of more. And he almost always succeeded. And that success was often overwhelming.

John Jones was preaching one Sunday at Holywell, Flintshire. For the afternoon service he had to go to a small chapel a few miles in the country. A student[3] who was then just starting his career as a minister accompanied him, and as they walked together they talked of preaching and the work of a preacher; and inasmuch as Mr Jones understood that the young man was beginning to preach, he gave him some valuable advice in that direction. He advised him to read well, and to endeavour to obtain thorough possession of whatever he read—to think his sermon out, and have a clear perception of it. He then said:

> When you enter the pulpit, be thoroughly self-possessed; and whatever you do, be sure to have six or seven bombs in every sermon, and after you have had them, take them with you into the pulpit. Then begin quietly and calmly, and pave the way slowly and gradually for the firing of your first shell. When the time comes, off with it. Mark the effect; it may be *nil*. However, be not in any way dismayed, and do not for a moment let the people think you are. As before, prepare the way silently for the second, and when you think the time has come apply the match. It is quite possible that this, again, will be a dead one. Nevertheless, be you as cool and unconcerned as possible about the effect, and let not the people in any way think that you are disappointed. Prepare the way again for the third, and fire. This may glance off like the others, doing no execution at all. Never mind; fire the fourth, and you may be perfectly sure that if you have six or seven, some of them will at last batter the walls.[4]

This advice, which he gave to Mr Cynhafal Jones, he followed unerringly himself; and the castles and the strongholds, before the close of the service, fell down before him in all directions.

Every time he ascended the pulpit, our preacher possessed an awesome sense of Christ, his 'Commander-in-Chief'. He

felt the enormous privilege and responsibility of being in
His Royal service. Indeed, no one had a more exalted view
of the glory and grace of our Lord Jesus Christ than John
Jones, Talsarn. For those who carelessly and foolishly made
light of the Gospel, he would remind them forcibly of Christ's
second as well as His first coming. Indeed, the backdrop of
the judgement to come made the ultimate sense of our
preacher's fervent evangelism from the beginning. In one of
his early sermons, which his brother David Jones called the
most powerful of all he ever heard from him, he said:

> We may well picture before our minds the state of things at
> the coming of the flood. Just as it begins to appear, a man runs
> to one of the cities, with fear and dread impressed upon his
> countenance, saying that one of the fountains of the great deep
> had opened in such and such a place, and that the water was
> shooting upwards with tremendous force. Another immediately
> follows, and says that one of the windows of heaven had opened
> in such and such a spot, and that the rain was coming down
> as one mighty river, sweeping everything before it. Just like
> one of those men have I come here to-day, a lad from the foot
> of Snowdon, to tell you that there is another deluge coming
> upon this world—a deluge of fire—and if you know of any
> place to flee to, flee; to tell you that there is a storm of hail,
> fire and brimstone gathering in the distance against the ungodly,
> and if you know of any place to flee to, flee; to tell you that
> God is whetting his sword and preparing His arrows against
> the wicked, and if you know of any place to flee to, flee![5]

After he had gone on for some time in this way, a man in
great anxiety shouted out from the congregation, "Tell us at
last where to flee to!" Then followed another glorious invitation
to take refuge in Christ.

On another occasion he varied the description thus. His
text was: 'Who hath warned you to flee from the wrath to

come?' (*Matt. 3: 8*). He described the state of things at the coming of the flood, and said:

A boy ran to the house and told his father and mother, 'Indeed, the deluge is coming, as Noah said; I saw the surge and foam of its waves breaking over the crest of the hill, far away. Let us flee for our lives!' Just so have I come to you, a neighbour of yours, and a friend well known; for I have seen the deluge of the wrath of God coming upon the world, and I am here to warn you in time. A boy on the streets of Sodom ran wildly for his father's house, saying, 'The shower of fire is come, for a spark fell at my side, until my clothes nearly caught fire. Is there any way of escape?' Though the warning came to Sodom, it was too late. But I have come here in behalf of my God to apprise you of it in time. I have seen the shower of brimstone, a live spark of it fell upon my guilty conscience, until I became almost all aflame. But I know to-day of a place of refuge, and there is time for you to flee there too. O Lord my God, may this people flee to Thee! Let us flee to Calvary— 'And a man shall be as an hiding place from the wind, and a covert from the tempest; as rivers of water in a dry place, as the shadow of a great rock in a weary land' [*Isa. 32: 2*].

Another time, John Jones reminded his hearers of the glory and majesty of the Judge of all mankind:

Imagine not, my friends, it was because of want of glory in Himself he fled before Herod. No; there was such a wealth of glory in him then as would have caused all the Roman governors of the time to pay Him the most humble homage; as would have cast that proud Herod down before Him to lick the very dust of His feet. Only it was not revealed. A glimpse of it appeared now and again. The veil moved a little when He was in the garden of Gethsemane, when those who had come to take Him went backward, and fell to the ground. But when He shall come to be glorified in His saints, and to be admired in all them that believe in that day, the heavenly windows of His Divine nature will be opened, and the deep fountains of

His attributes will be broken up, and such a flood of glory will come from Him as to deluge the universe with everlasting revelations of His person.

Not only did John Jones rejoice in the privilege of serving the King of kings and Lord of lords. He also rejoiced in the present *and* future fellowship of his fellow-servants. When speaking of preaching, he said:

There is no occupation in the world so delightful as preaching Jesus Christ the Saviour of sinners, and the ideal of human life for those who believe in Him. Old John Brown, of Haddington, used to say that he would be willing to beg his bread from door to door all the week long, in order to have the privilege of preaching Jesus Christ on the Sunday. And, indeed, I should be willing to do the same thing. My delight is often so great in the work that I do not know at all how I can be happy in heaven without preaching. But there is no need of anxiety. As for myself, I believe there will be a great deal of preaching in heaven. Oh! we shall have Associations without number there, far superior to any we enjoyed on earth. Enoch, the seventh from Adam, the first preacher we ever heard of, will be there; Isaiah, the greatest of the Old Testament prophets; Paul, the greatest of the apostles; Augustine, the grandest of the Fathers; Martin Luther, the mightiest of the Reformers; George Whitefield; Daniel Rowland; John Elias, and others;—they will all be there, and in a state of higher inspiration and ecstasy than ever they experienced here. And they will declare the wonders of grace, and praise the great Atonement of Christ. And I also hope to try what I can do there. Blessed be His name, however, because the work has been entrusted to me while here, and because of the pleasure I feel in performing it.[6]

Notes

1   For this extended extract, see *Great Preachers*, 507–11.
2   Ibid. 534.

3   Owen Jones identifies him as 'The Revd N. Cynhafal Jones, eminent minister
    of the Welsh Calvinistic Methodist Church at Llanidloes, Montgomeryshire'
    (ibid. 534).
4   Ibid. 535.
5   Ibid. 525.
6   Ibid. 531–2.

Pregethwr y Bobl,

NEU

FYFYRDODAU A ACHLYSURWYD

GAN FARWOLAETH

Y PARCH. JOHN JONES,

TAL-Y-SARN.

GAN GLAN ALUN.

Awdwr " Fy Chwaer," &c.

" YR YDOEDD GWR WEDI EI ANFON ODDI WRTH DDUW, A'I ENW IOAN."

WYDDGRUG:

ARGRAFFWYD GAN HUGH JONES.

—

1858.

Preacher of the People

122

31   **Miriam.**   8.7. D.

59

1 MARCHOG, Iesu, yn llwyddianus,
   Gwisg Dy gleddyf ar Dy glun ;
Ni all daear Dy wrthsefyll,
   Chwaith nac uffern fawr ei hun ;
Mae Dy enw mor ardderchog,
   Pob rhyw elyn gilia draw :
Mae Dy arswyd trwy'r greadigaeth
   Pan y byddost Ti ger llaw.

2 Tyn fy enaid o'i gaethiwed,
   Gwawried bellach foreu ddydd ;
Rhwyga'n chwilfriw ddorau Babel,
   Tyn y barau heiyrn yn rhydd ;
Gwthied caethion yn finteioedd
   Allan, megis tonau llif,
Torf a thorf, dan orfoleddu,
   Heb na diwedd fyth na rhif.

               W. WILLIAMS.

60

1 BABEL gwympa, er ei chryfed,
   Dagon syrth, er maint ei barch ;
Nid oes elyn ddichon sefyll
   O flaen Iôr a'i gadarn arch :
Hollalluog yw Duw Israel,
   Arglwydd lluoedd llawr a nen ;
Caerau Jericho a syrthiant
   Pan ddaw'r seithfed tro i ben.

2 Clywir swn yn mrig y morwydd,
   Deulu Seion, ymgryfhewch ;
Wele'r wawr yn dechreu codi ;
   Haleliwia, llawenhewch ;
Fe udgenir trwy'r holl ddaear
   Udgorn mawr efengyl hedd ;
"Syrthiodd Babel, syrthiodd Babel,
   Mwy nis gwelir ond ei bedd."

              DAVID HUMPHREYS.

29   Pen-yr-yrfa.   8.7.4.

55

1 WELE 'n sefyll rhwng y myrtwydd
   Wrthrych teilwng o fy mryd :
Er o'r braidd yr wy'n adnabod
Ei fod uwchlaw gwrthrychau'r byd :
   Henffych foreu
   Caf Ei weled heb un llen.

2 Rhosyn Saron yw Ei enw,
   Gwyn a gwridog, hardd Ei bryd ;
Ar ddeng mil y mae'n rhagori
O wrthrychau pena'r byd :
   Ffrynd pechadur,
   Dyma'r Llywydd ar y môr.

3 Beth sydd i mi mwy a wnelwyf
   Ag eilunod gwael y llawr?
Tystio'r wyf nad yw eu cwmni
I'w gymharu â'm Iesu mawr ;
   O ! am aros
   Yn Ei gariad ddyddiau f'oes.

ANNE GRIFFITHS.

56

1 I GALFARIA trof fy wyneb—
   Ar Galfaria gwŷn fy myd !
Y mae gras ac anfarwoldeb
   Yn dyferu drosto i gyd ;
   Pen Calfaria !
   Yno, f'enaid, gwna dy nyth.

2 Yno clywaf gyda'r awel
   Gerddi'r nef yn dod i lawr,
Ddysgwyd wrth afonydd Babel
   Gynt yn ngwlad y cystudd mawr ;
   Pen Calfaria,
   Gydia'r ddaear wrth y nef.

3 Dringo'r mynydd ar fy ngliniau
   Geisiaf, heb ddiffygio byth ;
Tremiaf, trwy gawodydd dagrau,
   Ar y groes yn union syth :
   Pen Calfaria,
   Dry fy nagrau'n ffrwd o hedd.

DYFED.

8
AT HEAVEN'S GATE

If we continued the account of John Jones's life for the next seven years, it would be very similar to what has gone before. His latter years were, however, characterized, if possible, by even greater consecration. Life was now drawing to its close; the other world seemed to him approaching nearer and nearer; and the solemnity of immortality and eternity appeared to engage and absorb his mind. John Jones often expressed profound thoughts on time and eternity. Preaching at Abergele, he compared 'time' to 'a small cloud, appearing for a season in the clear, dazzling sky of eternity, raining down for a while the purposes of the Most High, and then vanishing'.[1]

There is a remarkable anecdote about this sermon related years later by T. C. Williams in his biography of the preacher's son David Lloyd Jones:

> A lady living on the shores of the Menai—herself the daughter of one of our foremost ministers, and the widow of one of the most prominent elders of the Connexion—told me lately of a Sunday she spent many years ago at Abergele when Mr Jones, Talysarn, preached there. His sermon on the Sunday evening had been extraordinarily powerful. Its subject was 'Redeeming the Time' [Ephesians 5: 16], and it is included among his published sermons.[2] No one who heard it could forget the sublime flight of oratory in which Time was pictured as 'a small cloud rising in the clear sky of Eternity, to pour down the high purposes of the Almighty, and then vanish for

ever'. The power of his eloquence was irresistible, and it left
a lasting impression on the minds of the hearers. On returning
to the house, he was genial and happy, as was usually the case
with him after he had finished his Sunday's work. He went
into the kitchen to sit by the fire; and he was soon followed
by all who were in the house,—host, hostess, children, visitors,
and servants,—for every one seemed to feel his spell. That
night he gave an account of a journey he had made through
South Wales, and spoke of a hymn he had then heard for the
first time, from an old woman who repeated it with great
fervour and under great excitement. The voice of the great
preacher, as he related the incident, was indescribable; it sounded
like a great organ under the hand of a master. As he dwelt on
the story and repeated the hymn again, tears came into the
eyes of the listeners, and one old maidservant, who had remained
out of sight in a corner of the room, at last could restrain
herself no longer. She sprang into the middle of the room, and
went on to utter her praise and joy with such fervour that the
house soon rang with her voice; and the effect of the story
and the hymn by the fireside was greater even than that of the
sermon in the chapel.[3]

A new chapel was built at Talysarn in 1852. When he was
at home, he preached there always on Saturday night, and
three times on the Sunday; and during the week he went to
places in Caernarfonshire to hold services. The years 1853,
1854 were years of incessant labour in preaching the Gospel.
In 1855 his health was slightly beginning to give way. For a
great part of the year he remained at home, preaching regularly
on the Sundays, and going to hold meetings to places not
far distant. Towards the end of summer he went to South
Wales for another preaching tour. The year 1856 came, and,
though his health was not as strong as usual, yet his labours
were exceedingly great. He wished, it would appear, to wear
himself out in the service of his Lord. In the first month of
that year he went to Liverpool for two Sundays, where he

preached three times each Sunday, and on some of the
intervening nights. He left Liverpool for a meeting at Mold.
The months of February and March were again full of work.
In the month of March we find him in London, preaching
in the anniversary meetings at Easter. He seemed as vigorous
as ever, and his power was at times overwhelming. On Good
Friday, at Jewin Crescent Chapel, he preached on the words
'Of whom the whole family in heaven and earth is named'
(*Eph. 3: 15*). The people were bathed in tears. The woman
that was accustomed to clean the chapel said, "There will be
no need of *watering* the chapel after that sermon."

As was true of other Welsh preachers such as Robert
Roberts, Clynnog, Daniel Jones, Llanllechid and Thomas
John, Cilgeran, John Jones also felt his mind strongly attracted
by the vastness, the sublimity and the solemnity of time,
death, and eternity; some of his happiest sermons were on
these or cognate topics. The Sunday after the Friday mentioned
above he preached again in the evening at Jewin Crescent,
upon the words, 'Lift up your eyes to the heavens, and look
upon the earth beneath: for the heavens shall vanish away
like smoke, and the earth shall wax old like a garment, and
they that dwell therein shall die in like manner but My
salvation shall be for ever, and My righteousness shall not
be abolished' (*Isa. 51: 6*).

The preacher expanded upon this noble theme with flowing
ideas, beautiful rhythm of words, and with a most attractive
manner, voice, and intonation. The people could be seen
rising up one after another as the orator from Talysarn went
on, as if they wanted to get closer to him, and even possess
him, until for the last half-hour there was hardly a man sitting:

The heavens shall vanish away like smoke,' as sudden, possibly,
as smoke. If you were five or six miles away from London here,
on a clear spring morning, looking upon the dense column

of smoke resting upon the city, and reaching up to the sky, you might fancy, by its appearance, that it was a mighty mountain standing upon its sure foundations, and going to remain there to the end of the world. But, something draws your attention just for a moment—the lamb bleating on the slope of the hill, and the dam responding from the valley; the lark soaring on high, and singing his song of praise for God's care of him that morning; the little primroses just appearing, and the flowers just opening, and nature all around declaring the glory of the Creator. These catch your eye for an instant, and you look again at the dense column of smoke. It is gone! A breath of wind came and blew it away, leaving not a trace behind. It will be just so at the end of this world. When the voice of the archangel shall wake thee from the grave, and when thou lookest up to see whence the shout came, the heavens will shine as ever they did thousands of years before; the sun will burn as brightly as on the morning Jonah fainted under its beams, and Noah came out of the ark. But, possibly, the convulsions around thee—graves opening, rocks rending, creation dissolving—will draw thy attention for a moment; and looking up to heaven again, it will have vanished away like smoke, to give place to the immediate presence of infinite and eternal God. But, be it so; we know of something that will still endure. When this sun is gone, [Christ] the Sun of righteousness will shine as brightly, and pour forth its powerful beams as ever it did of yore. Then the rocks of earth shall melt with fervent heat, the Rock of Ages will then stand immovable and unchangeable in the solemn stillness of eternity. When the noble oak and the mighty cedar trees shall dissolve by the heat of that dreadful day, the Tree of Life will then be fresh as ever; its leaves as green; its fruit as sweet; and its delightful shade as sure and pleasant as ever before. 'My salvation shall be for ever, and My righteousness shall not be abolished'.

'And they that dwell therein shall die in like manner.' Put man wherever you will, he is sure to die. Though he be a mighty emperor,[4] ruling eighty millions of men, with hundreds of thousands of warriors at his call, ready to do his will, he will yet die like a fool, and you know not how soon. And so it is with the best of this world. 'Your fathers, where are they? And the prophets, do they live for ever?' I delight myself at times in painting in my fancy the old Associations on the Green at Bala, when I used to go there (as) a boy from Dolwyddelen. I picture before me the Green, the big waggon in the centre, containing the pulpit, and the other vehicles right and left. I see the old preachers rising one after another; I listen to them reading their texts; I hear them preaching their sermons; I behold their great fervour and enthusiasm; and I hear from the crowd the warm 'Amens' and 'Hallelujahs'; and I feel my soul refreshed every time after revolving those meetings over again in my imagination. But when I look for my old friends—they are gone! Nevertheless, we have others in their stead—as good as they, perhaps. But if the old preachers are gone, the Gospel is the same; God's salvation is ever with us, and shall be with us, and with our children, and our children's children, to the end of the world: 'My salvation shall be for ever, and my righteousness shall not be abolished.' And there are other preachers coming; upon the forehead of the age to come other spirits stand, burning with holy fire, angelic, seraphic. Here they are immediately behind us; they are pressing on just at our heels! Hear you not the tramp of their feet, and the sound of their voices? We also hasten away to give place to them. 'And they that dwell therein shall die.' But 'My salvation shall be for ever, and my righteousness shall not be abolished.'[5]

This was his last visit to London; and evidently his preaching was exceedingly effective. There was no diminution in the power or the grandeur of the Gospel as it came from him.

An instance of the same character as the above is seen in another sermon on Eternal Life upon the text: 'Lay hold on eternal life' (1 Tim. 6: 12). He preached this in Bedford Street Chapel, Liverpool, in the year 1848, and it was taken down in shorthand at the time:[6]

Everlasting duration is something that is ours already, and this, at times, fills me with awe. I am in a sense infinite in duration; I am like the Infinite God Himself in duration In anything else I am not like unto Him: in power, wisdom, and knowledge. But as to duration, I shall live as long as Almighty God Himself. When I compare myself with the sun, in many respects I find, in a sense, that I am nothing; but as to duration, I am greater than the sun. When his day's work is done, I shall be only starting my life; when his labour shall come to an end, I shall be only Just beginning to know that I am a man. Let the little bird sing on the tree—he has no eternity before him; let the little lamb prance on the mountain side—his life is short; and let the mighty inhabitants of the deep sweep and play in the ocean—it will all be over very soon. But, O my God! have mercy upon me and my hearers—we have an eternity of duration before us ...

Whatever is the difference between this world and Heaven, I am happy to think that Heaven must come down here all the while for its inhabitants. And, indeed, Heaven all along robs this earth of its best. If there happens to be a flower more beautiful than the rest, it is immediately taken to the regions beyond. Just as you do in your Sunday schools: if a boy excels in any class, you move him up higher; so if a man is better than another in this world, he is taken up yonder at once. O! Heaven has dealt unkindly with our poor world many a time. Many a warrior excelled in the fight; but as soon as his bravery appeared, he was called to the court above. 'Of whom the world was not worthy.' How happy would I have been to stand by the side of King David, when he fought so well, and many another commander beside, that I might also wax valiant in fight. But, as soon as they became heroes, they vanished from the field! Perhaps God wishes to carry on the fight by means of very raw soldiers, that He may have all the glory. Well, let the glory be His own for ever! They have, you know, vessels of gold adorning the tables of the dukes and lords of this world; but the metal was found in a country that was very, very poor— Peru—and in the dust of that country, too. The Lord of this earth has also collected together, in the world beyond, a large number of vessels of gold, more brilliant in glory than any that are there. But the raw material was found in a very poor country, this earth and the dust of this earth; and His eye is still on the quarry waiting for more. O, our God! take us also, take us also. ('Amen, amen'.) Ah, indeed, my friends, there is no harm in that Amen, and it is no breach of good manners to utter it, in a fashionable town like Liverpool here. O Lord, let us also be among their number!

After seeing the account of the labours of this great preacher, we might be inclined to ask, "How was he paid?" It is not difficult to answer. Dr Thomas has given in his biography,[7] a few facts upon this point. The diaries of the last five years of his laborious life contain all the particulars. In these, Mr Jones kept an accurate account of the places he visited, and the sermons he preached, together with, for the last four years, the sum paid him for his service. In the year 1854, for example, be preached 324 times, and this was only one portion of the work he did. He visited Liverpool, Runcorn, Manchester, Crewe; travelled over Anglesey, Denbighshire, Flintshire, Merionethshire. The total of his receipts for that year amounted to £112, all travelling expenses to be deducted out of it. Again, in the year 1856, which was the most laborious of his ministerial life, he preached 360 times; visited Liverpool, London, travelled the counties of Anglesey, Merioneth, Denbigh, Montgomery, in addition to all the work he did near his home, Talsarn, and in Caernarfonshire. The total receipts of the year were £149 9s. (approximately £10,900 in today's money),[8] out of which he had to pay all his travelling expenses. Clearly, the income provided through Fanny's Talysarn shop was indispensable (see chapter 3). Another inescapable conclusion is also obvious: John Jones wasn't in it for the money! How different were his truly apostolic labours from the outrageously-extravagant and covetous life-style of the Roman Popes as later exposed by his son, David Lloyd Jones.[9]

After returning from London in the year 1856 he continued

again to labour with untiring zeal. He went to several Anniversary meetings; and in the month of September, he went to Anglesey on a preaching tour of twelve days. And at the end of October, he started again through Montgomeryshire; and in December of this year he was in the Quarterly Association held at Mold. In all these places he discoursed with the same unfailing power; and the congregations were greatly blessed through him.

However, soon after the Mold Association, he caught a bad cold. As he had such a strong constitution, no one thought much of it in the beginning. But it grew worse and worse. Still he preached in the first months of the year of 1857. John Jones preached his last sermon at Moriah Chapel, Caernarfon on the Lord's Day, 22 March 1857. His subject was the believer's glorious transformation at the return of the Lord Jesus (*1 Jn. 3: 2*). Owen Jones relates that John Jones 'preached with [his] usual sweetness and beauty, pleasure and satisfaction to the congregation. But it was the last time the great orator from Talysarn ascended the pulpit'.[10] His health rapidly declining, a planned visit to Manchester at Easter had to be aborted at Rhyl where he stayed for about six weeks.

Back at home and confined to his bed, he reviewed his old sermons, his son David writing them down as he spoke. In this last illness, he told Dr Thomas, when he went to see him, "You are very happy, going about the country to preach Jesus Christ. I also long for it intensely; I should be exceedingly glad to be allowed to preach again. I look over my old sermons here in bed with some pleasure, mixed with sadness though, for I often fear I shall never try them again."[11] During these final weeks of his life, besides a few hymns John Jones also composed several tunes for well-loved hymns by William Williams, Pantycelyn and others. The noble tune 'Llanllyfni' is still found in modern hymn books.

During his illness his friends sympathized with him on every hand. Many visited him, and the presbyteries and the Association sent many consolatory and sympathizing letters. In the beginning it appears that he was oppressed with the fear of death. His mind and imagination was so strong, and he had been accustomed to paint the realities of the spiritual world before his eyes so much, that now, when drawing near the borders of that strange world, he was often filled with awe. It is possible also that some of the despondency he was in might arise from the nature of his complaint. Some years before he had met with an accident by which his liver was affected, and now the injury was developing itself into a fatal disease.

One day, his wife Fanny also being ill, he sent David to ask her opinion about his personal piety. "Your mother knows more about me than any one else in the world, go and ask her what she thinks of me." He went; her reply was, "Most pious, he was a pious man before I ever knew him; and I had never any reason to doubt his piety for a single moment during his life." After David had returned with this answer, he said, "And what do you think of me?" Receiving a similar reply, he seemed quite overcome, and turned his head towards the wall to weep. He then said, "And I also think that I shall never be lost. The old covenant which I made with God many years ago at Dolwyddelen, when I gave myself to the service of God and took Him to be mine for ever, comes most forcibly to my mind."

His old friend the Revd Henry Rees wrote to him, and said:

Are you afraid of appearing in the presence of God in the next world? If so, my dear friend, I can easily sympathize with you, for I also fear and tremble when I think of it. But let me ask you one question: Have you not been many and many a time before in the presence of God? Did his presence then cause you to fear? Was your spirit then filled with awe and dread before Him? Not in any way. God in Christ was the sublimest beauty you ever beheld. The dazzling brightness of His holiness consumed nothing in you but your sin and impurity. In His presence was fulness of joy, and at His right hand were pleasures for evermore. If so, my dear friend, why need you fear His presence in the next world? He is but the same; and His presence there will have but the same effect upon your spirit.[12]

By this and other letters he was greatly comforted, and especially by the visit of his brother, the Revd David Jones. Gradually he became perfectly resigned to the will of God. The path became easier, the way became clearer, the sky became brighter, till at last there was not a cloud between him and his God. To his anxious wife Fanny he said, "Don't break your heart, my girl, you will come to heaven to me." "Oh," she said, "What breaks my heart is the fear that I won't be able to spend eternity with you. I shan't mind if my Heavenly Father leaves me behind for twenty years, as long as I can come after you then, John bach." In full assurance, the dying preacher and loving husband replied, "Oh, you will, you will. Don't let the devil pain you, Fanny bach."[13]

Thus John Jones rested his soul in deep and calm confidence upon the great truths that he had proclaimed so earnestly, powerfully and joyfully for so long. When he died at Talysarn on Sunday, 16 August 1857, he proved the blessedness of all he had preached to others. Despite advancing weakness, his spirit was filled with rapture as he was heard repeatedly to whisper, "O! Iesu annwyl! O! Iesu annwyl! O! Waredwr bendigedig!"—"O dear Jesus! O beloved Jesus! Blessed be Thy name forever!"[14] When he passed away, young David, overwhelmed with wonder and grief, went to his mother, who was then herself confined to bed, and so unable to bid her husband farewell. "Mam, mam," he cried, "y mae fy nhad newydd fynd i'r nefoedd, y mae newydd gyrraedd yno, ydi yn wir; ac y mae wedi gweld yr Iesu yr oedd yn ei garu mor fawr"[15]—"Mam, mam, father has this moment gone to heaven; he has just reached there, and he has seen Jesus whom he loved so much!"[16]

When John Jones breathed his last, it was 10 am, the time when the services generally commence in the chapels of Wales; it was then that his great soul entered upon the worship of God in another world.

With great poignancy Owen Jones wrote: 'On Friday, 21 August, the day he was buried at Llanllyfni, the shops were closed in Talysarn and all the country around; and even in Caernarfon, which is several miles away; and the work in the slate quarries was at a stand that day. And in the eyes of some, great Snowdon seemed to wear a pall ...'

Before leaving the house in Talysarn, Henry Rees spoke to the large crowd of mourners:

> It is not becoming to say much now. Silence is the most eloquent. If you desire to have a real sermon today, look at the coffin, the funeral car, and the grave, and think of your sweet-mouthed preacher, who is now silent forever. His name was well known throughout the Principality for thirty or thirty-five years, and his eloquence roused and charmed the minds of Welshmen. But today there is no John Jones, Talsarn, in Wales. Far be it from us, however, to weep for him as men which have no hope. 'For if we believe that Jesus died and rose again, even so, them also which sleep in Jesus will God bring with Him!' [17]

In the funeral procession there were eight medical men, sixty-five ministers and preachers, three abreast; seventy deacons four abreast; two hundred singers, six abreast; six thousand men and women, six abreast, trending slowly on

the road from Talysarn to Llanllyfni, singing on the way some
of the old Welsh tunes, 'Yn y dyfroedd mawr a'r tonau',
'Ymado wnaf a'r babell', the hills around and Snowdon in
the distance echoing the sound. That day and for many a day
after a great gloom rested upon Wales'. Such sadness simply
reflected the widespread hiraeth for one whose life and
labours had radiated the love of Christ.

For John Jones's widow Fanny, the immensity of her loss
was indescribable. As we have noted, her entire life had been
devoted to loving and supporting God's servant. To be sure,
what he accomplished was impossible without her. Besides
providing a fitting tribute to her husband, Fanny's biographer
writes movingly of her grief:

> The death of John Jones affected her deeply, and she was in
> the depth of the valley of sorrow, depressed and gloomy, for a
> long time after his death. A remarkable fact in her history was
> that she was far above anyone in comforting those in mourning.
> She could give a word of comfort to those who were deepest
> in the moist land of tears, but when she herself was in the
> valley, it was difficult to meet anyone more grave. In her deep
> trial at this time she received scores of letters to sympathise
> and comfort her. From among the multitude it is possible that
> one from the Morgans of Dyffryn is among the best:

> Dyffryn
> August 21, 1857
> Dear Mrs Jones,
> I received a letter from your son, containing the sad news
> of the death of your dear husband. I wasn't, since some weeks,
> daring to hope to hear anything else; yet when this heavy news
> came, the fact, after all, was incredible to me; even now I cannot
> persuade myself that the world is without John Jones, Talsarn.
> But, oh, it is so. Oh unrestorable loss! There are tens of thousands
> in Wales whose hearts are bleeding because of it, and not
> without cause. One of the chief pillars of Methodism has been
> broken; one who did more, it cannot be argued against, nor

is there anyone living now, to draw the attention of the whole Principality to the great things that 'belong to peace';[18] one who was an instrument to stir more in the minds of thousands— who ended in eternal life. 'He turned many to righteousness'.[19] But the race is over; the prize is won; the crown is worn; no more fear for eternity; the last enemy is defeated; the palm's in his hand; and a tune more sweet than he ever composed, although some of them have great charm for us, on his lips. Almost we can imagine hearing him say to those he has left behind, "Don't weep; sorrow is over, joy has come in its place." But to you he is a great loss. Wales has lost an incomparable preacher. I have lost a dear friend; but you have lost everything that everyone else has lost and much more. I don't know what to say to you. It would be easier for me to weep with you than to say something to you. It was not a small privilege to have lived with such a seraphic man; but that makes the bitterness of the loss greater for you. Further, the world cannot be but a desert for you; but you are not without the knowledge that there is One who can 'speak to content your heart' that is troubled 'in the wilderness'. You are not without knowing that you need not die of thirst in the parched land you are in, because there is a fountain of living water nearby. But you must have One to lead to it. I can only desire this for you. No one but the 'Good Physician' can put the wine and oil on the wounds. But He is One so able for that today, and the One so ready to do it, as when He did that for Mary and Martha. There is no small consolation in the little verse you taught the children before their tongues spoke clearly, 'Jesus wept'.[20]

Mrs Morgan joins with me in sympathising with you all from the heart, and in greeting you and the whole family, in the kindest way. May the 'God of the orphans and the Judge of the widows'[21] keep you from sinking and sorrow 'as those without hope'.[22] I am hindered by a misfortune that my animal suffered from coming to the funeral. It would have been very good if I had been able to come there. Although that would have been nothing, it would have been all I could have done now, for one of the most excellent men who was ever on the earth, and one of those for whom I had more respect than anyone I ever knew.

I am, dear Mrs Jones,
Yours sincerely,
Edward Morgan[23]

The cloud of gloom and grief eventually lifted from Fanny's spirit. Outliving her husband by twenty years, she spent her days in the care of others. She died at Llandinam while staying with their son David, then recently widowed after three years of marriage. About five days before she died, she was present in the Methodist 'seiat' (experience meeting). The Revd Daniel Rowland, a visiting preacher from Bangor, asked her how she was. Her response was joyful and triumphant: "Oh," she said, lifting up her hand, "I am very glad, Mr Rowland, that I have such a God to trust in—the same God I have here as I had at home—a God whose faithfulness I can trust in every place. Blessed be His name for ever! for ever!"[24] Dying on 13 August 1877, Fanny is buried beside her husband in Llanllyfni churchyard, awaiting the resurrection!

While others—such as Henry Rees—laboured on faithfully and effectively, the loss of John Jones, Talsarn was incalculable. People throughout Wales and beyond were shocked and overwhelmed with grief, as two remarkable elegies indicate.[25] The first of seventy-seven stanzas in four parts, W. Ambrose's opening verse indicates the sense of national loss:

> GYMRU, GYMRU, dyma ddyrnod,
> Colli'r gwron DAL'SARN—
> Colli un fydd mewn anrhydedd,
> Pan agorir llyfrau'r farn.
> Gwaded pawb yr enw *Cymro*,
> Nad yw'n teimlo'r ergyd hon.
> Er fod genym lawer *Ioan*,
> Nid oedd genym ond un JOHN.[26]

> WALES, WALES, here's the day
> Of loss of the hero of TAL'SARN -
> Loss of one who will be held in honour,
> When the books of judgement are opened.

Let those disown the name of *Welshman*,
Who do not feel this blow.
Though we have many a *Ioan*,
We only had one JOHN.[27]

Beside the specific comfort of the Gospel, the passing of the 'People's Preacher' was relieved in measure by the very remarkable if less spectacular ministry of his son David Lloyd Jones (see Appendix 2). John Jones's faithful friend and famous biographer Dr Owen Thomas wrote of his hero:

We are disposed to think that he, during those years (from 1821 to 1857), made for himself a deeper home in the affections of his fellow-countrymen than perhaps any of his mighty predecessors or contemporaries—so deep a home, indeed, that the longing that is still felt for him in the breasts of his hearers is as keen and strong as if he had died yesterday'.[28]

Between his birth at Dolwyddelan and his death at Talysarn, was there any Welshman who brought more blessing to Wales through the preaching of Christ than he? Did any preacher present the Saviour of sinners more gloriously, eloquently and tenderly than he? Was there any minister whose heart throbbed with more love to Jesus and his fellow-men? Is there a better Spirit-anointed model for preachers today than the Christ-exalting John Jones, Talsarn?

"The memory of the righteous is blessed"
(Proverbs 10: 7)
SOLI DEO GLORIA

Notes

1   *Great Preachers*, 526.
2   See 'Amser' in Griffith Parry, Llanrwst (ed), *Pregethau Y Diweddar Barch. John Jones, Tàl-y-Sarn* (Dinbych: Thomas Gee, 1869), 639–42.
3   Hughes, R. (ed), *Memoir and Sermons of the Late Rev. David Lloyd Jones, MA, Llandinam* (Wrexham: Hughes and Son, 1912), 104–5.
4   Owen Jones's note is: 'Spoken in reference to Nicholas, the Emperor of Russia' (ibid. 515).

5   Owen Thomas, *Cofiant*, 728–31.
6   See Griffith Parry, Llanrwst (ed), *Pregethau Y Diweddar Barch. John Jones, Tal-y-Sarn* (Dinbych: Thomas Gee, 1869), Pregeth XXXV, 447–63.
7   Owen Thomas, *Cofiant*, 1006.
8   http://www.measuringworth.com/calculators/ppoweruk/
9   See 'The Indebtedness of Europe to the Protestant Reformation' in R. Hughes (ed), *Memoir and Sermons of the Late Rev. David Lloyd Jones, MA, Llandinam* (Wrexham: Hughes and Son, 1912), 348–60.
10   *Great Preachers*, 518–19.
11   Ibid. 531.
12   Ibid. 520.
13   O. Llew Owain, *Cofiant Mrs. Fanny Jones* (Machynlleth a Caernarfon, 1907), 57.
14   Ibid. 520; *Cofiant John Jones*, 755.
15   Elias Jones, John Williams, T. Charles Williams, *Cofiant a Phregethau Y Diweddar Barch. David Lloyd Jones, MA Llandinam* (Gwrecsam: Hughes A'i Fab, 1908), 15.
16   R. Hughes (ed), *Memoir and Sermons of the Late Rev. David Lloyd Jones, MA, Llandinam* (Wrexham: Hughes and Son, 1912), 16.
17   *Great Preachers*, 521, 399–400.
18   Luke 19: 42
19   Dan. 12: 3
20   Jn 11: 35
21   Deut. 10: 18
22   1 Thess. 4: 13
23   O. Llew Owain, *Cofiant Mrs. Fanny Jones* (Machynlleth a Caernarfon, 1907), 54–5, tr. Marian G. Clifford, cited from *Cofiant*, 763.
24   Ibid. 56.
25   See W. Ambrose, *Marwnad y Parch. John Jones, Tal-y-sarn* (Porth Madog, 1858) and Glan Alun, *Pregethwr y Bobl … Y Parch. John Jones*, Tal-y-sarn (Wyddgrug, 1858). See Owen Thomas's selection of the former in *Cofiant*, 779–82.
26   *Marwnad y Parch. John Jones, Tal-y-sarn*, 5.
27   Translation by Marian G. Clifford.
28   *Cofiant*, cited in Owen Jones, *Great Preachers*, 462.

Awelon Hedd. 6.6.4.

28

1 O! TYRED, Arglwydd mawr,
  Dyhidla o'r nef i lawr
    Gawodydd pur;
Fel byddo i'r egin grawn,
Foreuddydd a phrydnawn,
I darddu'n beraidd iawn,
    O'r anial dir.

2 Mae peraroglau'th ras
  Yn taenu o gylch i maes
    Awelon hedd;

Estroniaid sydd yn dod
O'r pellder eitha 'rioed,
I gwympo wrth Dy droed,
    A gwel'd Dy wedd.

3 Mae tegwch D'wyneb pryd
  Yn maeddu oll i gyd
    Ar ddaear las;
Mae pob rhyw nefol ddawn
Oll yno'n gryno lawn,
Yn tarddu'n hyfryd iawn
    O'th glwyfau i maes.

W. WILLIAMS.

Padarn. 8.8.8., 6ll.

71 1 GWNAED concwest ar Galfaria fryn,
　　Am dani canodd myrdd cyn hyn :
　　Fe faeddwyd uffern faith i gyd ;
　　Fe brynwyd gwael golledig ddyn,
　　Fe wnaed y ddwyblaid ddig yn un,
　　　A gwaed Iachawdwr mawr y byd.

2 Wel, dyma'r Cyfaill goreu gaed ;
　　Mae'n ganmil gwell na mam na thad ;
　　　Yn mhob caledi ffyddlawn yw :
　　Mae'n medru maddeu a chuddio bai,
　　Ac o'i wir fodd yn trugarhau
　　　Wrth bechaduriaid gwael eu rhyw.

3 Yr afon fawr o waed y groes
　　Yw iechyd f'enaid ddydd a nôs ;
　　　A thyna p'am yr wyf yn fyw :
　　Mae'r ffynon fywiol, fawr, ddi-drai,
　　Yn para byth i ddyfrhau—
　　　Anfeidrol haeddiant gwaed fy Nuw.

4 Ei haeddiant mawr anfeidrol Ef,
　　A lwyr foddlonodd nef y nef,
　　　A geidw'm henaid yn ddi-gryn ;
　　Yn ngwres y dydd a'r stormydd mawr,
　　Efe am daliodd hyd yn awr :—
　　　Gogoniant byth i Geidwad dyn.　　Morgan Rhys.

9
THE JOHN JONES LEGACY

It is now time to assess the legacy of John Jones, Talsarn. That he was, in several respects, an extraordinary Christian man is obvious from all that's gone before. The providence and grace of God equipped him remarkably for his unique place in God's purposes. Considering his physical endowments, one is reminded that the LORD looks at 'the heart' rather than 'the outward appearance' (*1 Samuel 16: 7*). Yet, while David was anointed for spiritual reasons in preference to Saul, we are still told that 'he was ruddy, with bright eyes and good-looking' (*verse 12*). If Holy Scripture says this regarding a man 'after God's own heart' (*1 Samuel 13: 14*) it is surely in order to note the physical features of John Jones's identity:

> He had a splendid constitution. He was one of the strongest men of his time. When working at home on the farm in his youthful days, or in the quarry as he did for a short time, he could do as much as any two men put together. After a hard day's work he would be none the worse; and after one kind of labour was over, he could with pleasure turn to another. Thus we found him, after being away for a week of toil at Capel Curig; and after walking over Moel Siabod for a long distance to his home at Tan-y-castell, beginning immediately to help them, or seeking the silence of Nantytylathau. But combined with this strength of body, he had symmetry of form and beauty of person. He was said to be one of the most handsome men of the time. His sweet and lovely countenance attracted the people everywhere. And when he was a young

man, just beginning to visit the chapels, they generally said of
him he was the handsomest man they had ever seen.[1]

Beside his good looks, John Jones was an oratorical genius.
His voice was clearly a God-given instrument, sanctified for
the work of effective gospel proclamation:

> It was strong and deep, and nevertheless capable of a vast
> compass. When he preached in the open air it was at the
> beginning very deep and low; but before the end it would
> sound like a trumpet, and rend the air, the hills around echoing
> it back again and again. It was, moreover, capable of endless
> variety and always under the most thorough command of his
> ideas, emotions, and will. He would preach the same sermon
> with a great variety of expression and voice, for he never made
> any illegitimate use of it; it would vary as the moods of his
> own spirit, as is most natural and reasonable. And here also,
> combined with great volume, there were the most charming
> sweetness and pathos.[2]

John Jones's personality was as attractive as his voice:

> His human nature was richly adorned with those qualities
> which make a man's presence interesting, influential, and
> delightful. On this account he ... might be said to be the most
> pleasant company in the world. His countenance beamed with
> the sweetest love and the most boundless benevolence. In his
> appearance and in his conduct he was a perfect gentleman,
> produced not by culture and art, but by Nature herself.[3]

John Jones was equipped intellectually as well as physically
for his calling. If 'the endowments of his head and heart were
of a very superior kind', says Owen Jones:

> His intellectual powers were of great natural strength. He
> had a memory of extraordinary capacity. He never forgot
> anything he had seen or heard. He could with ease remember

the smallest minutiae, and he had the power of reproducing with the greatest accuracy. In addition to this retentiveness of mind, he possessed reasoning faculties of great penetrating force. He had an eye not only for facts, but also for the great laws which govern them. Not only were the observing faculties strong, but also the generalizing powers. Not only was he an observer of Nature, but he could see her truths. His perception of similars was keen. He could perceive the most striking similarity, where another could only find contiguity. The scientific and philosophic qualities he possessed in great perfection; and if he had applied his talents in that direction he would have produced a natural or a transcendental philosopher of large calibre.[4]

Having defended John Jones from the charge of being more interested in philosophy than theology in Chapter 4, it is appropriate to add the following:

His sermons aimed always at the practical and useful; wherefore some have said of him that his qualities as philosopher and divine were not so great. This ought not to make any man the less of a philosopher; for the greater a man's powers are, often the more simple and useful he becomes. Nor is it the philosophy of a man that determines his character as a philosopher in the long run, but the philosophical qualities he exhibits in his investigations. ... So the great preacher of Talsarn, though leaning to the practical side of the Gospel, exhibits in abundance the faculties of a true philosopher and divine.[5]

In other words, John Jones was a reflective and thoughtful preacher rather than a mere reciter of texts and purveyor of clichés. For all his lack of formal education, no learned hearer could dismiss John Jones as a mindless ranter:

He was a man of great originality and independent power of thought. The great change he inaugurated in the preaching of his day could never have been effected but by a man of

great self-reliance and determined will. ... He was a keen
reasoner and accomplished dialectician. Never did his logical
powers appear to greater advantage than when attacking the
strongholds of error. He would set down his propositions, and
bring up his evidences from all quarters, all the resources of
nature and grace being at his command. He would pile argument
upon argument, and apply his reasons incessantly to the point
of attack, until at last the stronghold fell with a crash.[6]

We have seen evidence of this already. John Jones was not
slow to grapple with Unitarian error during his first visit to
South Wales. He also knew how to assault the bastions of
hypercalvinist antinomianism. He was ruled by a deep
attachment to God's truth, yet never without a touch of
humour and an abundance of compassion. He possessed
'humour that arises from the head and the heart, and whose
real essence is said to be love', wrote Owen Jones.[7]

Never did the tender emotions of love, pity, and sympathy
find a more congenial home than his bosom. And these fine
emotions had been touched by the love of God in Christ, and
they glowed with warm fervour. His passion did not burn with
the awful brightness of that of Robert Roberts; nor did it rush
with terrible wildness, like that of Christmas Evans, but it was
mellowed and toned with the most delightful sweetness. It ran
deep and strong, nevertheless, and vanquished with the most
subdued pathos the hardest congregations. It was often irresistible
and overwhelming. His voice, his intellect, his reason, his
imagination were all fused in the fire of his emotions.[8]

For all the warmth of his preaching, his intellectual cast
of mind prevented any tendency to sentimentalize. Indeed,
he possessed the philosophical capacity to produce a systematic
theology as well as effective and rousing preaching. One may
say that his choice of emphasis was an act of Christ-centred
self-denial. He wished only to impress his hearers with the

grace of God, rather than astound the learned world with erudition. This fact alone meets the criticism of those who questioned John Jones's seeming preference for 'philosophizing'. If anything, his determination to pursue biblical rather than confessional orthodoxy means that critics like John Elias were more guilty of 'philosophizing' than he was. After all, as I have demonstrated elsewhere,[9] the prevailing dogmatic High-Calvinist thinking of the early nineteenth century was undergirded by Aristotelian concepts of the kind John Jones had no time for. Besides, John Jones considered incursions into the academic sphere were unnecessary. Since Dr Edward Williams supplied him with theological direction, all that was needed was to get on with proclaiming the Gospel. This explains Owen Jones's accurate assessment of our preacher's truly apostolic preoccupations:

> As may be easily inferred from the above, the leaning of Mr Jones's mind was mostly to the practical side of the Truth. He preached the truths which have most directly to do with the conversion of sinners, more than those which bear directly upon the origin of the plans of God. He did not neglect these; but the stress of his preaching did not lie in this direction. The reason of this need not be found in the constitution of his mind, for his mind was as well adapted for the one as for the other. The reason of it may be found in the peculiar circumstances of the denomination in which Mr Jones was brought up. There had been previously a very strong tendency to dogmatic teaching, to which references have already been made. The sermons of the day dwelt mostly upon the other great truths, though, of course, not altogether. Mr Jones considered that the preaching was ineffective. He took the matter deeply to heart, and spent many a sleepless night over it, and many a struggle with God in prayer for wisdom and guidance. Gradually he was led to apply himself more to the practical side of the Gospel, to such an extent that he was the chief means of creating a revolution in the preaching of the day.[10]

Clearly then, the source of John Jones's greatness was his reliance on the Holy Scriptures rather than the tomes of the scholastics—which probably his monoglot Welsh culture mercifully shielded him from! Again, Owen Jones pin-points the focus of our preacher:

> The Bible was the chief book of his life. Though he had laboured assiduously and successfully to attain a proficiency of general knowledge, he had made all subservient and helpful to his Biblical studies. He had searched it thoroughly, and knew much of it by heart. This was the quarry of infinite resources where he found his materials. He believed it to be the Word of God; he rested upon its great truths; they were as real to him in the vigour of life as they were in his dying hour.[11]

While he clearly welcomed the sanctified scholarship of Edward Williams and others, John Jones demonstrated that such advantages are not absolutely indispensable. In this respect, we are reminded of John the Baptist in the wilderness[12] and Paul in Arabia,[13] as Owen Jones makes clear:

> He had no college training it is true, but he gave himself a training which proved not inferior. What is the great object of all discipline? To enable a man to obtain thorough command of his mind; to control it, and to concentrate his powers at all times. This is one of the chief ends of education, if so, Mr Jones had attained it. His college was the rugged mountains, the wild scenery around his home, and the various trials he passed through; and he availed himself of them in such a way as to attain a most thorough mastery over his thinking powers. Even University training has failed to accomplish this in a thousand cases. No amount of learning will make up for it; the quantify of facts a man carries with him from the University will be of little avail without it. Mr Jones, however, had attained the power of thought and meditation to a very high degree. He could think for hours without intermission on the truths of the Gospel. He could think out a sermon from beginning to

end, sitting silently in his room, or walking in the woods, or even in company.

Another feature of John Jones's truly apostolic life was his prayerfulness. His thought and reflection were conducted in an atmosphere of continual prayer. Here was an emphasis not generally associated with a university education, as Owen Jones rightly highlights:

> He was known to walk to and fro in his bedroom for hours, meditating upon some verse of the Bible, or some great truth. And, after thinking out a subject in this way, he could preach upon it in the next Association, without even committing the sermon to writing, or having a word of it in any way outside his own mind, such a thorough and masterly grasp he had of his thoughts on all occasions. Not far from his house at Talsarn there was a copse of wood, silent and lonely, except for the chirping of the birds. Here he used to go, and remain for hours together. There is a path in it to this day made by his own feet, where he used to walk backwards and forwards. He would remain here till the middle of the night, and even until the following morning. Here he often thought, meditated, and prayed. This is the kind of preparation that tells in the pulpit. Our Lord Jesus Christ had a great deal of it on the lonely mountains of Galilee; Elijah, the prophet, had it on the banks of the river Kidron, Ezekiel on the banks of the river Chebar, Daniel on the banks of the Hiddekel and the Ulai, and John the Baptist, on the banks of the Jordan. And we want just now, not less perhaps of the training of the universities, but a little more of the training obtained by the rivers and in the mountain wilds.[14]

Neither did John Jones confine his praying to private preparation. As we have seen, he felt an immediate need for God's blessing on the people during the delivery of his sermons:

A great peculiarity of the preaching of Mr Jones was the
ejaculatory prayers he intermixed with the delivery of his
sermons. And this more than anything else appears to us to
prove the great earnestness of the man. It was no mere declaration
of truth that he had in view; but after, *e.g.,* a long strain upon
the mercy of God, he turned to Him before the congregation,
and said, "O God, show unto this people the riches of Thy
mercy!" This would occur many times during the same discourse,
perhaps. And we are told that these fervent ejaculations added
intensely to the effect of his sermons. [15]

Such was John Jones's dependence on the Holy Spirit, that
he never resorted to dramatic arm-waving, jumping up and
down or similar gesticulations in the pulpit. But neither was
his style merely statuesque, as Owen Jones is careful to explain:

He took his position in front, fixed his eyes on a point
somewhere about the centre of the chapel, with his hands
steady upon the sides of the pulpit or taking hold of the desk.
He looked fixed like a statue. But from his mouth, nevertheless,
there rolled such eloquence that Wales has never since heard
the like of it. [16]

It seems impossible to exaggerate the impact of John Jones's
eloquence. Owen Jones cites the eye-witness account of his
chief source, Dr Owen Thomas:

As he went on, the feeling warms and deepens; the ideas
become more animated and elevated; the language richer and
clearer; the stream of his eloquence fuller, broader, and stronger,
until it becomes a mighty torrent, sweeping everything before
it. We saw him, scores of times, advancing swiftly, with such a
flood of eloquence, so high and mighty that nothing could
stand before him; and the whole congregation, unbalanced and
uncontrolled, swept away by the tide whithersoever it went. [17]

How did the congregations respond to such preaching?

On some occasions, when the orator was ecstatically-absorbed in his subject, the realities of life led to amusing consequences, not least in the era when his contemporary Michael Faraday's electrical discoveries were yet to make an impact:

> He does not appear to have depended much upon the congregation more than Daniel Rowland. The audience, in fact, to a great extent, escaped his immediate attention. There was only an underflowing consciousness of its presence. He was once preaching at Shrewsbury, and very long, as he often was; but, as it happened, the Welsh congregation here was made up mostly of young people who had come from Wales to serve as servants in families. The time going, they one after another went out, in order not to be late at home, until the chapel was comparatively empty by the time he finished. On another occasion at Llanuwchllyn, near Bala, he preached until the candles had nearly all gone out; and all this without observing it, owing to the absorption with which his theme took him. He would often preach for an hour and a half or two hours, the people not at all tired, but delighted and enchanted, and in raptures before the close.[18]

John Jones served the cause of Jesus Christ as a convinced Calvinistic Methodist, yet he rejoiced when his labours overflowed into the other communities of Welsh Christianity. While his pastoral labours at Talysarn—when he was not itinerating—were devoted to the local church according to the presbyterian faith and order of the Methodist Connexion, John Jones was pre-eminently an evangelist, as Owen Jones is careful to point out:

> The nature of the ministry of Mr Jones must also be taken into consideration, for he was a minister not [just] for any special church, but for the whole of Wales, especially for Caernarfonshire and North Wales. He was an evangelist. This again was a special reason why he should continue with those truths rather than with any other—i.e., with those that bear

directly upon the return of sinners to God. Undoubtedly, if
he had been more stationary, and labouring for the same
particular people, as Mr Rees at Shrewsbury, his mind would
have dwelt more upon other phases of the truth.[19]

Unjustly criticised for his 'New System' theology and
'philosophizing' approach, John Jones has been charged with
starting a dubious style of preaching intonation. Dr Eifion
Evans says our preacher 'in some measure must be held
responsible for the 'hwyl'/intonation in preaching which
later became a substitute for careful exposition'.[20] Writing
in the 1880s, Owen Jones explains the nature and significance
of this phenomenon:

> It was in the Revd John Jones that one of the characteristics
> of the Welsh preaching of the last 150 years appeared in its
> greatest prominence. When he was thoroughly warmed by his
> theme, when he was inspired and in the 'hwyl', his speech
> acquired a most pleasing intonation. When a poet is in a certain
> state of elevation, there is nothing that will satisfy that inspiration
> but the rhythm of lines, cadence, and harmony. Let a man be
> inspired by his subject, his sentences in writing will have a
> certain rhythm and flow. So when a man speaks, as he enters
> into certain moods, as he warms and becomes aglow with
> emotion, not only is there a certain run in his sentences, but
> also a certain flow in his speech. It is perfectly natural that
> something should correspond to this in his voice. So was often
> the case in Wales during the great revivals of religion which
> started in the year 1735. It was a swing of the voice, or an
> intonation, not made, nor taken up, but a development of
> speech and tone which arose from the great enthusiasm and
> deep emotions of the preachers of the time. It continued for
> a long while in Wales, and is not yet extinct.[21]

While the 'hwyl' phenomenon had its general features,
there were individual variations from preacher to preacher.
In this respect, John Jones was apparently unique:

It was not the same, in different men; each had his own. David Morris, Ebenezer Morris, Christmas Evans, Daniel Jones, Llanllechid, Cadwaladr Owen and John Jones had each his peculiar intonation. Nor had they this at all times; it was only when they were in a certain state of emotional warmth that it came. Mr Jones had a most beautiful and varied sweetness of intonement, superior to all the rest.[22]

The chief concern over the 'hwyl' seems to be the ease with which it was abused. Prayerless pulpiteers were often guilty of artificiality in their efforts to arouse and impress congregations. Owen Jones treated this 'trickery' with the contempt it deserves:

The phenomenon seems to be dying away from the Welsh pulpit at the present day. If it arose, from the height of religious feeling, it is a thing to be regretted. As was natural enough, those great preachers had their imitators. Many thought that the effect they saw upon the multitude was due to the accident of intonation; they, therefore, intoned. It is however, condemned by all intelligent congregations, unless when there is real feeling, and it appears as a development of it.[23]

On the other hand, there was nothing of contrivance in the sacred oratory of John Jones, Talsarn:

In Mr Jones [the 'hwyl'] was simply the flower and bloom of his own intense emotions; and the influence upon the congregation was completely subduing. Dr Thomas says that the effect of some of the notes was indescribable; that he could not imagine anything more sad and heartrending than the Ow, Ow! (Alas! Alas!) which he had when describing any irretrievable loss or calamity that had taken place from neglect [of the Gospel]. On the other hand, when expressing the believer's delight over the riches of God in Christ, there was such a heavenly sweetness in his voice as electrified every congregation.[24]

Owen Jones seems entirely justified in his conclusion regarding the 'Preacher of the People':

> As to power, flexibility, sweetness, and beauty of voice, the Welsh pulpit no doubt reached its climax in the orator from Talsarn. ... The sermons of Mr Jones were often nothing but a continued flow of eloquence from beginning to end, ... however, [he] enchanted his hearers by the greatness of his truths. The wealth of language he possessed and the rich tones of his voice were altogether subordinate. When the truth itself did not move him, his language and voice seemed to have lost their beauty.[25]

Before we make a closing comparison between John Jones and John Elias, a word about the former's musical compositions are in order. While Owen Jones remarks on the hymn tunes of John Jones more than once, whether he ever saw or heard them is uncertain. However, a selection was published in 1908 by D. Emlyn Evans.[26] The fact that the original tunes were referred to in Edward Morgan's letter of condolence to Fanny Jones indicates their significance. While 'Tan-y-castell' and an abridged version of 'Llanllyfni' appear in modern hymnbooks, forty others possess considerable interest, at least for those who appreciate the tunes of the nineteenth century.

Whatever musical influences inspired John Jones (apart from earlier Welsh hymn tunes), no composers names appear in the index of Owen Thomas's *Cofiant*. Yet our preacher's musical contemporaries were Haydn (1732–1809), Beethoven (1770–1827), Hummel (1778–1837), Schubert (1797–1828), Mendelssohn (1809–47), Chopin (1810–49), Liszt (1811–86) and Schumann (1810–56), to name but a few. In 1846, Mendelssohn crowned a series of visits to England by directing his oratorio *Elijah* in Birmingham, and 'his music set the canons of mid-Victorian taste'.[27] Mozart's pupil and teacher of Mendelssohn, J. N. Hummel visited England (the third of four visits in all) in

1831, performing at Manchester and Liverpool in July of that
year.[28] It is not unlikely that, in the course of his preaching
appointments in London, Manchester and Liverpool John
Jones might have met musically-minded Welsh people who,
having possibly heard these composers, might also have told
our musical preacher of their experiences, showing him some
acquired sheet music in the process. Certainly, the melodiousness
for which Hummel and Mendelssohn were famous seems to
find an echo in his compositions. More important is the distinct
dimension of Christian joy in John Jones's tunes. Comparing
the two groups of Welsh Methodist, the Calvinist and the
Wesleyan, John Roberts writes that the 'Calvinist was inclined
to speak more of the old bondage from which he had passed,
and the Wesleyan to sing the songs of his new freedom'.[29] If
his tunes are anything to go by, our preacher-composer clearly
did both! As a further 'window into the soul' of John Jones,
back-to-back specimens of his tunes appear as chapter breaks
in this book.

    Without ignoring the warning of the famous phrase
'comparisons are odious',[30] it is difficult not to compare
John Jones, Talsarn with John Elias. Indeed, regarding the
galaxy of preachers of the period, the literature does this
kind of thing frequently without acrimony. While enough
has appeared in this tribute to draw certain conclusions, more
may be said. Notwithstanding Dr Owen Thomas's obvious
admiration for John Jones, he still declared that regarding
'those special qualities in which he excelled', John Elias 'was,
without a doubt, the most popular preacher, taking the whole
Principality, that ever rose in Wales'.[31] This could, of course,
simply relate to the period ending with Elias's death in 1841,
the time when John Jones's influence was peaking. If not, it
is a revealing fact that Owen Thomas chose to write a
biography on John Jones rather than on John Elias.

Considering the tensions and differences already alluded to, it is difficult to find the kind of blemishes in the younger preacher that were evident in the earlier one. Not to ignore his strong political conservatism (as regretted by Drs Lloyd-Jones[32] and Tudur Jones[33]), Elias's tendencies to theological extremism (ignored by his biographer, Edward Morgan[34]), his authoritarian and intimidating manner (noted by Owen Thomas[35]) detract from his reputation. Even as a preacher, his depictions of hell could perhaps be excessive, on one occasion prompting a terrified hearer to shout, "Oh, for Mr Richardson, if it were only for five minutes!"[36] With his dramatic preaching style, he has been charged with 'acting',[37] an accusation never levelled at John Jones that I am aware of. Without questioning his immense evangelistic success, his zeal for missions and his opposition to hypercalvinism, he was deficient in humour, creative thought and the high imaginative powers evident in John Jones, Talsarn.[38] Suggesting a correlation with Elias's adoption of a commercialistic view of limited atonement (that Christ's sufferings were a 'payment' for the 'debts' of the elect alone),[39] Edward Morgan indicates that John Elias's later ministry never quite matched the brilliance of his early preaching.[40] However, John Jones progressed (as we have noted already) year by year. 'Thus', wrote Owen Jones, 'he improved himself from time to time, until gradually he became the most efficient and most popular preacher of the age in Wales. The epithet is applied to him to this day, 'The preacher of the people' '.[41] Not to forget that these two pulpit princes enjoy the perfect harmony of heaven, a fellowship John Jones looked forward to,[42] yet Owen Jones's verdict is entirely justified by—here repeated for the second time!—Owen Thomas's commendation with which this tribute began:

> We are disposed to think that he, during those years (from 1821 to 1857), made for himself a deeper home in the affections

of his fellow-countrymen than perhaps any of his mighty predecessors or contemporaries—so deep a home, indeed, that the longing that is still felt for him in the breasts of his hearers is as keen and strong as if he had died yesterday.[43]

Without ignoring the valiant and faithful contributions of all his brethren, there can be no doubt that John Jones, Talsarn provides a model for ministry in every age. He is both a rebuke and an encouragement for all who take seriously the Church's ongoing witness to the world. True, he laboured long before the advent of electricity and the resulting distractions of radio, television and the internet. There were, of course, distractions of another kind even in his day. Yet I defy anyone to read his sermons without being gripped and edified by them. If we prayed and preached as he prayed and preached, nothing but shameful unbelief would conclude that it would be a waste of time in the 21st century. The challenge is clear: are we prepared to trust, love and serve God as did John Jones, Talsarn? Of this we may be sure that, hard on the heels of the liberal-ecumenical Christian apostasy of the post-John Jones era, paganism, materialism and humanism—expressed in the politics of both 'left' and 'right'— have left a decadent trail of spiritual, moral and cultural devastation in Wales and the rest of the United Kingdom. Instead of today's superficial 'entertainment evangelism', man-centred spirituality, 'dumbed-down' preaching and multi-faith madness, only a mighty outpouring of the Holy Spirit can reverse our tragic decline. Bearing in mind the kind of man God made him, truly we may say, "John Jones, you are needed in this hour!"

THE END

Notes

1   *Great Preachers*, 522.
2   Ibid.
3   Ibid. 523.
4   Ibid.
5   Ibid. 523–4.
6   Ibid. 524.
7   Ibid. 527.
8   Ibid.
9   See my *Atonement and Justification: English Evangelical Theology 1640–1790—An Evaluation* (Oxford: The Clarendon Press, 1990/2002).
10 *Great Preachers*. 535.
11 Ibid. 528–9.
12 See Luke 3: 2.
13 See Galatians 1: 17.
14 *Great Preachers*, 528.
15 Ibid. 532–3.
16 Ibid. 533.
17 Ibid. 536–7
18 Ibid.
19 Ibid. 535–6.
20 E-mail, 29 September 2011.
21 *Great Preachers*, 537.
22 Ibid. 537.
23 Ibid. 537–8.
24 Ibid. 538.
25 Ibid.
26 D. Emlyn Evans, (ed), *Tonau Talysarn: Sef Casgliad o Donau y Parch. John Jones, Talysarn, Gydag Emynau* (Machynlleth a Gwrecsam: Hughes A'i Fab, 1908).
27 J. A. Westrup and F. Ll Harrison (eds), *Collins Music Encyclopedia* (London and Glasgow: Collins, 1959), 420.
28 See Mark Kroll, *Johann Nepomuk Hummel: A Musician's Life and World* (Lanham, Maryland, Toronto and Plymouth, UK: The Scarecrow Press, Inc., 2007), 142.
29 J. Roberts, *The Calvinistic Methodism of Wales* (Caernarvon: The Calvinistic Methodist Book Agency, 1934), 46.
30 If not directly used by Shakespeare, it is found in John Donne and others. See Martin, G. (n.d.), *Comparisons are odious: The meanings and origins of sayings and phrases*. Retrieved 27 March 2013, from http://www.phrases.org.uk/meanings/Comparisons%20are%20odious.html
31 Cited from *Cofiant*, 854 in *Great Preachers*, 244.
32 See D. M. Lloyd-Jones, 'The Christian and the State in Revolutionary Times' in *The Puritans: Their Origins and Successors* (Edinburgh: The Banner of Truth Trust, 1987), 337.
33 See R. Tudur Jones, *John Elias: Prince Amongst Preachers* (Bridgend: The Evangelical Library of Wales, 1974), 32.
34 See Morgan, Edward, *John Elias, His Life and Letters* (Edinburgh: The Banner of

Truth Trust, 1973).

35 *Atonement Controversy*, 326.See Morgan, Edward, *John Elias, His Life and Letters* (Edinburgh: The Banner of Truth Trust, 1973).

36 He was a preacher from Caernarfon 'whose sermons were always upon the bright side of the Gospel' (Owen Jones, *Great Preachers*, 247).

37 See R. Tudur Jones, *John Elias: Prince Amongst Preachers* (Bridgend: The Evangelical Library of Wales, 1974), 9.

38 See *Great Preachers*, 281–2, 291.

39 See R. Tudur Jones, *John Elias: Prince Amongst Preachers* (Bridgend: The Evangelical Library of Wales, 1974), 16 and 28.

40 See Morgan, Edward, *John Elias, His Life and Letters* (Edinburgh: The Banner of Truth Trust, 1973), 40–1.

41 *Great Preachers*, 532.

42 Ibid.

43 *Cofiant*, cited in *Great Preachers*, 462.

PICTURE GALLERY

Castell Dolwyddelan

Dolwyddelan (from the castle)

Birthplace and monument, Tan-y-castell

Moel Siabod

Nant-y-tylathau (with the author)

John Jones (1830s)

Fanny Jones

The Jones's home and shop, Talysarn

John Jones (1840s)

John Jones (1850s)

Esch auheilung and Effnant Brawd,

John Jones.

John Jones's signature (1841)

John and Fanny's grave, Llanllyfni

John Jones's epitaph

Fanny Jones's epitaph

David Lloyd Jones

Dr Edward Williams

Map of North Wales

26   Arvonia.   8. 6.

50

1 MAE'N llon'd y nefoedd, llon'd y byd,
    Llon'd uffern hefyd yw ;
Llon'd tragwyddoldeb maith ei hun,
    Diderfyn ydyw Duw ;
Mae'n llon'd y gwagle yn ddigoll,
Mae oll yn oll, a'i allu'n un,
Anfeidrol annherfynol Fod
    A'i hanfod ynddo'i hun.

2 Un hunanfodol ydoedd Ef
    Cyn llunio nef na llawr ;
Yn nhragwyddoldeb maith yn ol,
    Yn Dduw anfeidrol fawr ;
Heb ddechreu dyddiau iddo'n bod,
Na diwedd einioes chwaith i ddod,
Tragwyddol a rhyfeddol Fod
    Yn Drindod uniawn drefn.

3 Clyw, f'enaid tlawd, mae genyt Dad
    Sy'n gwel'd dy fwriad gwan,
A Brawd yn eiriol yn y nef
    Cyn codi'th lef i'r lan :
Cred nad diystyr gan dy Dad
Yw gwrandaw gwaedd dymuniad gwiw,
Pe byddai d'enau yn rhy fud
    I'w dd'wedyd ger bron Duw.

ED. JONES, Maesyplwm.

Clanllyfni. M. B. D.

31

1 FY ngweddi, dos i'r nef,
  Yn union at fy Nuw,
A dywed wrtho Ef yn daer,
"Atolwg, Arglwydd, clyw!
Cyflawna'th 'ddewid wych,
I'm dwyn i'th nefoedd wen;
Yn Salem fry par'to fy lle
Mewn llys o fewn i'r llen."

2 Pererin llesg a llaith,
  Dechreuais daith oedd bell,
Trwy lu o elynion mawr eu brad,
  Gan geisio gwlad sydd well;
Am ffoi mae f'enaid tlawd
At f'anwyl Frawd a'm Pen;
  Yn Salem fry, &c.

3 Yn nglŷn wylofain trist,
  Lle bu fy Nghrist, 'rwy'n byw;
Ac wrth ryfela a'm gelyn caeth
Fy nghalon aeth yn friw;

Iachâ bob clwyf a brath
A dail y bywiol bren;
  Yn Salem fry, &c.

4 Mae 'mrodyr uwch y nen
  Yn canu ar ben eu taith;
A minau oedais lawer awr
Ar siwrnai fawr a maith;
Ond bellach tyn fi'n ddwys,
Ar Grist dod bwys fy mhen;
  Yn Salem fry, &c.

5 'Rwy'n gwel'd yr oriau'n hir
  I fod o dir fy ngwlad;
Bryd deuaf at fy mrodyr fry
Sy'n canu'n nhŷ fy Nhad?
Gael gorphen ar fy nhaith,
A'm siwrnai faith îs nen;
Yn Salem fry par'to fy lle
Mewn llys o fewn i'r llen.

W. WILLIAMS.

APPENDIX I
FANNY JONES

Extracts from

Cofiant Mrs Fanny Jones, Gweddw y Diweddar Barch. J. Jones, Talysarn

by

O. Llew. Owain of Talysarn. [1]

Translated

by

Marian G. Clifford (née Edwards)

As Welsh people we are under a great debt to this woman, and we can never put a price on her service nor measure the work she did in being an instrument to give 'the People's Preacher' to the people ... In her self denial, Wales heard a message from Heaven—her efforts facilitated the way for Wales to be drenched by the irresistible eloquence of the 'hero from Talysarn'. [2]

B iographies of women are not common in Wales, however much many deserve it. Undoubtedly that is a loss to the country; it is a priceless service to commemorate those who are worthy.

Although I have had some information here and there, it is to my mother that I am indebted for her story in its wide extent, since she was born and bred in this area, therefore had knowledge of Mrs Jones's movements and her private life. From my mother's reminiscences, I could have written a volume about her twice the size, and if any letter of praise comes from the work, she has the first claim to it.

BIRTH AND EARLY YEARS

Frances Edwards, or rather as she was more commonly known, Fanny Edwards, was a daughter of Thomas and Anne Edwards. She was born at Cefn-faes, Ffestiniog, in May 1805. ... From Cefn-faes, the family moved to Llanllyfni (to Llwydcoed farm). They moved from there to a farm called Taldrwst. Thomas Edwards was looked upon as a cultured man of a cultivated mind who was very knowledgeable with regard to slate quarries. He was among the first in Dyffryn Nantlle to hold the office of overseer. He was a very zealous Methodist, ... taking a great interest in the cause in Talysarn.

[Fanny's] mother, Ann Edwards, is portrayed as a woman of strong common sense ... and of strong religious convictions. She possessed an exceptional and melodious singing voice, and since it was so penetrating, it could be heard throughout the whole chapel. Ann Edwards died in March 1816 at the early age of 35 years and Fanny Jones loved to speak often of her mother, and the longing (hiraethus) memories were intensely felt. She admired her mother's piety and remembered the sad moments when she died—so peacefully and without struggle, calling her children together to kiss them and exhort them to godly living.

By this time we see young Fanny bereft of her mother at the time of her awakening—that time which is so full of life and vivacity—a restless time common in young people. Here she was in this situation without home guidance at the most important time of her life, the period of awakening to self-knowledge. The young girl is face to face with the world, and the world is dangerous for her, having lost the one who would have guided her. But we shall see the effect this had on the life of Fanny Edwards.

When she came to a suitable age, she was sent to school at Caernarfon, and during this time, her circle of acquaintance widened. She tended to be friendly and affectionate—naturally therefore, she was a character who drew people to her. She had a good education in Caernarfon, and since she learned quickly, she benefitted greatly—more possibly than others who didn't have such a keen mind. While on this course of instruction she came into contact with several important people in society, and the association with some lasted to the end of her life. One of her best friends was Miss Roberts, Castell, Bangor, and she frequently went to her home to spend the Sabbath with her. Miss Roberts married Mr Owen Roberts, Dinas, near Caernarfon, but their friendship did not cease while they lived. In addition to her school, she had another important advantage through the woman with whom she lodged, Sussi Roberts. She was industrious, noted for her cleanliness, orderliness and economical ways, and was very wise and provident. She taught Fanny Jones how to behave properly and modestly, and she responded to the instruction. Since she was naturally ladylike, and as was noticed earlier, quick to learn, she soon became quite polished and an adornment to the circle she served.

After returning from school, she was given the total care of her father's home, and she played her part to great satisfaction. She showed providence in her care of her father's possessions and circumstances at this time of his life. Thrift was instinctive in her character. It was not for show. This element or feature remained prominent all her life. Providence and thrift were her chief characteristics but they did not develop into stinginess or miserliness. She controlled them to be beautiful and acceptable virtues in her character, since she showed so much compassion towards those in needy circumstances. She used them to her praise in her youth, in her family responsibilities and in her old age. Her life was leavened with them to be of service, and widened her popularity.

She was spoken of when she ran her father's home as one remarkably kind to the poor and compassionate to the needy. She believed that those who were merciful to the poor would not be in need while on earth, and her beliefs were revealed in this more than once.

It so happened during her time at home that there was a year of scarcity, and necessity drove scores of the poor to go from house to house to beg, and each one took care to call at every farmhouse, since they thought it would be easier to get a bit of food there. Although crowds called at Taldrwst, Fanny Edwards could not refuse to give alms to any of them. She knew that 'the God of Providence' above saw all her kindnesses and that she through these kind deeds was working according to the Commandments. She had a religious upbringing, and without realising it, her love for her Saviour grew intensely, and that love was rooted through every part of her life, until it flowered in beauty and fragrance. She used to say that she did not know of any time in her life that she did not love Jesus Christ. In addition to the religious home she had, her religious leanings were nurtured from within; she possessed circumstances which gave every advantage to show the love that was in her heart and to warm the flame which was burning and growing gradually. She appreciated these advantages and said toward the end of her life that these very circumstances were of enormous advantage to her in increasing her devotion.

One of the people who were a help to Fanny Edwards in nourishing this reverence for religious things was Ann Parry, Ty-Capel, Llanllyfni. She was an especially godly old woman—

her godliness made her well-known and famous among the ministers of Wales. This elderly sister kept the chapel house at Llanllyfni for fifty years and there are many interesting stories about her. She prayed much, and there are facts to prove that some ministers had powerful meetings at the very moments when she prayed for them, that God would own their message.

In the old days, preachers would travel on horseback, and every one who passed through Llanllyfni would be sure to call on Ann Parry for some refreshments. Many men of reputation and influence would come to Llanllyfni to preach at this time and everyone knew it was the old lady who succeeded in getting them since she used to keep a journal. This was the environment which influenced Fanny Edwards— it was under the mantle of this old sister that she was brought up, and who gave her guidance.

Fanny herself promised that she had listened to her advice and that it would be a help to her all her life. Other circumstances which left their mark on her whole life were the presence and victory of the old godly people in the religious meetings, and the words of Fanny Jones toward the end of her life were: "I would never tire of the godly old people jumping up and rejoicing in Llanllyfni, when they were on fire, praising God, and the influence that was in their lives at that time has stayed with me all my life." She was drawn like that to strong spiritual characters—Welsh characters, old-fashioned, sincere, until she increased in the virtues they had.

COURTSHIP AND MARRIAGE

[After John Jones's arrival in Talysarn, he established singing meetings—see chapter 3]. Among the young people who gathered like this was a bright young girl, lively and pretty—

therefore special, a young girl who drew everyone's attention with her beauty and cheerfulness ... This girl drew the attention of John Jones and his love began to stir when he saw her; and if heaven leads in life or provides in marriage, these circumstances worked for this. A secret inner turbulence came to the bosom of Fanny Edwards—she couldn't describe it—she didn't know what it was. She hadn't spoken to the young stranger, and yet there was something wonderful and mysterious between them—something she could neither describe nor explain. At the same time there was a stirring in the heart of the young man, though he looked calm and unmoved, so unperturbed that no one knew from him outwardly that he had noticed anyone more than anyone else in the singing meetings; yet, something spoke inside him, and his thoughts always ran to the bright and beautiful one at the singing meeting.

What could explain the mystery? Neither knew what the other was thinking—they didn't have an opportunity to make known the fervency of their hearts to each other—they didn't converse in such a way as to convey their thoughts and wishes to each other. What therefore caused these stirrings in the hearts of each, one for the other? We have to conclude that Heaven was intervening to lead them to each other, and the value that one was to the other in their lives confirms this idea. It was the choice of God to care for one of the 'strong of Wales' and to prepare him for the service of his country, and as Ioan Eifion said with great vivacity in a 'cywydd' (alliterative poem) about the subject:

> John Jones oedd long—oedd long lawn
> O ddoniau'r Nefoedd uniawn.
> Fanny dda a'I llywiai'n llon,
> Hwylus, rhag creig gofalon.
> Duw a'i rhodd—gododd o gant
> Ar gyfer y gwr gwiwfant.

John Jones was a ship—a ship full
Of Heaven's upright gifts;
Good Fanny merrily steering,
Sailing along in spite of rocks of care;
God gave her—raised her up out of a hundred
For the sake of the worthy man.

More than once John Jones himself found his eyes drawn toward the young girl without knowing it; Fanny Edwards from the other side was fixing her eyes on him in amazement. In this unwitting meeting of eyes, each one awoke as from a dream, and in a twinkling turned their eyes in another direction. This eye contact happened often, and it is odd that both fell into the same mistake as the other, without ever saying a word to each other, yet something spoke in each heart that there was some strange meeting together of the two hearts. Fanny had stolen John Jones's heart and John Jones had stolen Fanny's heart. These strange feelings increased in the heart of John Jones and the spark began to be a burning flame—burning so much that he himself took note of the young girl one night in the chapel house, and the fact that John Jones—quiet, deep and serious—noticed [her] gave him strong proof that she had totally won his heart. He asked the family who kept Ty Capel (the chapel house), "Who was that young girl?" "Oh!" they said, "Fanny Edwards, daughter of Thomas Edwards, Taldrwst, a respected farmer and overseer in Cloddfa'r Lôn Quarry." "Well," he replied, "she's a very lively girl." That was all he said that night.

Somehow he had felt inadequate in her company during the conversation at Ty Capel, and he noticed her again at his lodging, i.e. in the home of his cousin, the wife of Mr Griffith Williams, overseer of the Talysarn Quarry, and Mr Williams understood at once that Fanny had won his heart. He said, "She'll make you a good wife, John Jones," appealing to a stranger who was in the house who knew Fanny well, for a confirmation of his observation. He confirmed it with the sentence, "She'll make a very excellent one for him."

After this conversation the matter was left alone, and they continued with other ordinary things, but as Emerson said—"All mankind loves a lover." So it was with John Jones, and he went to the stranger who was at his lodgings the following day, revealing to him the tumult in his bosom, how the girl had won his heart.

At the end of the second singing meeting, John Jones went to Fanny Edwards with the purpose of escorting her a little way in the direction of her home, and before leaving, put a letter into her hand. Fanny Edwards went home, and going straightaway to her bedroom opened the letter, asked for guidance from Heaven in the circumstances and placed herself in the Lord's hands. John Jones went there for her answer at mid-day the next day, and although Fanny Edwards was certain of her own feelings, she couldn't give an answer until she had spoken with her father, so he had to come away a little stunned. In the meantime, he went to see Dr Griffith Roberts, bone doctor, Llanllyfni (the stranger) and asked him to say a word on his behalf to Thomas Edwards, and also to ask Fanny Edwards for a definite answer to his letter ... Not knowing what her feelings were, the obliging man went, quite anxiously, because he did not in the least understand how she felt, and conveyed to her the request of John Jones; and in spite of her great surprise, Fanny was totally ready and ripe for the question, answering in the affirmative without hesitation. In this reply the two felt that they had had in the agreement a basis for the comfort of their lives, ...

In the story of the two we see an intellectual mystery coming to light—the association of minds or the influence of thoughts on each other. Each one worked unknowingly on the thoughts of the other. Fanny Edwards thought about

John Jones whether in her sight or out of her sight, before ever speaking a word to him, and John Jones thought about Fanny Edwards before he ever spoke a word to her. Indeed we could say that there was some leading from above in guiding them towards one another—touching their thoughts until it produced feelings that inclined them towards each other. It was said—indeed Fanny Jones herself told the story—an amazing little tale about her before she ever saw John Jones. Her father and step-mother were in Caernarfon at the time of the 1822 Session [of the Calvinistic Methodists], and after coming home, they told of a strange man of a preacher, a modest young man who was having tea at the same time as them, and they described him as one full of virtues, and the most pleasant that they had ever had in their company. As she heard this story told, something struck Fanny's mind (though she hadn't seen him) that he would be her husband. From that moment, she couldn't get rid of that idea—it followed her everywhere.

Soon after this, Fanny Edwards heard of the young man's coming to Llanllyfni to preach, and she made a decision to go to hear him and see him. Unfortunately, she failed to fulfil her household duties in time to go to the chapel punctually, and she had to be satisfied to hear a little of him from the door; although she didn't see the preacher, there was something in his voice that touched her heartstrings a little, and for the life of her she couldn't stop thinking that he would be her husband.

We see through this that Providence was working in the background and working for her good in preparing the two hearts for each other. From the viewpoint of Heaven, Fanny Edwards was the 'perfect helpmeet', the most suitable from all aspects to help John Jones to prepare himself to be God's messenger, and to deliver with irresistible strength the great message entrusted to him from Heaven.

In the meantime, before John Jones messenger came to Fanny, any word or glance, every movement of his would have a deep impression on Fanny, and caused a turbulence in her heart; it was not surprising then, when the message came from him, that she received it with a ready acceptance. Some sweet power had made her tender to the situation— some power or influence she couldn't explain. Having consented to the proposal in this way, they spoke in a friendly way for a while, and having the consent of her father, they agreed to marry, and the agreement was sealed in an afternoon in April between 4 and 5 o'clock.

The custom at that time was very different from the situation today. After completing the agreement mentioned, John Jones went, exactly as the custom was then, to the fellowship to announce his purpose (even though the girl he loved was present) and asked for the prayers of their fellow Christians for them. He believed that the situation was too important to embark on without Divine strength and guidance, and he implored them earnestly, as members of the Church of God, to take their cause often to the 'throne of God'.

The Saturday following this announcement in the Seiat, John Jones went to Caernarfon to buy a license; but to his great shock he couldn't get it, since his intended wife was too young—she hadn't yet reached her eighteenth birthday. He was thrown into a bit of a quandary, as he was *en route* to Ynys Môn (Anglesey), but he suddenly thought of a plan to get himself out of the difficulty, and that was to write a note to the Parish Clerk to announce the banns the following Sunday, and he persuaded a friend from Llanllyfni to take the note to the Clerk. The banns were announced the following Sunday, and that unknown to Fanny Edwards. She came to know of it through some friends who happened to be in church at the time. According to the Parish register, they were married on Wednesday, 14 May 1823, not in 1824, as it seems that some have said. The Clerk noticed that there was sincerity and honesty to be seen in the wedding arrangements—everything was done openly with nothing stealthy in the preparations.

WIFE & MOTHER

Now we see Fanny Jones starting on the most important part of her life—a period when she had to put into it much wisdom, foresight, diligence, effort and thrift; and her life, her connexions, etc, asked for an abundant degree of the features named. She wasn't yet fully eighteen, but she undertook the responsibility, and the success of her life depended on her strength with the help of the virtues noted. She understood her husband's position and also her obligations in the circumstances. She believed, like one of the English authors that true love is 'having self-sacrifice for another object' (Theodore Watts-Dunton). ... She must have pondered greatly on the cost before coming to the decision since it was such an important step, and that she had a great part in making John Jones the 'Preacher of the People' in Wales. She drew on all her resources to put her understanding into action.

One of the first things she felt was that John Jones wouldn't have peace and quiet to study and compose while continuing to work in the quarry, and she resolved to get him from there quickly. She proceeded after marrying to build a shop in Talysarn, in a place convenient to the quarry. Some at that time said that the owner of the quarry built the shop for them, while others said it was her father who did it, but whoever is correct—it doesn't make much difference which—the work was done.

Her life began with great responsibility—we connect Fanny Jones with these revolutionary things, since she was the direct cause of them—the responsibility of building a house and a shop. She built them near to the Talysarn quarries and by the chapel.

For a year after the wedding, John Jones still went to the quarry, and he preached on work-nights and on the Sabbaths, and his wife didn't complain at being alone, but took care to let him spend his time reading and studying. Having begun their lives together, Fanny Jones persuaded her husband to give up his work at the quarry, not only because of the dangers, but so that he would be enabled to spend all his time preparing for the Ministry in seeking to save sinners. She succeeded in getting him out of the quarry and committing all his time to the Ministry, and this was a cause of rejoicing for her throughout all her life. She had been an instrument for her husband to consecrate his whole life to the cause of his Saviour.

By her endeavour with the shop, and it was a very great effort, she succeeded in supporting John Jones and the family, and she gave him every opportunity to prepare for his great mission. She took all the responsibility for the business, so that John Jones didn't have to worry or bother at all with the work. Fanny Jones possessed plenty of will-power in undertaking the task, and also plenty of ability for it to work out successfully. She feared in case earthly circumstances should have an effect on John Jones's spirituality, since she was totally convinced that he was specially set apart for the work. As Welsh people we are under a great debt to this woman, and we can never put a price on her service nor measure the work she did in being an instrument to give 'the People's Preacher' to the people … In her self denial, Wales heard a message from Heaven—her efforts facilitated the way for Wales to be drenched by the irresistible eloquence of the 'hero from Talysarn'.

Her endeavour was a means for John Jones to have leisure
to produce his great thoughts; her efforts allowed him to
travel throughout Wales to declare the message with such
strength. He acknowledged this often while on his journeys,
and he spoke of how much of a comfort Fanny was to him,
and how she was such a blessing to him in his inner being.
"Fanny," he said, "is a great help to me in going on through
the journey of my life." He was altogether wholly to thank
his wife for this quietness from earthly care. She accepted
the pains and burdens of life so that he could enjoy 'the
quietness of the mountain of the Lord'; and, to draw from
the Divine thoughts, his soul drank from the great inexhaustible
fountain which is everlasting in its springing and its continuing.
O glorious wife!

Although John Jones became very popular, his earnings
were very small, and although his labour was endless and his
calls were frequent and many, he was not much 'nearer the
shore' in a financial sense, since his income was shamefully
weak. Since they had increasing family pressures, … it was
necessary for [Fanny] to double her efforts, and she did that
rather than hinder, nor at all prevent, her husband going on.
She thought highly of him, and that his success and his service
to his country and the Lord depended much on her effort.
Also, she possessed very high views of the talent of her
husband—she believed that he was a special gift from above
and that her responsibility was to ease the way so that his
talent had every facility to be revealed. She admired his
honesty and conscientiousness, and his pure and unsullied
character; and since her belief in her husband was so deep,
she gave him her sympathy in the hardships of life, and she
assisted him in chasing away every weariness by reminding
him of parts of the Scriptures—most commonly the Psalms.

Her exceptional acumen and keenness of mind—and here

was one of the strongest features of her character—was an advantage to her, in view of her unselfish nature, and were the basis of her right and pure purposes. If it had happened that her husband had failed on the national stage, he would have gone against the wishes and assistance of his faithful wife—one who rejoiced in his success, one who had confidence concerning his future, one who did everything possible for him toward his lifting of fallen humanity, and of gathering the lost sheep of Christ. If it hadn't been for the effort of Fanny Jones, doubtless John Jones would have failed, since he could never have provided for his family with the small earnings he had from preaching, and Wales would have lost the most important message in the world. They had twelve children and his earnings were too little to be able to keep the family but for the industry and thrift of Fanny Jones. If it had happened that she had been different from what she was—wasteful, thoughtless and lazy, John Jones would have had to set apart his time for temporal needs; but she was otherwise, and Wales should—not only Dyffryn Nantlle— raise her up as a woman worthy to be remembered.

Had it not been for the valuable virtues of her character, John Jones would have had to give his genius to work for earthly things, and through that, Wales would have lost a vital message, and he couldn't have raised his fellow-men nor given them spiritual edification. O noble, splendid work! A woman who was spiritual enough to hear the message entrusted to her, and had plenty of grace, wisdom and love in her heart to carry it out for the benefit of a country and the pleasure of her Creator.

However busy and hurried were her business troubles and her earthly demands, they did not affect at all her faithfulness and punctuality at the means of grace. She closed up her shop on work-nights, i.e. for the Seiat (fellowship meeting) and the prayer meeting, and took care that all the children came to all the [services] without exception. Fanny Jones came there in her black, the children being driven like an army in front of her to the seat so that they didn't stop and loiter in front of the chapel.

When John Jones was at home, all the children had to get up early to do their chores; and in the evening again, they were expected to be ready with a [Bible] verse each, and the mother wouldn't be slow with her verse. She took that as a habit for herself, since she believed that to be an example like this had great influence.

BUSINESS WOMAN

Soon, the scope of her business widened, so that she had to keep servants and maids; and her chief mark at this time was to take care to keep them all busy. She was privileged with the talent of winning customers, and also with skill and peerless wisdom to keep them after getting them, and they remained faithful customers to her while she was in business. They kept a blacksmith's forge to be convenient to all rural needs in the area and they hired a craftsman for this service. Thus they succeeded to have some comfort, and this help along with other things was enough to enable them to live more easily. Also they kept all sorts of materials and tools for the workmen together with [gun] powder for use in the quarries. Bit by bit, the shop developed and that under Fanny Jones's management alone, until her circle widened. In the end the business became a General Drapery, Grocery, Ironmongery, etc. on a rather abundant scale.

Since she kept a shop with such a variety of articles, and the population was growing as the quarries were developing, the calls for different goods in the business were great. To meet the hosts of requests, and to make up the usual supply, she would go all the way to Chester and to different towns in England. Sometimes she travelled by coach part of the way, other times she would ride the whole way to Chester [on horseback], and this meant—at that inconvenient period— undoubted determination and courage. Look at the picture—a woman who had denied herself the temporal luxuries of life, who had undertaken its burdens, its pains, its troubles—had gone out to the field as if to wrestle with circumstances in the heat of her love for her husband, and with the help of Heaven had succeeded in overcoming her difficulties, and had withstood their assaults. Her love for the success of her husband was the means for her to tread on the rocky objections of the world and to fly from them higher to the cloudless blue sky of success. Who would not say as they looked at this picture, "O excellent woman, splendid wife!" The blessing of her life was to strive for her husband's sake. She sucked comfort from the stuff that was a grief for some. She rejoiced in cares that would make some people complain—her character strengthened and developed in circumstances which would weaken and ruin some wives.

Because of the growth of her business, the development of the region and the inconvenience of the shop in the face of this increase, they built a new house and shop in a central place in the Talysarn area, and they moved there, and doubtless this move was better for the shop no matter how widespread was the sphere of her business in the old place. While in the new place she was very kind to the poor, and tender to those in distress. She aimed hard to better the circumstances of the area and one of the prominent marks of her life was to want to guide the poor in how to live, and to encourage them to economise. These were her works and her words in accord with each other—she acted out what she preached, or more rightly, perhaps, she preached in her actions.

Although she was thrifty and economical, and attempted to prepare for the future, she could not, because of the element of tenderness in her nature, leave anyone in want; and she contributed tens of pounds through this. She offered work to the poor children in the area, and gave them belly-fulls of food for doing it. She didn't believe in giving pennies to children, in case they got used to being wasteful in their childhood.

Though she was stubborn and tough with regard to circumstances in the world, she wasn't allowed to avoid drinking from the bitter cup of the trials of the world, and the severity of the storms had this affect on her—the whirlwinds blasted a little the edge of her joy. She lost three children, and in August 1857, lost her husband, who was so dear in her eyes, and the one for whose sake she had devoted her life. She remained faithful to him and was kind to him to the last moments.

The death of John Jones affected her deeply, and she was in the depth of the valley of sorrow, depressed and gloomy, for a long time after he died. A remarkable fact in her history was that she was far above anyone in comforting those in mourning. She could give a word of comfort to those who were deepest in the moist land of tears, but when she herself was in the valley, it was difficult to meet anyone more grave. In her deep trial at this time she received scores of letters to sympathise and comfort her. From among the multitude it is possible that one from the Morgans of Dyffryn is among the best:

Dyffryn
August 21, 1857
Dear Mrs Jones,
I received a letter from your son, containing the sad news of the death of your dear husband. I wasn't, since some weeks,

daring to hope to hear anything else; yet when this heavy news came, the fact, after all, was incredible to me; even now I cannot persuade myself that the world is without John Jones, Talsarn. But, oh, it is so. Oh unrestorable loss! There are tens of thousands in Wales whose hearts are bleeding because of it, and not without cause. One of the chief pillars of Methodism has been broken; one who did more, it cannot be argued against, nor is there anyone living now, to draw the attention of the whole Principality to the great things that 'belong to peace';[3] one who was an instrument to stir more in the minds of thousands— who ended in eternal life. 'He turned many to righteousness'.[4] But the race is over; the prize is won; the crown is worn; no more fear for eternity; the last enemy is defeated; the palms in his hand; and a tune more sweet than he ever composed, although some of them have great charm for us, on his lips. Almost we can imagine hearing him say to those he has left behind, "Don't weep; sorrow is over, joy has come in its place." But to you he is a great loss. Wales has lost an incomparable preacher. I have lost a dear friend; but you have lost everything that everyone else has lost and much more. I don't know what to say to you. It would be easier for me to weep with you than to say something to you. It was not a small privilege to have lived with such a seraphic man; but that makes the bitterness of the loss greater for you. Further, the world cannot be but a desert for you; but you are not without the knowledge that there is One who can 'speak to content your heart' that is troubled 'in the wilderness'. You are not without knowing that you need not die of thirst in the parched land you are in, because there is a fountain of living water nearby. But you must have One to lead to it. I can only desire this for you. No one but the 'Good Physician' can put the wine and oil on the wounds. But He is One so able for that today, and the One so ready to do it, as when He did that for Mary and Martha. There is no small consolation in the little verse you taught the children before their tongues spoke clearly, 'Jesus wept'.[5]

Mrs Morgan joins with me in sympathising with you all from the heart, and in greeting you and the whole family, in the kindest way. May the 'God of the orphans and the Judge of the widows'[6] keep you from sinking and sorrow 'as those without hope'.7 I am hindered by a misfortune that my animal suffered from coming to the funeral. It would have been very good if I had been able to come there. Although that would have been nothing, it would have been all I could have done now, for one of the most excellent men who was ever on the earth, and one of those for whom I had more respect than anyone I ever knew.

I am, dear Mrs Jones,
Yours sincerely,
Edward Morgan

As it can be seen it was a very suitable letter for one of Fanny's state of mind. Her life spoke of how dear John Jones was in her eyes and how faithful she had been to him.

LAST DAYS

After giving up her shop [Fanny] was for many years in a private house—Brynafon, and she spent her time seeing her friends and the old saints of the area. Also she went from place to place visiting her children who were married and spread about.

In May 1877, she went to Llandinam to comfort her son, the Revd D. Lloyd Jones, MA, who had newly lost his wife. When she had been there for about three months, she got an inflammation of the lungs, and after being in bed for a short while, she died at the fair age of 72 years—twenty years after her dear husband, i.e. 13 August 1877.

While in Llandinam, she was quite calm and cheerful and yet, one day she said she thought she had come there to die. It was as if she had received a private message from the spiritual world. Around five days before her death, as spiritual as ever, she related her experience to the Revd Daniel Rowlands, MA, Bangor. In the seiat (fellowship meeting) that night, the reverend gentleman came to her and said, "Well, Mrs Jones, bach, what is on your mind tonight?" "Oh," she said, lifting up her hand, "I am very glad, Mr Rowlands, that I have such a God to trust in—the same God I have here as I had at home—a God whose faithfulness I can trust in every place. Blessed be His name for ever! for ever!"

And she told her daughter Fanny one day, "I came here, my girl, because I am anxious for you. Thomas told me you were poorly, and I was afraid for you to come home and leave your brother in his trouble, and his two little children in the care of strangers, I will help you to raise this dear little baby." On the last Sabbath of her life, she said to her daughter Fanny, "The time has come to an end." "What do you mean?" asked her daughter. "Don't you know that it is twenty years since your father died; yes, the twenty years are up." It is appropriate to mention here the strange coincidence relating to the twenty years. When John Jones was approaching death, he called Fanny Jones to his bedside, and naturally she was greatly troubled, and seeing her, he said, "Don't break your heart, my girl, you will come to heaven to me." "Oh," she said, "What breaks my heart is the fear that I won't be able to spend eternity with you. I shan't mind if my Heavenly Father leaves me behind for twenty years, as long as I can come after you then, John bach." "Oh, you will, you will," he said, "don't let the devil pain you, Fanny bach."

It is glorious to see God's saints sailing to their home from the wilderness of this world—turning their backs on the tears and sighs, and facing endless blessedness, leaving a world of great afflictions and going to eternal paradise, ending mourning and beginning bliss. Our subject when leaving this world was like a noble vessel going into the heavenly haven from the stormy ocean of life; and the virtues flowered so beautifully in her life like white banners on the vessel, waving quietly under the gentle touching breezes of the land 'where the sky is always clear' ('lle mae'r wybren fyth yn glir').[8]

When as if on the doorstep of another world, she called her daughter Fanny, and said to her, "What do you think of your mother's faith?" "Oh," she said, "It is a true faith,"— and Mrs Fanny Jones added, "I had three rocks to rest on through the night," and raising up her right hand she said, "here they are—'and I give unto them eternal life',9 and the other," she said, lifting up her left hand, "'and they shall never be lost',10 and the third," she said, while beating her hand on her heart, "'none shall pluck them out of my hand' 11— Blessed be God—Oh my dear Jesus."

At this, David entered, and she said to him again, "I was telling your sister that I had three rocks through the night," and then she began shouting—"Glory for ever for the unshakeable plan [of salvation]." "What do you think of your mother's faith, David bach?" "It is a splendid one," he said. At that time, Mr Davies, Llandinam came in, and seeing him, she raised her hand and said, "Yes, Mr Davies, everyone in these circumstances are on the same level, aren't they—'*on equality*', isn't it?" "They are, Mrs Jones," he replied, "but you will soon be on higher ground than I." On going down the stairs, he said with tears running down his cheeks, "*Pray for the Lord to take her to Himself, she is too good for this world— yes, too perfect indeed—let her go.*" Isn't it a glorious death?—to die with every certainty that 'the everlasting arms were under her', and her entrance abundant into the glory of her Lord.

This is what the Revd D. Lloyd Jones, MA said of her death: "One night, the door of my room was knocked and I was told she was worse. I got up and went to the room, and going behind her, I lifted her up to a sitting position by putting my arms under her armpits; and while I was holding her up, she looked towards heaven, and her immortal spirit flew to the unseen world."

By this time her industrious and troublous life was over—

a life of faithfulness and incomparable comfort to her husband. Her spirit flew to the 'One who gave it',[12] and she left the world with the Great Sun of righteousness shining on her soul.[13]

Histories are speckled with men of philosophy having been destroyed by petulant wives, like Titian, Carlyle, Dickens, Thackeray, etc, but here is one whose wife was every comfort to him. One who had been a blessing to him, and not a curse, one who had helped and not hindered him. 'Fanny' kept thoroughly pure to him, and she assisted him in all the circumstances of his life. She did not give one minute of hindrance to her husband but aimed to facilitate every part of his life. After all the weary work, a life full of effort, in a troubled age, her spirit was taken away to 'float in love and peace' ('nofio mewn cariad a hedd').[14]

Notes

1 O. Llew. Owain, *Cofiant Mrs. Fanny Jones, Gweddw y Diweddar Barch. J. Jones, Talysarn* (Machynlleth a Caernarfon, 1907).
2 Ibid. 43.
3 Luke 19: 42
4 Dan. 12: 3
5 Jn 11: 35
6 Deut. 10: 18
7 1 Thess. 4: 13
8 See the hymn 'Gwêl uwchlaw cymylau amser'/'See above the clouds of time' (Islwyn).
9 John 10: 28a.
10 John 10: 28b.
11 John 10: 28c.
12 Ecclesiastes 12: 7.
13 Malachi 4: 2.
14 From the hymn 'O fryniau Caersalem ceir gweled'/'From heavenly Jerusalem's towers' (David Charles).

APPENDIX 2
DAVID LLOYD JONES

David Lloyd Jones (1843–1905) was the youngest son of the famous Welsh Calvinistic Methodist preacher John Jones, Talsarn (1796–1857) and his wife Fanny. A teenage lad at the time, David spent many hours with his father during the great preacher's last weeks and days on earth. Among many moving exchanges between father and son, David was asked, "My dear boy … are you determined to cling to your faith?" "Yes, father, for ever and ever," was David's reply. Both of them affirming their dependence on the grace of God, dying John Jones said, "Remember to keep your promise to remain true to the faith, true to the end." In his last hours, David's father was often heard to whisper, "O dear Jesus! O beloved Jesus! Blessed be Thy name for ever!" When he breathed his last on the Lord's Day, 16 August 1857, 'The sunset glow of that great soul sank into the boy's heart, leaving a memory which the passing years could not efface. When his father had passed away, the boy, overwhelmed with wonder and grief, went to his mother, who was then herself confined to bed, and so unable to bid her husband farewell. "Mother, mother," he cried, "father has this moment gone to heaven; he has just reached there, and he has seen Jesus whom he loved so much!"'[1]

These experiences could not fail to make a deep impression on the youngest son of John Jones. As surely as the preacher's ministry affected the lives of thousands of others, it also

influenced his son David. The great revival of 1859 reinforced
these early impressions. 'The revival made itself felt with
extraordinary power in the neighbourhood of Talysarn; and
David was among those who were most profoundly moved
by it'.[2]

David early sensed God's call to walk in his father's footsteps.
So, towards the close of 1860, he entered the old Grammar
School at Clynnog run by Ebenezer Thomas, 'a quiet and
modest man of rare culture and poetic genius'.[3] This school
served to prepare young men to enter the theological college
at Bala. It wasn't long before young David was exhibiting
the character traits of his famous father. When he began to
preach in 1862, albeit informally at this stage, interest was
aroused over a wide area:

> When it became known that a son of John Jones, Talsarn,
> was preparing to enter the ministry, the whole countryside
> was in a state of eager expectancy. The memory of his father
> was still vivid in the hearts of multitudes; and in congregations
> throughout that part of the country there was an ardent desire
> to see the son of one who, in so peculiar a sense, was the
> 'People's Preacher'.[4]

This great sense of expectancy is easy to understand. The
mere sight of him brought many to tears. While there were
obvious disadvantages for anyone attempting to following
the seraphic John Jones, congregations were seldom disappointed
when they heard David Lloyd Jones:

> Old admirers of his father would exchange significant glances
> as the young preacher proceeded; and when some remark or
> illustration was made which bore the characteristics of the
> father's style, they could be seen looking round and nodding
> to one another in a way that unmistakenly meant: "That is it
> ... That was indeed one of the old Talsarn strokes."[5]

For all the similarities with his father, young David began to win wide popularity on his own merits. 'Some of his sermons at this period give evidence of much originality, and his delivery of them was often powerful in a marked degree'.[6]

David entered the college at Bala in 1861. He proved himself a diligent and accomplished student, finishing top of the year in 1865. Moving to Pembroke Dock in 1866, he served as chaplain to the workmen employed by Messrs Davies & Roberts in the construction of the Pembroke and Tenby Railway. From there David went to Edinburgh University where he attained his MA degree in 1869. Reflecting the 'Scottish presbyterianizing' influence introduced by Lewis Edwards (1809–87),[7] this development indicated a shift of thinking regarding training for the ministry among the Calvinistic Methodists. There were dangers in these changes, that academic respectability might erode the spirituality and power of earlier generations. In David's case this proved sadly to be so for a while:

> His style in the pulpit was more scholarly and scientific, and he had, to a considerable extent, lost the fervour and fire which had formerly filled his spirit, and his popularity suffered. Many agreed with what the old deacon, Robert Jones, Tan'rallt said to Mr Lloyd Jones's sister: "Dafydd began to preach with the same manner as your father had, full of a burning earnestness, and his voice was as a trumpet, but he went to these colleges, and they have spoiled him; he has lost your father's 'home strokes'. It's those wretched schools and colleges that have done it."[8]

It is worthy of note that David Lloyd Jones was himself aware of what was happening. He was clearly disturbed and exercised in his spirit by the time he received a call to the Calvinistic Methodist pastorate at Llanidloes in 1870. He was soon shaking off the deadening influences of academia, and growth in the congregation demanded the building of a new and larger chapel. Immersed in the realities of life and the pastoral care of his growing flock, David began to dig deep for the resources he needed. His father's example was increasingly evident. 'The woods became Mr Lloyd Jones favourite resort. Here, with that love of solitude which was so marked in his father, he would every day spend hours in meditation'.[9] As surely as John Jones met with God in the woods of Talysarn, so his son David enjoyed the divine presence in the woods of Llanidloes:

> Many a time, we are told, while he was meditating, in the quiet of the wood on what he was to preach, the congregation on a Sunday morning had to wait for him. And often, too, the miners, as they went to or from their work, morning and evening, would hear his melodious voice echoing through the woods which lay on the other side of the glen by which they passed. "That little plantation," says one who knew him well, "is to us, to this day, a hallowed place. We feel, as we draw nigh to it, as though we could draw off our shoes from our feet, because it is holy ground, a place where God's servant gazed with reverent awe on the wonders of the bush."[10]

Clearly, the God-inspired vision of the father was now gripping the son. The evidence for this appears in David Lloyd Jones's address to the church which appeared with his Report for the year 1874, the very year Dr Owen Thomas's monumental biography of John Jones was published. The father would have rejoiced to see the spiritual priorities of his son in the following extract, priorities which remain as valid for the 21st century as when they were first uttered:

> We find from these statistics that Christ's cause among us, in all its outward aspects, is in a most flourishing and satisfactory condition. Few churches in the Principality possess such valuable

property, freehold and free of debt, as we have. The most pessimistic can hardly discover any dark cloud which darkens our prospects. The ship seems well made and fully equipped. No rocks or quick-sands are within sight. It is true that we cannot expect a passage which shall be perfectly calm and free from storms. Yet, notwithstanding the troubled waves and wild commotions of the sea, the vessel is bound to land safely if only we have Him on board who calmed the troubled sea of Galilee. If He is at the helm, and if all the workers carry out His commands, the voyage will be one without much damage or hurt, either of our own lives, or of the lading and ship.

One of our dangers in the present day is to be satisfied with the external aspects of religion, with grand edifices and elaborate ceremonial, with a system of creeds, rules, regulations, and observances. There can be no more dangerous error. A church may have all such outward adornments in the highest perfection, and yet be entirely void of what constitutes a true and living church. We must at all times strive to keep before our minds the ideal of a Christian Church. The true church has always been, and ever will be, made up of men 'called out of the world.' The disciples of Christ must be separated from the world. 'They are not of the world,' says Christ, 'even as I am not of the world.' They are in the world, but are not of the world. The Christian is intended to be as a drop of oil in the ocean, touching it on every side, yet not mingling with it.

The prosperous church is that in which all her members partake of the Spirit of Jesus, and follow in His footsteps. Never was there a time when more prominence was given to Ritualism in all its aspects than in our day. But we must never forget that good, holy, devoted men are immeasurably more important for the prosperity, nay, even for the existence of the church than any elaborate organizations or established orders. All schemes and regulations, however well adapted for their work, are bound in the long run to be failures in the hands of unholy men. On the other hand, ordinary and comparatively obscure men,—men with little worldly wisdom or power or influence,— if they possess the Spirit of Christ and are moved by holy enthusiasm for the glory of His name, will prosper; they cannot but prosper, for He himself is with them. You have then a

Church of Christ, a real Church, with His own Divine presence filling it with light and life and joy."[11]

For all the similarities between father and son, David did not possess his father's talents for music and poetry. Neither was he as forthright a campaigner[12] as the 'hero of Talysarn'. However, the kindness of his father combined with the tenderness of his mother to produce a deeply compassionate and sensitive personality. A seemingly trivial incident illustrates this. Being more bookish than his father, he had little inclination for outdoor pursuits. However, one day his friend Thomas Jones induced him to go shooting. Our biographer takes up the story:

> Mr Lloyd Jones took hold of a gun and fired at a crow. To his great astonishment, his shot took effect, and brought the crow down. He was much concerned at this, but it was a great delight to him to find that the shot had not been fatal. Nothing could then keep him from taking the crow to the house, and trying to heal its wound; and to his great joy, his treatment was successful. It was a great relief to him to be delivered from the burden of passing through life conscious of having killed a crow. The incident, trivial though it may seem, is an indication of his sympathy and tenderness of heart, and of the extreme care which marked him throughout his life not to hurt or give offence to any one.[13]

Augmenting the spiritual happiness of the Llanidloes ministry, this same year (1874) witnessed David's marriage to Sophia Williams. However, though blessed with two sons, Egerton and David, their wedded life lasted only three years. Never possessing robust health, Sophia actually died a year after David Lloyd Jones had been called to the church at nearby Llandinam. Anxious to comfort her son and two grandsons, Fanny Jones travelled from Talysarn. She stayed in Llandinam for three months until she herself died—in great faith and assurance—of inflammation of the lungs on 13 August 1877.[14] The double grief David experienced had a wonderfully-deepening effect on his ministry. He was also comforted when, six years later, he married Annie, daughter of the Revd and Mrs Evan Jones.

Beside the pastorates at Llanidloes (1870–5) and Llandinam (1875–1905), David Lloyd Jones served the cause of Christ with great distinction in Wales. Honoured by his brethren in the Calvinistic Methodist Connexion, he was Secretary of the General Assembly in 1883–4, Moderator of the North Wales Association in 1899 and Moderator of the General Assembly in 1904. His wider ministry in urban centres and rural districts was warmly appreciated and greatly blest. 'Never was his bearing more gracious, his voice more winning, and never was his message delivered with greater unction than at these gatherings'.[15] A true son of John Jones, Talsarn, David's sermons 'were full of protests and warnings against all kinds of religion which consisted in mere forms and rites. He emphasized the utter inadequacy of all ceremonies to make up for the lack of spirituality'.[16] His impact was not unlike his father's: 'It is no exaggeration to say that, during the last twenty years of his life, no preacher was more popular with all classes'.[17]

There can be no doubt that the father's mantle rested upon the son. Though being more of a scholar than his father, David inherited much of his father's pulpit eloquence: 'None of his sermons, possibly, could be compared in depth of thought, and width of scope, with the best discourses of his father, since he had constantly to preach to the same people'.[18] In fact, he was happier as a pastor than filling the role of an 'ecclesiastic'. His care of the young was exemplary; he was diligent, considerate and patient. Besides being personally involved with the Bible Classes, the Llandinam church had a flourishing Band of Hope.[19]

David Lloyd Jones was also a zealous supporter of the 'Forward Movement' of the Presbyterian Church of Wales. He was accordingly involved with efforts to establish English-speaking churches in the non Welsh-speaking parts of eastern Wales. While his preference for the Welsh language was unquestioned, his chief loyalty was to the Gospel rather than to the language.[20]

In his reading and sermon preparation, David Lloyd Jones's preferences were for the old Church Fathers and the Puritans. He especially reverenced Matthew Henry as a commentator. "The ancient writers stand far higher than our modern theologians."[21] At the time when Darwin, Huxley and Spencer were beginning to assault Christianity with their speculative infidelities, David Lloyd Jones 'was never so far carried away by any speculations of this character as to experience any wavering in his faith. He remained strong in his conviction, through the turmoil of that exciting period, that 'the firm foundation of God standeth sure', and that it would continue so to stand in the face of all assaults'.[22] Sadly, as if bewitched by the growing liberalism, not everyone shared his faithfulness.

Besides the intense spirituality and biblical fidelity of his preaching, David Lloyd Jones employed copious illustrations of Gospel truth from history, geography, science—especially astronomy—and technology. He gave lectures on subjects such as 'The Great Buildings of the World' and 'The Famous Bridges of the World'.[23] After the Tay Bridge railway disaster of 1879, he declared: 'After the hurricanes of the Judgement have laid the old pyramids level with the ground, the bridge of God, from misery to glory, will stand'.[24] Many people remembered his explanation of the Saviour's sacrifice on Calvary: 'The Father blasting the Rock of Ages, to make a breakwater between man's soul and the storm'.[25] Much as he had applauded the father, the Revd Owen Jones, Newtown praised the son: "I always thought of Mr Lloyd Jones as one who belonged to the highest class of thinkers. There was nothing common about him. Like his father,—John Jones, Talysarn,—his mind was of the Miltonic type'.[26] He was a thorough-going Welshman, aware of the rich heritage of his people. While he showed much interest in the history of Persians, Greeks, Romans and Saxons, 'the history which gave him most delight was that of the Celts and the Welsh. The story of the Welsh people and of the Methodist Fathers had a special charm for him. He was a warm admirer of Griffith Jones, Llanddowror; Howell Harris, Daniel Rowland, William Williams, Pantycelyn; David Jones, Llangan; Thomas Charles of Bala, and of the excellent men associated with them'.[27]

David Lloyd Jones made some interesting ethnic comparisons between the English and the Welsh:

Another subject on which he talked much was the position of the Church of England in Wales. He was strongly in favour of the disestablishment of this Church; and he believed that in her present form she would never succeed in regaining possession of the nation. "She will never do," he would say, "for the Celts; she is too deficient in emotional warmth to appeal to the lively and warm temperament of the Welsh people. The liturgy of the Church of England does not suit them; it is not sufficiently emotional. The high ritualism of the Church of Rome is more likely to appeal to them. This is what accounts for the success of the Romish Church in France and in Ireland; and this is why the Welsh were at one time such ardent Papists. This longing for the emotional which lies so deep in the nature of our Welsh people is met in some measure by the warmth of the pulpit and of our sacred songs. My firm conviction is that if the enthusiasm and intensity which have been so marked a feature in Welsh preaching are lost, it will lose its hold and influence on the hearts of the people."[28]

That said, one wonders how accurate such stereotypical statements are. After all, one has met dour, unemotional Welshmen *and* highly-emotional English people. And not all the English are Anglicans. Is it not the case that England's Rome-inspired, Latin-based imperial culture tends to suppress spontaneity in a manner rightly resisted by the kind of 'grass-roots' features prominent in both Welsh *and* English Nonconformity? From a liturgical perspective, it may be said that the balance inherent in Calvin's Genevan Liturgy provides a check on the dangers of over-mechanical forms of worship and unregulated spontaneity alike.[29]

In the wake of earlier debates over Calvinism and the consequent amendments of 1874 to the *Confession of Faith*, there's no mistaking where David Lloyd Jones stood. Following in the theological footsteps of his father, he also anticipated the evangelistic theology of Dr D. Martyn Lloyd-Jones (1899–1981). Happy to affirm that Christians are 'chosen in [Christ] before the foundation of the world' (*Eph. 1: 4*),[30] his sermons indicate that he had no sympathy with the ultra-orthodoxy of John Elias. While Stressing that 'the salvation of sinners is due to God's benevolence and mercy' and that 'salvation is always the work of Sovereign grace', he was comfortable in preaching John 3: 16 without restrictive overtones.[31] Indeed, his 'free offer' Gospel preaching was uninhibited:

> You can approach God in Christ without darkness and despair. He inspired all who approached him with confidence and peace. 'God was in Christ reconciling the world unto himself not imputing their trespasses unto them' [*2 Cor. 5: 19*]. To see God in Christ is eternal life.[32]
>
> By his sufferings and death he was qualified to be the great corner stone of the church, and the foundation of eternal hope to all men.[33]

He who declared himself a Divine Person, and claimed for himself a sinless human nature, entered into such a connection with the sins of the world that he 'was made sin for us'.34

Through his Incarnation and death he has become the Saviour of the world.35

On this subject, David Lloyd Jones's contemporary, friend and fellow-Moderator of the Presbyterian Church of Wales (1901) Dr J. Cynddylan Jones (1840–1930) is probably the most articulate Welsh theologian of the late nineteenth/early twentieth century. Contrary to John Aaron's 'Owenite' perspective, Dr Cynddlylan Jones published in 1912 an 'authentic Calvinist' statement on the extent of the atonement which John Calvin, Richard Baxter and John Jones, Talsarn would happily identify with.36 This biblical stance was thus mediated to the twentieth century. Dr Cynddylan Jones also provided 'wise advice' (according to Iain H. Murray) on preaching to young Dr D. Martyn Lloyd-Jones in 1927.37 There can be no doubt that the younger man agreed with the older man's view of the Atonement (see Appendix 8).

There was scarcely an Association or a General Assembly during the last twenty-five years of his life to which David Lloyd Jones was not specially invited as preacher. Dr Cynddylan Jones said of him that he was the most popular preacher that visited South Wales from the North, and that the question asked in all parts of South Wales, when the news came of his sudden death in 1905, was, 'Who could be found to fill his place in the Associations and the Anniversaries?' Many a time he delivered powerful sermons which left indelible impressions on the memories and hearts of the great audiences which he addressed.

A good example—and worthy of extended quotation— is seen in an account of a sermon preached by him at the General Assembly held at Merthyr in 1888. It was a sermon of unusual impressiveness, but it may be taken as an example of the power which often attended his preaching at the great gatherings which were so notable a feature of Welsh religious life. The description is given in the words of the Revd T. J. Edwards of Merthyr:

> I was prevented from being present at the services except on the last day of the Assembly. At the 10 o'clock service, the late Revd William Jones, Trawsfynydd, and Dr Owen Thomas were the preachers at Pontmorlais Chapel; and having heard the Revd William Jones (then minister of David Street Church, Liverpool) and Mr Lloyd Jones announced as the preachers at Soar Independent Chapel at the afternoon service, I decided to go and hear them.
>
> The first sermon was preached by Mr William Jones. After him Mr Lloyd Jones preached, taking as his text,—'Nevertheless, when the Son of man cometh, shall he find faith on the earth?' (*Luke 18: 8*). His movements at first were slow and heavy. He took a very depressing view of the strong forces of infidelity in the present day, and of the possibility that unbelief might continue to grow in the future. "The probability is," he said, "that unbelief will grow and increase to an alarming extent in the world. If infidelity is even now so strong and powerful, what will it be in the remote future, when men will be separated from the historic facts on which Christianity is based by periods of many thousands of years? If the brief, dim, imperfect glance which we possess now into the infinite extent of the creation produces such doubt and infidelity, what may we expect to result when all the veils which now cover the secrets of nature are removed, when the veil of the Shekinah is rent, and man can arrogantly gaze on what had been supposed to be a Divine glory? Shall He find faith on the earth? Are not the scientific researches of our day a peril to faith? As man draws aside one veil after another from the mysteries of nature, is he not in danger of losing sight of the great First Cause which lies behind the whole? Speculations on the physical creation are being taught which lead directly to pure atheism. It is the unwavering

conviction of some of the ablest of our men of science that all that really exists may be resolved into matter and energy.

So the preacher went on for a long while in this strain, and spoke of the powerful forces which seem as though they would completely destroy Christian faith. Something like depression had spread over the audience, and every one seemed to expect that the sermon would end in a mood of deep melancholy. But suddenly, after a brief silence, he began to ask, with a deep solemnity in his countenance,—"When the Son of man cometh, shall He find faith on the earth?" As soon as the question was asked, Mr Jones, Trawsfynydd, who sat immediately before him in the pulpit pew, cried,—"Yes, He shall! He shall!" "He shall," responded the preacher. Then he asked the question again, with greater emotion even than before,—"When the Son of man cometh, shall He find faith on the earth?" And this time, answers came from all parts of the audience,—"Yes; He shall, He shall!" The whole audience was by now profoundly moved, and tears were falling from the eyes of many.

Then, with an abrupt charge, the preacher proceeded in a leisurely manner to give a description of the mountains talking with the Jordan on the day when its waters stood in a heap [see Josh. 3: 13–17]. "Do you see,'" he said, "the Jordan over there stopping one day on its journey, and how the mountains begin to question her,—"What, O Jordan, is wrong with thee today? Why dost thou not run to-day as on all the other days? We never saw thee still before. Go on thy course, why dost thou stop?" And the Jordan replies,—"Do what I will, I cannot go on today. Do you see that small chest, that ark, with a few men standing by the side of it? I cannot pass beyond that chest and the men who guard it. You must move that chest away, or else I can never go on.

At this point, the preacher with great earnestness addressed his audience,—"Will the wave of infidelity spread over the land? It threatens us. But will it cover the land?" "No! No!'" said the preacher. "No! No!'" echoed many voices from the audience. "Why not?'" the preacher asked, and in a voice full of triumph and joy, and with irresistible power, he answered,— "The Levites stand by the ark! The Levites stand by the ark!

As long as they stand there, the swelling waters will be driven back.

I shall not attempt to describe the scene, or to give expression to the impression which was made on all who were present. It was truly 'unutterable,' something beyond the power of man to produce, or even to express in words. It was the brightest and most glorious ray of the Divine that ever dawned on my soul.[38]

As his father had done sixty-five years before, David Lloyd Jones preached at the Bala Association on 14 June 1900. Replete with appropriate illustrations reflecting his wide interests, the son set forth the glory and grace of Christ just as vividly and powerfully as the father. His text was, 'And to know the love of Christ which passeth knowledge' (*Ephesians 3: 19*). Speaking of the fulness which is treasured up in Christ, streaming forth to meet the needs of man, he said:

> You know that the inhabitants of the great towns in England are in need of water for drinking, and for the cleansing of their houses and streets. What do they do? They come to Wales. Here we have a large rain-fall, and there is no smoke to pollute the rain. So the wise people in Liverpool and Birmingham,— and I should not be surprised to find some day that the London people will follow their example,—have resolved to come to the mountains of Wales for water. They have already constructed one reservoir, and they are busily making another in the central parts of Wales. There is one for the inhabitants of Liverpool in Montgomeryshire, and there will soon be another for Birmingham in Radnorshire. But, as you know well, though thousands of pounds were spent on the construction of these reservoirs, and though the rain might fill them to the brim, the people of Liverpool and Birmingham would not get a drop of water unless pipes were laid down to carry it to their towns. And that requires a vast capital. They would get no benefit from that lake Vyrnwy in Montgomeryshire, or from that lake which will soon be seen near the borders of Breconshire and Radnorshire and Cardiganshire, if it were not that the

capital of the citizens of Liverpool and Birmingham is spent
on laying down the pipes. Ah! God, too, had purposed from
eternity to make a reservoir. He sent His beloved Son into
this world to construct it. And on Calvary, lo! a great cloud
bursts, and fills it to overflowing. But, my friends, though Jesus
was full of righteousness to the brim, no sinner could ever be
justified on the ground of that righteousness if the Holy Spirit
had not come to give him faith. And, there, on Pentecost, the
Father sends Him forth. He sent the Spirit to lay down the
mains through which the Divine fulness might flow for the
supply of the needs of three thousand souls.

Another way by which we may know something of the
Divine fulness is through the great revolutions which it effects
in men's character. I remember visiting, many years ago, the
Government Dockyard in Pembroke Dock, where I saw great
steel plates ten inches thick,—I believe they now make them
fifty-five inches thick. I thought as I saw them that no power
could ever bend these; but in a short time, I saw some of them
bent in a hydraulic press just as if they had been sheets of tin.
Ah! my friends, more wonderful things have been done by
love. Look at Saul of Tarsus. There, indeed, you have a steel
plate; but he was brought under the hydraulic press, and he
was bent to the shape required for the vessel, and not all the
forces of hell could bend him back to his old shape. Have you
been bent by the love of God? ... Then we must know the
love of Christ through our having an experience of it in our
hearts. Do you know anything of the Divine love from
experience? I have begun to love Christ, and I cannot now
cease to love Him. I sometimes think of many of the old
farmers in the heart of Wales,—in Radnorshire—say that
though they know so little about the ocean, yet they have
some knowledge. If you were to ask an old farmer from those
parts how much he knew about the sea, he would have to
confess that his knowledge was very small. 'Then you do not
know the depth of the sea between Ireland and America, or
off the coast of Japan? Well, you know nothing about it'. 'Oh,
yes', he would say, 'I do know something. I have been a shepherd
with the sheep on the mountain, and I have seen the sea from
the slopes of Plynlimon,—that great expanse of water stretching

far away. And I have stayed by its shores, have bathed in it, and have waded to a depth of five or six feet, and could feel it lifting me off my feet'. Oh, my friends, before you pass over into the great Eternity, do you know something, something of the love of Christ? 'To know the love of Christ which passeth knowledge'. It will ever lie beyond our comprehension. Some years ago, expeditions were sent out to measure the depth of the ocean, and they succeeded in finding the depth over practically the whole bed of the sea. They are equipped with instruments which can bring up matter from a depth of five miles. If an expedition were sent from heaven to sound the depth of the Divine love, it would never find the bottom. Its members would cry out,—'It is unsearchable; it is past finding out'. And then, with the angels and saints, they would fall down and worship, saying, 'Worthy is the Lamb that was slain'.[39]

The last Association David Lloyd Jones attended was at Caernarfon in 1905. Enthusiasm for the nationwide Revival was in full flood and the revivalist Evan Roberts was also visiting the area.[40] David Lloyd Jones's sermon had a remarkable effect, his text being 'Simon Peter went up, a drew the net to land, full of large fish, … and for all there were so many, yet was not the net broken' (*John 21: 11*). In the context of concern that unwelcome and man-centred features were evident in the revival movement, David Lloyd Jones's emphasis was timely: 'We see in these days how the Revival has broken forth in manifestations of great power in districts which have not been visited by any of the professed Revivalists. The great condition is that we should feel our dependence on Jesus'.[41] The preacher proceeded to focus attention on the power of the Gospel. It is able to transform the most depraved sinners; it meets the need of the entire human race and is able to establish in holiness all who believe. It is reported that 'the influence of the spiritual world was felt in an

extraordinary degree throughout that Association at Caernarfon;
but no part of it produced a deeper impression than Mr Lloyd
Jones melodious voice declaring that 'for all there were so
many, yet was not the net broken' '.[42]

David Lloyd Jones was clearly aware of the dangers of
over-familiarity with the Gospel. In a powerful sermon, 'The
Spirit of the Lord leaving Saul' (based on 1 Samuel 16: 14),
he showed how stubborn hearers become 'Gospel-hardened':

> I remember some years ago speaking with an old soldier
> who had been in the battle of Waterloo. I could see at once
> that the old veteran was very deaf, and I asked him how he
> had come to losing his hearing. "Was it at Waterloo?" I asked.
> "Yes'", he replied. "Ah! I suppose you were wounded, or had
> a severe chill." "No, sir", he said, "it was the booming of the
> big guns that did it." That is how the Gospel has a hardening
> effect on disobedient hearers. 'Their ears become dull of
> hearing'. I have seen many of those who heard John Elias
> preach, and some of them had become terribly dull of hearing.
> Why? 'Oh! the booming of the big guns'.[43]

The last time he entered the pulpit was at the Monthly
meeting at Llanfair-caereinion on 10 November 1905. The
automobile era being in its infancy, he travelled there by car
with his friend the Revd. T. C. Williams, who wrote an
account of the service:

> On this last occasion, he preached with great freedom and
> effect (on Zechariah 14: 20–1). ... No word was lost. As to
> structure, the sermon was one of the best we ever heard from
> him. ... He spoke with visible effect of the beneficent results
> of the [1904] Revival in the greater consideration shown to
> the ponies in the coal-pits. And his magnificent intonation in
> reciting like a refrain the words,—'Holiness unto the Lord
> upon the bridles of the horses'—still rings in my ears. ... He
> began to speak of 'the dear old preachers', as we heard him
> do scores of times, and of the deep longing he felt for them:

'But God has made up for the loss of the great bowls by boiling
the little pots wholesale. God prefers a small pot, if it is boiling,
to having some great cold boiler in his Church'. It seemed to
me that on that night he was more like his father than at any
other time when I heard him, particularly in the playful way
in which he set the truth before the people. ... At his request,
the tune *Llanllyfni*, composed by his father, was sung to the
closing hymn. So the service ended in a spirit of reverence
and praise, and the most melodious of our silver trumpets was
silenced.[44]

After supper at their host's house, he with Dr Cynddylan
Jones and others conversed on the variety of denominations
in Wales and the world of spirits. He had what must have
been a heart attack, from which he recovered. On returning
home the next morning, he had another attack, recovering
enough to prepare his next Sunday sermon on 'Be thou
faithful unto death, and I will give thee a crown of life' (*Rev.
2: 10*]. The sermon was never preached but he was shortly
to receive the crown. A few days later, 'about 7 o'clock on
Wednesday [15 November] he had another attack, and then—
while he was within two months of completing his sixty-third
year, his spirit fled to the land where the inhabitants shall
not say 'I am sick'.[45] The day of the funeral, 20 November,
was 'cold and wintry' with hundreds of mourners gathered
at Llandinam. 'From early morning, each train had brought
friends from all directions to the quiet village by the Severn.
Every preparation had been made for the strangers at the
Village Hall. By 2 o'clock, the road from the station towards
Vron Haul and towards the village was dark with people.
The time appointed for the funeral was 2 o'clock, and by
then a large number of relatives and friends had gathered
together in and around the house'. Several ministerial brethren
took part in the impressive and deeply-moving service. 'The
procession to the churchyard was exceptionally long and

very orderly. ... The service closed with the singing of one of Mr Jones's favourite hymns,—'O, Iachawdwr pechaduriaid', to [his father's] tune *Tan-y-castell*.[46]

There was a sense that the passing of David Lloyd Jones was the end of an era.[47] Something similar was felt with his father's demise in 1857. However, in several respects, the son extended the father's influence in a remarkable manner. His friend, the Revd T. C. Williams went as far as saying, 'I felt he was different from any other preacher. ... When the Power from on high was upon him, he surpassed, in my estimation, all the preachers I have ever heard'.[48] Another friend, the Revd John Williams, cited a mutual friend and one time fellow-student of the son of John Jones, Talsarn:

> I am glad that I heard him preach a few months before his death. I had many times heard him preach, but could never convince myself that he deserved his great reputation. But at a preaching meeting held at Wrexham a short time before his death, his sermon was such that I can never forget it. I then felt certain that he was fully worthy of his fame; he was so magnificent that I felt that whatever praise had been lavished on him, 'the half was not told me'.[49]

Besides his preaching and pastoral care, his moderatorial valedictory address[50] given at Birkenhead on 6 June 1905 was a splendid affirmation of Protestant conviction at a time when resurgent Roman Catholicism was adding to the growing liberal assault on the Reformed Faith:

> When Luther nailed his theses on the Church door at Wittenberg, he tells us that they were known in a fortnight throughout Germany, and in a month they were read in Rome and in every school and convent in Europe. An honest study of the Bible by the masses of the people, which gave rise to the Protestant Reformation, will promote Christian truth and check the spread of Roman Catholicism in our days. This is

the great remedy,—a thorough acquaintance with the contents of the inspired volume. Let us all cling to the impregnable position occupied by Luther at the Diet of Worms,—"Unless I am convinced by the testimony of scripture, or by the clearest reasoning, I cannot, and I will not retract. May God be my helper, I can retract nothing."[51]

His presentation on the Christian ministry[52] is a model of consecration to the cause of Christ for ministers in every age, lived out by the author to the end of his days:

> Self-consecration to the work of the ministry is further shown by cultivating unselfishness, courage, and honesty in clinging to the truth, and not allowing ourselves to deviate a hair's breadth from it under the influence of the tides and currents of society around us … If others desert the truth, let us cling to it and be willing to die rather than forsake it … Allow not 'learned men', 'democracy' or 'aristocracy' to have a dominant influence over our souls, but let us try to muster sufficient moral courage to be thoroughly loyal to the truth and to Christ.[53]

Recalling the vow he made to his dying father, there can be no doubt that David Lloyd Jones had—by the grace of God—been faithful to the end.

POSTSCRIPT

Dr Cynddylan Jones on the Atonement

What answer does the great body of Calvinists give to the question? For whom did Christ die? Without doubt, their first answer would be that Christ died for all. It would be folly for any to query the truth of this response for it is taught clearly in the Holy Scriptures. [He then quotes John 3:16, 17; 1 John 2:2; John 1:29; and 1 Tim. 2:16.] We have no part in limiting the unambiguous statements of the Bible. Because the divine revelation teaches that Christ died for all, we Calvinistic Methodists have always offered salvation to all. Our being Calvinists does not hinder us in our proclamation of a salvation as wide in its extent as all humanity. Perhaps one or two preachers in the old days—the days of the religious controversies—more careful of their Calvinism than of the nurture of their hearers, taught a limited Atonement and a particular Redemption. ... [but] we will have no part in any limitation of the Atonement. It is an infinite Atonement and, as such, it is an Atonement for the whole world. We rather suspect that we differ a little here from Dr Lewis Edwards. He taught the sufficiency of the Atonement but we doubt whether he taught the universality of the Atonement. But we hold to both—its sufficiency and its universality. In our judgement its sufficiency ensures its universality ...

Dr Lewis Edwards, and all Calvinistic divines of any note, used to say that the Atonement had made the salvation of all men possible. What did they mean by this statement? This—that the death of Christ was a sufficient Atonement for all, and that no greater or worthier Atonement is needed were all to be saved without distinction. They defended and proclaimed categorically the possibility of the salvation of the whole world by virtue of the Atonement of the Cross, that there were no obstacles on God's part to the salvation of all. But they were not all as categoric and open as one would wish in their proclaiming that there are no obstacles either on man's part, other than his own unwillingness. In their systems, God did very little, if anything, to break down man's unwillingness or to heal his moral inability, inherent due to the original corruption of his nature. to exercise faith in the Saviour. But it is clear to all that it is not enough to teach that there is a sufficient remedy in the Atonement to heal all the sufferers of the Fall, if they are unable to stretch out a hand to receive that remedy—they will die just as if no remedy existed.

The Atonement makes it possible on God's part to save all the hearers of the Gospel. Does it also make it possible on men's part? Does it remove man's natural inability to believe? Calvinistic divines have not been so clear and open on this as might be desired. We therefore venture to reply that it does. By that which is known as 'Common Grace' it removes the innate inability of sinners to believe. Both Calvinism and Wesleyans acknowledge this Grace. Dr Hodge's Systematic Theology contains a chapter on it, though he does not give it as much attention nor as much emphasis as Wesleyan theologians … the Atonement has ensured Common Grace for all—the secret influence of God's Spirit on all hearers of the Gospel sufficient to remove the moral weakness which results from original sin, and sufficient to enable them to believe in Christ when he is presented to them as a Saviour. No-one in Gospel lands is condemned because he cannot believe, but because he will not though he might. … It is an influence upon them, not an influence in them—God's Spirit working on their minds and pushing them in the direction of faith; and the only reason why they will not believe is the stubbornness of their wills. Not inability but unwillingness … This is the reason, although often possibly quite unconsciously, why we invite unbelievers to believe and come to Christ. We are not exhorting them to do that which they cannot, but encouraging them to do that which they can with the help of the influence of God's Spirit on their mind, which influence is never absent in a religious service any more than the air is absent from the building. It may be seen therefore that we hold as firmly as our respected brethren, the Wesleyans, to the universality of the Atonement, and we stand on the same ground as they in appealing to an ungodly world to believe in Christ.[54]

Notes

1 R. Hughes (ed), *Memoir and Sermons of the Late Revd David Lloyd Jones* (Wrexham: Hughes and Son, 1912), 15–16. Hereinafter *Memoir and Sermons*.
2 Ibid. 16.
3 Ibid. 18.
4 Ibid. 22.
5 Ibid. 23.
6 Ibid.
7 See *Atonement Controversy*, 368.
8 *Memoir and Sermons*, 29.
9 Ibid. 35.
10 Ibid. 36.
11 Ibid. 36–7.
12 Ibid. 56.
13 Ibid. 38–9.
14 See O. Llew Owain, *Cofiant Mrs. Fanny Jones* (Machynlleth a Caernarfon, 1907), 56.
15 *Memoir and Sermons*, 60.
16 Ibid. 58.
17 Ibid. 73.
18 Ibid. 100.
19 Ibid. 50.
20 Ibid. 70–1.
21 Ibid. 83.
22 Ibid. 84.
23 Ibid.
24 Ibid. 106.
25 Ibid.
26 Ibid. 83.
27 Ibid.
28 Ibid. 81–2.
29 See the Reformed Liturgy of Norwich Reformed Church (www.nrchurch.co.nr).
30 'The White-robed Multitude', *Memoir and Sermons*, 190.
31 'The Fulness of God', ibid. 139–41.
32 'The Unsearchable Greatness of God', ibid. 160.
33 'The Son of Man Glorified', ibid. 197.
34 'The Uniqueness of Christ's Claims', ibid. 233.
35 Ibid. 236.
36 See Postscript.
37 Iain H. Murray, *D. Martyn Lloyd-Jones: The First Forty Years 1899–1939* (Edinburgh: The Banner of Truth Trust, 1982), 182–3.
38 Ibid. 74–77.
39 Ibid. 118–20.
40 Eifion Evans, *The Welsh Revival of 1904* (Port Talbot: Evangelical Movement of Wales, 1969), 144.
41 *Memoir and Sermons*, 113–4.

42 Ibid. 115.
43 Ibid. 121–2.
44 Ibid. 91–2.
45 Ibid. 93
46 Ibid. 94–5.
47 Ibid. 101.
48 Ibid. 103.
49 Ibid. 110.
50 'The Indebtedness of Europe to the Protestant Reformation', ibid. 348–60.
51 Ibid. 358.
52 'Self-consecration to the Work of the Ministry', ibid. 315–47.
53 Ibid. 329–31.
54 J. Cynddylan Jones, tr. John Aaron, *Cysondeb y Ffydd* (Cardiff, 1912), iii. 286–7, 289–90, 291–3.

APPENDIX 3
JOHN JONES'S THEOLOGY

DEDICATORY

T he following recently-delivered paper serves to elucidate this subject. I Dedicate it to the memory my doctoral tutor, the Revd Dr R. Tudur Jones (1921–98), formerly Principal of Coleg Bala-Bangor, and Honorary Professor in the School of Theology and Religious Studies, the University College of North Wales, Bangor, Gwynedd, North Wales. He kindly endorsed the theological analysis and conclusions of my doctoral thesis, conclusions which inform the perspective of the following paper. The thesis was eventually published by Oxford University Press in 1990,[1] a copy being presented to 'Dr Tudur' in appreciation of his guidance and help. In the Preface, I wrote:

> Believing that I had the best tutor available in 'Dr Tudur' (as his students affectionately address him), I will always be grateful to him for his knowledge, wisdom, and kindness. He was always just and generous in assessing my work. Since I was in pastoral charge of a Norfolk village church—I was a part-time, external student—Dr Tudur's prompt and encouraging postal responses to my efforts were all the more important.

In his letter of thanks of 9 April 1991 (which remains a precious document in my possession), he wrote:

Dear Alan: it was most kind of you to present me with a copy of your book. It is an impressive and attractive volume. I shall treasure it, not only for its admirable contents, but as a reminder of the pleasure I had supervising your research. I sincerely hope that it sells well, as it deserves to do.

But above all, I am deeply moved by your gracious references to me in your "Preface". I hardly deserve what you say. Many, many thanks.

I trust that the family flourishes and that you feel your ministry is being blessed.

With cordial Christian greetings,

Yours appreciatively,

Tudur.

A REFUGE FOR THE GUILTY RACE

AMYRALDIAN FEATURES IN WELSH CALVINISM

(5) DANIEL ROWLAND & JOHN JONES, TALSARN
A paper given at the 9th Amyraldian Association Conference (Norwich Reformed Church) on Friday 12 April 2013

Dr Alan Clifford

Introduction

Since some kind of connection may be demonstrated between Daniel Rowland and all the other subjects of our conference, what link is there to justify the special 'coupling' implied by my title? After all, Daniel Rowland (1713–90) died six years before John Jones, Talsarn (1796–1857) was born. It may be claimed that these two Welsh servants of Christ were the greatest gospel preachers of their respective centuries. One difference is obvious. While thousands travelled from all parts of Wales to hear Daniel Rowland at

Llangeitho for about five decades, John Jones, Talsarn travelled thousands of miles all over Wales for over thirty years in much-blest evangelistic endeavour. Among other things, and driven by the love of Christ, the two men shared an extraordinary degree of 'hiraeth' for the salvation of the Welsh people. Consistent with this, and in tune with the perspective of this conference, it might surprise some to know that this pair of Calvinistic Methodists expressed 'Amyraldian features' in their gospel theology.

To clarify terminology used in this paper, 'High Calvinism' is properly defined as the theology of Theodore Beza, the *Westminster Confession* and John Owen, as distinct from the original teaching of John Calvin which Amyraut claimed to reaffirm as 'authentic Calvinism'. Losing Calvin's biblical balance, 'High Calvinism' was the prelude to the antinomian hypercalvinism which blighted Wales for a while, as it did England and elsewhere. In short, the Owenite 'limited atonement' teaching created evangelistic and pastoral havoc, as it still does.

I begin my case for linking the two preachers by citing the testimony of a preacher and historian from Caernarfonshire, one Robert Jones, Rhoslan (1745–1829).[2] He had heard the seraphic Daniel Rowland during several visits to Llangeitho. An old man in his seventies when he first heard John Jones, Talsarn, he remarked: "Well, indeed, here is a preacher like old Rowland, with a voice much more melodious, and, possibly, talents more bright."[3]

Whatever might be true of Wales in general, Daniel Rowland is undoubtedly better-known today than John Jones, at least in Reformed and Nonconformist circles. What better way is there of refreshing our memories of Daniel Rowland than to quote the dust-jacket blurb of Dr Eifion Evans's superb biography?[4]

Daniel Rowland (1711–90) has been described by J. C. Ryle as 'one of the spiritual giants of the eighteenth century'. Lady Huntingdon considered him to be 'second only to Whitefield'. Howel Harris wrote of him, 'In his pulpit he is a second St Paul', while others acclaimed him as 'the greatest preacher in Europe'. Yet he has been one of the least known leaders of that age. The loss of manuscripts shortly after his death, the Welsh language barrier, the remoteness of the scenes of his ministry, and the fact that all his closest friends were also preachers rather than authors, all contributed to leave only a shadowy impression of his greatness. Now, after many years of work, Dr Eifion Evans has succeeded in breaking through a multitude of difficulties and in presenting for the first time a full-scale biography.

Here is a record of revivals, of friendships with other leaders, of persecutions and divisions, and the birth of a new age for Wales. Amidst it all, Dr Evans excels in showing what made Rowland the preacher and the humble Christian that he was.

Rowland was a man of abounding energy. He walked to London for ordination, ran beside his native River Aeron when turned 70, and travelled nearly 3,000 miles a year on foot or on one of his 'little nags' for more than 50 years. At death, when reminded that he had been instrumental in the conversion thousands to Christ, he protested, 'It is nothing. I die as a poor sinner, depending fully and entirely on the merits of a crucified Saviour'.

J. C. Ryle writes of Rowland: 'Never, perhaps, did any preacher exalt Christ more … No British preacher of the 18th century kept together in one district such enormous congregations of souls for fifty years as Rowland did'. And Dr D. M. Lloyd-Jones asks, 'Has there been preaching which has had anything like the effect of his preaching since those days?'

Who then was John Jones, the preacher with 'a voice much more melodious' than Rowland's and possibly more talented? Unfortunately for English readers, no one has done for John Jones what Eifion Evans has done for Daniel Rowland. The chief source for John Jones remains the scholarly Dr Owen

Thomas's impressive 1,000-page *Cofiant Y Parchedig John Jones, Talsarn,* a work 'unhappily, never translated from Welsh into English', wrote Iain Murray in 1990.[5] First published in 1874, the work is considered to be 'the best biography ever written in Welsh. ... No Welshman can consider himself to be cultured unless he has read it'.[6] However, Owen Jones's *Some of the Great Preachers of Wales,* published in 1885, provides in English a substantial final chapter on John Jones, Talsarn. Using Dr Thomas's biography and other sources, the author thus provides a fairly full and vivid account of John Jones.

Born on 1 March 1796 at Tan-y-Castell near Dolwyddelan (5 miles west of Betws-y-Coed), John Jones experienced the power of God's grace around the time of the famous Beddgelert Revival (1817–22). Coming from a family remarkably blest by God, John became an extraordinary preacher. Greatly admired by the illustrious veteran preacher John Elias,[7] the late Dr R. Tudur Jones also described him as one of the princes of the period.[8] These appraisals are reflected in the impressive monument to the Jones family at Tan-y-Castell. The column for John Jones reminds us that he was a composer of hymn tunes (and a few hymns) as well as an eloquent preacher. Of course, John Jones is famously remembered as 'John Jones, Talsarn' [9](or more correctly Talysarn, about 10 miles south of Caernarfon, his home from 1823 until his death in 1857). He is buried in the churchyard at Llanllyfni (the name given to one of his tunes), where a fine and moving epitaph records the amazing impact of his ministry. Close communion with God was the source of his pulpit power. Indeed, writing thirty years after the death of John Jones, Owen Jones wrote that 'not far from his house there was a copse of wood, silent and lonely, except for the chirping of the birds. Here he used to go [and pray], and remain for hours. There is a path in it to this day made by his own feet, where he used to walk backwards and forwards'.[10]

John Jones's nationwide ministry—from Bangor to Swansea, from Mold to Carmarthen (not to forget preaching in London)—helped lay the foundations of the glorious events of 1859. Significantly, his preaching after 1835 was marked by a personal directness often lacking among his brethren. Revealing the influence of Dr Edward Williams, Rotherham on his thinking, he identified the growing dangers of antinomian hypercalvinism. In short, he criticised a tendency among some Calvinists to stress the exposition of God's sovereign grace at the expense of application and human responsibility. Coupled with deeply felt conviction, John Jones's 'practical' sermons possessed a compelling immediacy few could resist. Not surprisingly, wrote John Aaron, 'many thousands [ascribed] their conversions to the influence of his preaching'.[11]

When he died at Talysarn on Sunday, 16 August 1857, John Jones proved the blessedness of all he'd preached to others. Despite advancing weakness, his spirit was filled with rapture as he was heard to whisper, "O dear Jesus! O beloved Jesus! Blessed be Thy name forever!"

As depicted by Owen Jones, John Jones's funeral indicated the impact of his ministry:

> On Friday, 21 August, the day he was buried at Llanllyfni, the shops were closed in Talysarn and all the country around; and even in Caernarfon, which is several miles away; and the work in the slate quarries was at a stand that day. And in the eyes of some, great Snowdon seemed to wear a pall … Before leaving the house in Talysarn, Henry Rees spoke to the large crowd of mourners: "It is not becoming to say much now. Silence is the most eloquent. If you desire to have a real sermon today, look at the coffin, the funeral car, and the grave, and think of your sweet-mouthed preacher, who is now silent forever. His name was well known throughout the Principality

for thirty or thirty-five years, and his eloquence roused and charmed the minds of Welshmen. But today there is no John Jones, Talsarn, in Wales. Far be it from us, however, to weep for him as men which have no hope. 'For if we believe that Jesus died and rose again, even so, them also which sleep in Jesus will God bring with Him!'" In the funeral procession there were eight medical men, sixty-five ministers and preachers, three abreast; seventy deacons four abreast; two hundred singers, six abreast; six thousand men and women, six abreast, trending slowly on the road from Talysarn to Llanllyfni, singing on the way some of the old Welsh tunes, 'Yn y dyfroedd mawr a'r tonau', 'Ymado wnaf a'r babell', the hills around and Snowdon in the distance echoing the sound. That day and for many a day after a great gloom rested upon Wales.[12]

Such sadness simply reflected the widespread hiraeth for one who radiated the love of Christ. While others—such as Henry Rees—laboured on faithfully and effectively, the loss of John Jones, Talsarn was relieved in measure by the remarkable if less spectacular ministry of his son David Lloyd Jones (1843–1905).[13]

Dr Owen Thomas wrote that 'We are disposed to think that he, during those years (from 1821 to 1857), made for himself a deeper home in the affections of his fellow-countrymen than perhaps any of his mighty predecessors or contemporaries—so deep a home, indeed, that the longing that is still felt for him in the breasts of his hearers is as keen and strong as if he had died yesterday'.[14]

Owen Jones himself wrote that John Jones 'consecrated all the powers of his soul for the Gospel of Christ. Preaching absorbed all the energies of his life … He became the most efficient and most popular preacher of the age in Wales. The epithet is applied to him to this day, "The preacher of the people." And no one since his time has arrived at anything like his popularity'.[15] Of course, this author was not to know that, less than fifteen years later (1899), a boy named David Martyn Lloyd-Jones was born in Cardiff whose influence, by the grace of God, was possibly to demand a revised assessment?

From a strictly theological perspective, English readers are indebted to translator John Aaron and the Banner of Truth Trust for providing a window on the views of John Jones, Talsarn. Published in 2002, *The Atonement Controversy in Welsh Theological Literature and Debate, 1701–1841*[16] is simply Chapter 11 of Owen Thomas's original biography, comprising about a third of the entire work! This substantial section provided a comprehensive historical and theological background to the author's subject. Covering a period of nearly two centuries, the chapter's very existence indicates the problematic and vexed nature of continual controversies over the atonement. Following his very illuminating but highly-critical introduction, the translator follows the author's division of the subject matter thus: Part 1 charts the debates between Calvinists and Arminians, 1707–1831. Part 2 covers debates among the Calvinists of all denominations, 1811–41. Part 3—with which we are chiefly concerned—focuses on internal debates among the Calvinistic Methodists (later known as the Presbyterian Church of Wales), 1814–41.

This book has an intriguing feature. Judging by his highly-biased introduction, the translator is largely at odds with the material he translates. Anxious to alert us to the 'weaknesses' of the author's own standpoint, his 'Word of Caution' is in effect a 'health warning' against the author's so-called 'moderate Calvinism'![17] Concerned to expose the governmental theory of the atonement, he totally ignores the flawed commercial or mercantile 'price for price' view rightly rejected by many who otherwise subscribe to Dr John Owen's doctrine of limited atonement.[18] For a while, even the veteran Welsh colossus John Elias embraced this erroneous and 'unscriptural position'.[19] Revealing his strongly-Owenite bias, Aaron laments that 'Owen Thomas's heart is with John Jones ... He wishes the 'New System' [of Dr Edward Williams, Rotherham] to prevail'.[20] Among other things, he is accused of lacking 'objectivity in his arguments' in thinking that heroes such as John Elias and Henry Rees—both opponents of hypercalvinism—sympathised with the need to 'modify' the older Calvinism.[21]

John Aaron's dubious analysis tends to deflect the reader from the heart of the problem being addressed by Owen Thomas. The author and many of his brethren were convinced that the High-Calvinist 'Owenite' doctrine of limited atonement involved an 'unscriptural limitation'[22] which, besides its faulty biblical exegesis, discouraged active and compassionate evangelism.

Thomas and his friends were persuaded that by stating that '[Christ's] Person [stood] in the stead of those persons (and those only) who had been given him to redeem', Article 18 of the Calvinistic Methodist *Confession of Faith* (1823)[23] was 'wise above what is written'.[24] Indeed, no biblical text supports such an explicit view. Indeed, this article *Of Redemption* is arguably more 'particular' than the *Westminster Confession of Faith* equivalent. These arguments had significant effect. In 1874, the year Thomas's biography was published, the General Assembly of the denomination (Carmarthen, 1874; Portmadoc, 1875) amended the interpretation of the article with an appendix stressing the infinite sufficiency of the atonement.[25] In this way, a long-standing problem was in great measure (but not entirely[26]) resolved. That said, it is hardly right to say this 'sufficiency' is an 'opposite' truth; 'complementary' is surely better.

In short, the whole controversy concerned a right

understanding of the Gospel and the true character of Calvinism. Aaron's assumption that 'Calvinism' really means 'limited atonement Owenism' prevents him from appreciating this. Despite the translator's criticisms, Owen Thomas had done his homework well in an extensive and highly-accomplished historical-theological survey. For instance, he was thoroughly aware that John Calvin and many other reformers both Continental and British did not teach the doctrine of limited atonement and that the Canons of Dort maintain a universal dimension in the atonement. In his highly-biased critique (conditioned by an uncritical reliance on Paul Helm[27] and others), the translator fails to perceive the integrity and accuracy of the author's case. As we shall see, by blaming 'moderate Calvinism' as 'Calvinism in decay',[28] Aaron is effectively saying that 'Calvin's Calvinism' is dangerous!

As a not-insignificant aside, there is a surprising omission in Dr Owen Thomas's survey. I have in my possession his personal copy of Thomas Chalmers's *Institutes of Theology* (1849). It is worth noting that Thomas had studied under Chalmers in Edinburgh. As John Aaron indicates, the two men corresponded and continued to be very close.[29] Now, in the course of his historical survey of the atonement controversy, before he looked—very sympathetically—at France and Amyraut, Owen Thomas does not quote Thomas Chalmers in the section dealing with Scotland. Yet under his nose—in Chalmers's *Institutes*—was a statement which supports John Jones, Owen Thomas and other brethren in Wales who sought to express a more biblical and non-Owenite Calvinism. The Scottish colossus stated:

> I cannot but think that the doctrine of Particular Redemption has been expounded by many of its defenders in such a way as to give an unfortunate aspect to the Christian dispensation. As often treated, we hold it to be a most unpractical and useless

theory, and not easy to be vindicated, without the infliction of an unnatural violence on many passages of Scripture ... Its ministers are made to feel the chilling influence of a limitation upon their warrant. If Christ died only for the elect, and not for all, they are puzzled to understand how they should proceed with the calls and invitations of the gospel. ... Now for the specific end of conversion, the available scripture is not that Christ laid down His life for the sheep, but that Christ is set forth a propitiation for the sins of the world. It is not because I know myself to be one of the sheep, or one of the elect, but because I know myself to be one of the world, that I take to myself the calls and promises of the New Testament.[30]

Doubtless, Owen Thomas heard statements like this from Chalmers's own lips. This one undoubtedly justifies his assessment and verdict on the entire controversy. Interestingly, the Free Church leader was never seemingly-challenged for exceeding the soteriological limits of the *Westminster Confession of Faith*! Chalmers and Thomas clearly believed that Christian evangelism would be more biblical and healthy if it avoided the distortions of both Arminianism and Owenism. In addition, was Owen Thomas ever aware that, on his death-bed, Chalmers expressed considerable sympathy with the views of Richard Baxter[31] whose undeniably-important stance he also omitted in his survey? Baxter's name nowhere appears in the index of Dr Owen Thomas's *Cofiant John Jones, Talsarn*. A possible reason for this is that Baxter was ignorantly dismissed as an Arminian by William Williams, Pantycelyn.[32] Hence he wouldn't have been regarded as a sympathetic supporting authority. Whether or not he ever read his works, John Jones was one with the seraphic 17th-century English Puritan Richard Baxter.[33]

The simple fact is that Owen Thomas and his friends saw the need to 'moderate' not Calvin's teaching but the 'ultra-Calvinism' of the day in order to return to a Bible-based

'Authentic Calvinism'. One may say that they sought to rescue the denomination from 'Owenistic Methodism' and to be true to correctly-defined 'Calvinistic Methodism'. In this respect, contrary to the standpoint of both translator and publisher, the author—despite ignoring Chalmers and Baxter—produced a persuasive, praise-worthy and illuminating study in historical theology.

Another intriguing feature of this book is a dust-jacket appeal to Dr D. Martyn Lloyd-Jones's enthusiasm for it. One can only conclude that Dr Lloyd-Jones preaching was indeed influenced by Owen Thomas's monumental work, but not in the manner assumed either by the translator or the publisher.[34] While I share Mr Aaron's concerns over several liberal theological developments in the post-Thomas era, my enthusiasm for *The Atonement Controversy* does not extend to the translator's over-reactionary introduction.

This brings us to John Jones and the 'New System' of Dr Edward Williams, Rotherham, first introduced into Wales in 1814 by one of his students at Oswestry, John Roberts, Llanbryn-mair. Wrongly accused by Aaron of forging a compromise between Calvinistic and Arminian views,[35] Roberts's and Williams's position may be styled as a *via media* between Owenism and Arminianism. Owen Thomas expresses surprise at the strong opposition to John Roberts and his broadly biblical views compared with the 'strange, narrow and unscriptural' mercantile or commercial view of the Atonement advanced by the Baptist preacher Christmas Evans in 1811. He concludes that 'the land' had been 'to a significant degree leavened with very High Calvinist ideas'.[36] As we have noted already, such was the stance eventually taken by John Jones, Talsarn. Owen Thomas provides a vivid and highly-significant account of young John Jones's studies with other youths led by an educated young man named Evan

Evans [Ieuan Glan Geirionydd], a member of the Calvinistic Methodist church at Trefriw in the Vale of Conwy:

In the meetings, to which we referred, they went over much of the work of Dr Edward Williams, *On the Equity of Divine Government and the Sovereignty of Divine Grace,* and also his *Defence of Modern Calvinism,* being his answer to *Refutation to Calvinism,* that was published by Bishop Tomline. Mr Evans read part of Dr Williams to them in Welsh. Then great research was done into the meaning of that area, when they had decided on that standpoint as a topic for conversation, and commonly as a text for discussion, some taking the opinion of the Doctor and the remainder opposing. If it contained a topic of great importance that stood as a topic of discussion in the Christian world, they would spend several meetings on it. And great would be the searching and meditation on it by the next meeting. The two main books of Dr Williams, would be under the same detailed investigation by them, tortuously setting them sentence by sentence, some pulling one way and others the other to test the power of the assertions that were taught them. These meetings, as can be easily thought, and as he himself acknowledged with gratitude to the end of his life, were of immense advantage to Revd John Jones, not only because he didn't understand the English himself, but also, at that time, he only had very few Welsh books. A new field opened wide in the forefront of his mind at this time, and after that he meditated diligently on it for many years. *He couldn't bear anyone say anything derogatory about Doctor Williams's work. He would be particularly surprised to hear men of Calvinistic ideas doing that; and always judged that they had not read the writings themselves, or had done so prejudicially or else inappropriately by virtue of their mental disability to place fair judgement on such writings.*[37]

What was it about the so-called 'New System' of Edward Williams that so impressed John Jones, Talsarn? Two things stand out. *First,* as a Bible man first and foremost, he was persuaded that Williams was faithful to the Scriptures, and *second*, he was persuaded that Williams taught nothing contrary to properly-defined Calvinism. On the first point, Edward Williams's affirmation of the Gospel reflects biblically-rooted 'Amyraldian features', viz. that the Gospel makes a universal provision of mercy for the entire human race, notwithstanding the sovereign purposes of God to save the elect, and that such an understanding facilitates evangelistic enterprise:

> We conclude, therefore, that the rectoral design of the death of Christ (whatever higher speciality there is in it) extends to all the human race; not merely to those who have been, or actually shall be, but also such as may be evangelised or discipled—that is, all the nations, past, present, and future; and with St John we may affirm, without either trembling for the cause of orthodoxy, or throwing dust in the eyes of its enemies by far-fetched criticisms: 'He is the propitiation for our sins, and not for ours only, but also for the sins of the whole world' (*1 Jn 2: 2*). And with St Paul: 'We thus judge, that if one died for all then were all dead; and' (we further judge) 'that he died for all', with the same rectoral intention by which He gives His promises and Himself to all, to the end that they may have the means of being obedient and happy; and with the higher and more specific end, 'that they who live' (as justified by sovereign grace, and made alive by virtue derived from Christ) 'should not henceforth live unto themselves, but unto Him who died for them and rose again' (*2 Cor 5: 14–15*). Thus, in a word, Jesus Christ is, in the plan of DIVINE GOVERNMENT, the appointed and intended 'Saviour of all men, but, especially', with a decretive infallible speciality, 'of those that', through gracious influence, 'believe' (*1 Tim 4: 10*). 'There is one mediator between God and men, the man Christ Jesus, who gave Himself a ransom for all, to be testified in due time' (*1 Tim 2: 5–6*).[38]

On the second point, Edward Williams was confident that his theology was in tune with John Calvin's actual views, whatever so-called Calvinists of later generations have thought. Indeed, his admiration for Calvin is emphatic and unambiguous:

That illustrious reformer and admirable writer, Calvin, has treated much of predestination and the doctrines of special grace; but though his works consist of nine volumes folio, I do not think that there is one sentence in them all that militates against the above representation; and in many places he expresses himself in a manner that abundantly justifies it, particularly his comments on several passages of the New Testament. To instance only the following: 'The word 'many' does not mean a part of the world only, but the whole human race' (*Comm. Mark 14: 24*).—'Although Christ suffered for the sins of the world, and is offered by the goodness of God without distinction to all men, yet not all receive him' (*Comm. Rom 5: 18*).[39]

Edward Williams was concerned to demonstrate that authentic Calvinism did not commit its advocates to the doctrine of limited atonement. He made this clear in the second treatise studied by John Jones, Talsarn. In response to an attempted refutation of Calvinism by the Bishop of Lincoln, Edward Williams appeals to Calvin against the bishop's assumption that all Calvinists teach the doctrine of limited atonement:

His Lordship I hope will excuse me for asserting, in return, that this eminent reformer did not 'directly' oppose the doctrine of universal redemption, in the sense now explained, as far as I have been able to collect by a frequent search into his voluminous writings. He admitted a universal price of redemption; but he had reasons innumerable against the notion of an actual redemption of all men from sin and misery. He maintained that the remedy was universal, and that it was universally proposed to mankind, according to God's rectoral design; but not that it was the sovereign design of God by it to make mankind universally and indiscriminately submissive, and compliant with the terms on which the blessings resulting from it were to be enjoyed.[40]

While Williams's views on double predestination are thought

to be at variance with Calvin's, the discrepancy is more between a caricature of Calvin's views than the reformer's correctly-perceived teaching. For all that he has been charged with 'double predestination', Calvin requires a carefully nuanced interpretation, in line with Williams's general endorsement plus minor qualifications about some of Calvin's ill-digested expressions.[41] While seeking to be a faithful servant of the Word of God, Calvin still acknowledges the decree of reprobation to be 'dreadful' (*Inst.* 3: 23: 7), clearly taking no improper delight in teaching it, as Williams is careful to point out.[42] Calvin's unequivocal affirmation of it was blended with humility and caution. He plainly taught— while affirming an ultimate agnosticism over the advent of sin—that while God providentially arranges all the factors behind human choices, *without being the author of sin*, the 'cause and matter' of reprobation is foreknown human guilt rather than a naked supralapsarian decree (see *Inst.* 3: 23: 7– 9). Williams clearly agrees with such an interpretation of Calvin.[43]

Despite 'High-Calvinist' Geoffrey Thomas's rather negative portrayal of Edward Williams,[44] there can be no doubt that the latter had a high regard for 'that illustrious writer' John Calvin.[45] Furthermore, despite other literary influences, and feeling 'uneasy' at the excesses of some Methodist revivalists, John Jones's 'mentor' was perfectly 'at home' with the evangelical authors of the seventeenth and eighteenth centuries including George Whitefield, John Newton[46] and others. Warmly commending 'honest' Richard Baxter's 'glowing heart',[47] Williams especially admired Philip Doddridge and Jonathan Edwards, even producing editions of their works in 1802–5 and 1806 respectively. It is worthy of note that one of Doddridge's favourite Northampton pupils, Benjamin Fawcett of Kidderminster (where Baxter had laboured gloriously in the previous century) preached at Williams's ordination at Ross-on-Wye in 1776. Williams's early enthusiasm for John Owen's *Exposition of Hebrews* (an edition of which he published in 1790) evidently did not extend to the Puritan's 'limited atonement' treatise *The Death of Death*. Williams quotes at length another Puritan whose understanding was obviously permeated with 'Amyraldian features':

> The great Mr Charnock, who for depth of penetration and accuracy of judgement was equalled by few, expresses himself, in his *Discourse of the acceptableness of Christ's death*, thus: ... The blood of Christ is a stream, whereof all men may drink; an ocean, wherein all men may bathe. It wants not value to remove our sins, if we want not faith to embrace and plead it' (Charnock's *Works*, ii. 564 (London, 1699)).[48]

Such were the influences on young John Jones, Talsarn. Williams's theology became his theology. Only ignorance could smear Edward Williams's theology as some defective 'New System', a kind of liberal departure from the 'Old System' of John Owen and his 'High Orthodox' friends— 'Calvinism in decay'.[49] If anything—as Dr R. Tudur Jones agreed[50]—it was largely a return to an 'older system'—that of John Calvin's 'authentic Calvinism' and, more importantly, the Bible! Thus it is entirely incorrect for John Aaron to argue that this stance was a 'compromise' between Calvinism and Arminianism,[51] and to repeat[52] W. T. Owen's restatement of R. W. Dale's criticism of Edward Williams that his so-called 'Moderate Calvinism' was a failure to 'begin and end with Calvin!'[53] On the contrary, he 'started' and 'ended' with Calvin without going beyond him as his High Calvinist critics did! The reality is that 'authentic Calvinism' is the biblical middle ground between Owenism and Arminianism.

Just as Edward Williams was a leading light in mission and

evangelism in England, so his theology directed and animated John Jones, Talsarn's mission in Wales. Recently translated for the first time, the sermon quoted in Chapter 2 is one of John Jones's earliest sermons, preached in 1823. It is a glorious example of uninhibited evangelistic preaching at its best.

W.T. Owen is right to conclude that 'Among the Methodists no one did more to free his denomination from the grip of hypercalvinism than John Jones of Talsarn.[54] That said, as noted earlier, the *Confession of Faith* was adopted in the same year his sermon was preached. Sadly, the confession bore the stamp of John Elias's 'High Calvinism'. Matters become clear when we scrutinize the standpoints of both John Jones and John Elias whose views represent the polarized positions among the Calvinistic Methodists of the period. While both preachers rejected Arminianism, John Jones may be called a *biblical* 'authentic Calvinistic Methodist' whereas John Elias was a *confessional* 'Owenistic Methodist'. Whereas for the former, 'The Bible was the chief book of his life',[55] the latter was governed by an undue attachment to the objectionable phrase (limiting Christ's atoning death to the elect) 'and those only' ('a hwy yn unig') in Article 18 of the 1823 *Confession of Faith*. His extreme reaction to Robert Roberts, Rhosllannerchrugog's objection was, "I would prefer to lose my right arm than to lose these words from our Confession of Faith."[56] Such a reaction to an unscriptural, man-made phrase is appalling for a Protestant. Calvin would never say such a thing, although Beza might.[57] Well might John Jones have said concerning the universal wording of John 1: 29, 3: 16, 1 Timothy 2:6 and 1 John 2: 2, etc, 'I would prefer to lose my right arm than to lose these words from the Holy Bible'. There is a precedent for such a thought, since Dr John Davenant, one of the English delegates at the Synod of Dordt said as much.[58]

Although he was strongly-opposed to hypercalvinism and was wonderfully and fruitfully evangelistic, Elias and his brethren would have been wiser in following the stance of Thomas Jones of Denbigh who argued for the 'moderate orthodoxy' of the Anglican formularies. Dr Eifion Evans is right to remark that the North Wales Methodist leader's 'great contribution lay in steering the Methodism of the [19th] century safely between the rocks of Arminianism and High Calvinism … both Thomas Jones and Thomas Charles [Bala] were following in the tradition of Rowland and Williams'.[59] However, despite the concerns of Thomas Jones of Denbigh and the similar parallel teaching of Edward Williams, their biblical stance was not reflected in the 1823 *Confession of Faith*. Sadly, although there was little *practical* difference between Elias and John Jones, Article 18 provided a seed-bed for fatalistic hypercalvinism, against which both men and others rightly protested. Tensions would have been eased had John Elias been consistent with his agreement with John Newton, that 'election' (like Calvinism) 'is to be preached, not on its own, but as permeating though our whole ministry, … just as sugar sweetens tea'.[60] Was Elias aware that John Newton rejected the very Owenite particularism insisted on by the Welsh veteran?[61]

Sadly, John Elias was a divided man. He was torn between confessionalism and biblicism.[62] So, after a passionate and ground-breaking sermon by John Jones which brought blessing to thousands present, John Elias was not at all happy.[63] How sad that he should disapprove of that wonderful Gospel sermon. Hence John Jones and others who shared his stance became objects of suspicion, as Dr Owen Thomas made clear:

John Jones, in particular, was one; especially after his sermon in the Bala Association of 1835. His ministry at this time was in evident opposition to the narrow and extreme views held by some on the atonement of Christ, and he would lay particular emphasis on the sufficiency of the provision in Jesus Christ for sinners, as sinners, and indiscriminately; and would impress specifically upon the consciences of all his hearers that if they were lost at the last, the fault for that would be theirs alone, and that their blood could never be required at the hand of Almighty God.[64]

Let us sample the anointed heavenly oratory of the hero from Talsarn. The text of *Coming to Christ* was 'No man can come to Me except the Father which hath sent Me draw him: and I will raise him up at the last day' (*John vi. 44*):

If the Government of England were to send an order to the British Admiral to bring the Fleet home from the Mediterranean Sea, you would not suppose that the Government intended that the Admiral and his men should carry the ships home? Nothing of the kind. We all know full well that the meaning of the order would simply be that the Admiral should make the proper preparations; that they should employ the proper means in order to bring the ships home—weigh the anchors, turn their prows towards the deep, that they should put them in the way of the great forces of nature: spread the sails, and steer the vessels home; let the winds play upon them, and the waves and the tides carry them. Meanwhile, the men on deck might take it easy; they could enjoy themselves, and sing their native songs, while the mighty elements co-operated to bring them home.

In the same manner, God in the Gospel calls upon you to repent, to believe, and to lead a pious and godly life. But He does not mean that you should do all this of your own individual resources. No; He intends that you should put yourselves as you are under the operation of the mighty forces of the Gospel; that you should faithfully employ the means which He has commanded. Turn the prow of thy little vessel to the deep; let it sail upon the wide ocean of Christ's Atonement; spread the sails, and steer it on by the guidance of the Word of God. The winds will blow, the mighty forces of redemption will play

upon thy vessel; the tides will carry it, and thou shalt find thy
little bark one day in the haven of eternal rest.

You have, my friends, something yourselves to do, and it is
of no use at all to expect the operations of the Spirit of God,
while we ourselves neglect our duty. 'But what can I do?' Canst
thou not read? Open thy Bible; look at it, read it bring thy
mind into contact with the great saving forces, and wait for
help from above. 'But I cannot pray.' Canst thou not try? Canst
thou not bend thy knee, and put it down on the ground? 'But
I must pray from the heart, and this I cannot do.' Wouldst thou
give Him thy heart? Give Him thy body, give Him thy tongue;
and if thou canst not say a word, there is One up there who
can open His lips to intercede for thee. Try fairly; do your best
for your own salvation. Do not, at least, rush headlong into
perdition. I, indeed, have made up my mind long ago that I
shall not go there so. If I must go to hell at all, I shall not go
there straight along. No; I shall loiter a good deal about the
Garden of Gethsemane; I shall go many a round about the hill
of Calvary; I shall bend my knees daily at the throne of grace.
I shall be good enough for hell, if I have to go there, after all
these efforts. But, blessed be the name of God, we have every
reason to believe that this is the high road to heaven, and that
no one ever went to hell in that way, and that no one ever
will.[65]

While most of John Jones's material is locked away in
Welsh, we are indebted to John Aaron for translating an
important letter from Owen Thomas's biography,[66] written
just before decades of damaging debate were happily ended
at a Calvinistic Methodist conference in Mold, Flintshire in
March 1841. It was a lengthy plea to Thomas Richard of
Fishguard to attend the conference, since John Jones believed
his very presence would help restrain John Elias and his ilk
from imposing their oppressive opinions on others. Bearing
on the issues of hypercalvinism, this letter reveals John Jones's
deeply-felt, pastorally-driven theological concerns. After
complaining about an ill-digested and excessive prominence

given to predestination, and a preoccupation with an over-refined orthodoxy, he exposes the causes of widespread barren evangelism:

> In a word, for some years they have been preaching in a polemic, controversial way, and not in the most appropriate way for convincing a sinner of his danger and of exhorting him to flee from the wrath to come. If the wickedness and misery of man is under consideration, the sermon tends not to stress that the fault is completely due to man, but rather shows *how it is he became* a sinner and then refers to the covenant of works. If the atonement is the subject, the tendency will be to stress the particularity of its appointments rather than the fact that it is the only refuge for life for the sinner and he be urged to flee to it; if the work of the Spirit is preached, the emphasis will not be on the encouragement to seek him and the directions given as to how to find him in the means by which he works, but rather that everything attempted or sought is in vain until the Spirit come; etc., etc.

John Jones believed that many of the problems he identified were due to an over-reactionary response to Wesleyan Arminianism in North-eastern Wales in the early 19th century resulting in something akin to Islamic fatalism:

> Our fathers made such an attack upon Arminianism here in north Wales that the common people were led to harmful extremes on the contrary side. They are full of Antinomian views which have as disastrous an effect upon them as Mahometanism has upon the Egyptians. What is most necessary therefore, in my view, before such an attitude of mind and judgement, is to drive them out of their false hiding places, to tear away their excuses, and to press them in the most importunate way to give themselves to the Saviour.

Assured of his theological foundations, John Jones felt

liberated to preach in a 'practical' rather than a polemical and excessively-doctrinal manner:

> We do not choose to preach practically in order to oppose our brethren or from a contentious spirit, but, before my Judge, I can testify that it is from the demands of conscience and from seeing the good effects produced that I have so purposed.

John Jones also believed the content of preaching has a vital bearing on fruitfulness, that a close biblical correlation exists between style and success:

> Know, dear brother, and I mention it with tears, that many of our older brethren in the ministry preach many of their sermons with the purpose of persuading their listeners to believe in things that are not necessary to salvation. It is as clear to me as that the sun is in the sky that they are not producing any good effect. In contrast, I can declare with confidence, and prove it by many evident facts from at large, that practical, convincing and exhortative preaching has been, under the blessing and unction of the Holy Spirit, the means of returning many hundreds in Caernarvonshire this last year. It is believed that between 1800 and 2000 have been added to our churches in the area during the year, and it is acknowledged that it is the change in the style of ministry, with less topical sermons and a more practical, persuasive emphasis, that was instrumental in this. But such is the jealousy of these for preaching their own narrow views that they cannot acknowledge these conversions as being the work of God's Spirit and they then declare boldly in the Associations that they suspect the genuineness of the work. How it grates upon my ear to hear such words and in such a place, more or less blaspheming the work of God's Spirit in the souls of sinners. At Rhosllannerchrugog there was the addition of some hundreds to the church last year. It is well known that the labours of our faithful friend, Mr Robert Roberts, were the means of bringing forward this revival—his warnings and encouragements to the church to pray for revival and to maintain frequent meetings for prayer

amongst themselves, pleading for a visitation from the Lord. Gradually the church was brought to a state of deep longing for such a visitation, and they did not have to wait long after that.

In the providence of God, John Elias was too ill to attend the conference. In fact, it proved to be his last illness. While John Jones and his brethren deeply lamented the loss of the mighty preacher, events proved propitious for a biblically-balanced view of the Gospel. In short, the complementary twin 'Amyraldian features' of the atonement's universality and particularity were widely embraced. As we noted earlier, such an understanding found eventual confessional expression in 1874, the very year Owen Thomas's biography of John Jones, Talsarn was published.

Owen Thomas's claims that John Elias and Henry Rees diluted their High Calvinist views in their later days are dismissed as 'wishful thinking' by John Aaron.[67] However, besides the evidence of his lovely hymn 'And was it for my sin that Jesus suffered so',[68] it is certain at least that Elias repudiated his attachment to the commercial theory of the atonement after a heated discussion with Thomas Jones of Denbigh in 1814.[69] As we have seen, such a view had been advocated by Christmas Evans in 1811.[70] Yet John Aaron fails to engage with this detail[71] (albeit identified in Owen Thomas's account[72]). Sadly, despite Elias's repudiation of the commercialistic error, it made no difference to his limited atonement thinking. He continued to insist that our Saviour's death 'was appointed for the Church alone'.[73] As for Henry Rees, whose essay *Christ Suffering the Punishment of His People* (1831) is undeniably Owenite, there is some evidence that by the 1860s his emphasis had shifted to embrace a wider sufficiency in the atonement. As Owen Thomas indicates, this was probably due to Rees's acquaintance with works by

Richard Baxter's Amyraldian friend John Howe, Andrew Fuller and others.[74] In a sermon preached at Mold in 1864 and repeated at Bala in 1867, ideas of Owenite limitation are absent:

> It was God that appointed Christ as Saviour … And as the authority of God was with him, there was infinite value and merit in what He did. So that now, by that perfect obedience which Christ gave, the greatest sinner can safely venture to believe … The Spirit of God can give us [all riches of the full assurance of understanding], and may He give unto us some degree of it before we die. The language of such a man would be this: 'Whatever God and holiness may be; whatever the law and its demands may be, I am perfectly sure that there is infinite value in Christ's death in my behalf.[75]

This tends to confirm a statement by Robert Ellis, Llanddeiniolen that 'the Mr Rees of 1841 was very different from the Mr Rees of 1861'.[76]

By way of conclusion, let us return to the fascinating similarities between John Jones and Daniel Rowland detected by Robert Jones, Rhoslan. Indeed, we may ask, what would the preacher of Llangeitho think of the preacher of Talysarn? While the former would humbly rejoice that the latter possessed 'a voice much more melodious, and, possibly, talents more bright', are there any grounds to suggest that Rowland would approve of John Jones's theological stance?

As Eifion Evans makes clear in his excellent biography, Daniel Rowland was undoubtedly a Calvinist: 'Rowland followed Calvin in his understanding of grace'.[77] While Calvinistic Methodism 'had its own distinctives' of 'fervent spirituality' and 'lively proclamation', it 'bore unmistakable resemblance to the teaching and piety of Augustine and Calvin'.[78] Indeed, Rowland's sermon on our Saviour's words to the dying thief, *Free Grace indeed*,[79] confirms such claims.

His acceptance of the doctrine of election is unmistakable: 'By saving one thief, and leaving the other to receive the due reward of his deeds, is signified to us, that the election prevailed …'[80] The fact that Rowland's sermons are 'practical' rather than polemically-doctrinal is important. In this respect, he anticipated the concerns of John Jones, Talsarn in the next century. In short, an 'unmistakable resemblance' is evident in this respect too. Indeed, Rowland deliberately shuns a controversial discussion of election, since 'God's judgements are very secret, and unsearchable. It is our duty to honour, and reverence them, rather than to dispute about them'.[81] Dr Evan's rightly highlights this feature thus: 'In Rowland's view, these deep truths were for the eye of faith to admire, rather than for the skill of reason to judge'.[82]

However, another question is: does Rowland's understanding of grace bear an 'unmistakable resemblance' to the High Calvinism of John Owen? On this issue, Dr Evans sheds no light. That said, judging by the only available published sermons of Rowland—the translated *Eight Sermons* of 1774 and the *Three Sermons* of 1778, the answer seems to be 'no'. While Rowland states in the later sermons that Christ 'was the Lamb intentionally slain for his people before the world was made',[83] there is no Owenite qualification that He was slain *only* for 'his elect people'. Indeed, later in the same evangelistic sermon, Rowland affirms *generally*: 'Though you are lost and wandering sheep, yet here is a good shepherd, who laid down his life for you, that he might save you from perishing'.[84]

What is striking about this sermon is the assurance given to 'encourage every poor sinner to repent and come to Jesus Christ' because the good shepherd's 'shoulders imply strength— and in this parable they represent the all-sufficiency of grace and merit that there is in Christ Jesus to justify the guilty and uphold the weak'.[85] In a sermon concerned to challenge both

Arminians and Antinomian High Calvinists alike,[86] Rowland stresses *particularly* that Christ 'hath often snatched his chosen ones' from the mouth of the devil, yet He is *generally* 'the Saviour of the lost and perishing'.[87] The emphasis on Christ's general provision of all-sufficient grace is ubiquitous in Rowland.[88] For this reason he feels free to make his evangelistic appeals: 'Here are strong shoulders which can carry us *all* to heaven. O that many of us may be laid on them this day'.[89] Clearly these sermons exhibit 'Amyraldian features'.

What is clear in the *Three Sermons* is even clearer in the *Eight Sermons*. In fact, while Dr Evans rightly appealed to the second sermon *Free Grace indeed* for Rowland's teaching on election, what might he have said about the first entitled *The Redeemer's Voice*? Based on the text 'Behold! I stand at the door and knock' (*Revelation 3: 20*), Rowland's sermon is remarkable for at least three reasons. *First*, because he obviously attached great importance to what was a widely-appreciated publication. According to the editor Thomas Davies, 'The first sermon was published ten years ago, and met with great reception; it has lately been enlarged by the Author'.[90] *Second*, this truly-gripping sermon is remarkable for an important theological clarification. While it is intended as a 'practical' evangelistic message rather than a theological essay, yet something akin to a single footnote appears towards the end. Probably a late addition inspired by concerns over hypercalvinist tendencies among Calvinists, it speaks for itself:

> Every faithful ambassador of Christ will preach the gospel unto every creature, and spread forth as far as he can, the infinite compassion and excellencies of the Lamb. He will declare the richness of his atoning blood, and in a pointing manner, show the sinner his danger and remedy, will invite the indigent to become rich, and the guilty to accept pardon, and with the Apostle beseech and intreat sinners to be reconciled

to God—without this how can Gospel ministers be free from
the blood of all men, if they warn them not? ... If salvation
by Jesus Christ is not to be offered—how can sinners be said
to refuse and reject? Yet God says, 'because I have called and
ye have refused'—again—'Ye have put away the word of eternal
life'. How can a thing be refused if not offered?—If it is not
the duty of a sinner to believe—how can unbelief be a sin?
That mankind are dead in trespasses and sins is no objection,
because the Spirit of God is Almighty to quicken—and 'tis his
usual method to work in the way above mentioned.[91]

Third, the sermon is remarkable because of the preacher's
exegesis of his text. Judging by the context, Revelation 3: 20
has more to do with a 'back-slidden' congregation of professing
Christians than an audience of unbelievers. Yet Rowland uses
the text in a totally evangelistic way. Whatever the character
of his hearers, he proclaimed God-in-Christ as a 'pleader',
much in the manner of the Old Testament (see Ezekiel 33: 11,
the text of Richard Baxter's famous *Call to the Unconverted*).
While there are Calvinistic precedents for this,[92] Reformed
commentators are generally agreed that such a use of Rowland's
text is inadmissible.[93] Some would say Rowland's approach
is thoroughly Arminian! Indeed, how can Rowland defend
himself from such a charge in view of the climax of his
sermon? Since he has no inhibitions about telling his hearers
that Christ died for them, his rousing conclusion seems to
break every 'Reformed' rule:

> Consider in whose stead, and to whom it is that I beseech
> you to open your hearts. It is to him who gave and preserves
> your lives—to him who shed his blood for you, and is kind
> to you every moment—even 'to the Lamb of God who taketh
> away the sins of the world' [*Jn. 1: 29*] ... Lamb of God! patient,
> spotless Lamb of God! set up thy throne in our hearts and
> enable us to cry before thee 'Hosannah to the King of saints'
> ... To this happy state may God of his infinite mercy bring us

APPENDIX 3: JOHN JONES'S THEOLOGY

all through Jesus Christ, Amen.[94]

In reply to Lee Gatiss's criticism of R. T. Kendall,[95] does Rowland's language need defending? Since the Saviour of the world declared that God loves the world, how dare we *not* say 'God loves you and Christ died for you'? As Calvin, Baxter and many others have made clear, God's special love for His elect does not exclude His general love for all.[96] If Rowland is out of order on this issue, what would Gatiss[97] and Aaron say about a 'whiff' of the Governmental theory in Rowland?[98]

All this evidence points in one direction. In steering a course between Arminianism and High Calvinism, Daniel Rowland's gospel grasp fits the contours of the Amyraldian *via media*. Of the three most eminent preachers of the Methodist revival, this makes Daniel Rowland sounder than the 'sub-orthodox' Arminian Wesley and sounder than the 'ultra-orthodox' High Calvinist Whitefield. The Welshman had an edge over the two Englishmen! His understanding of the biblical message possessed a balance missing in his two brethren. It is surprising that, in his essay on Rowland, 'Amyraldian' J. C. Ryle[99] never highlighted the 'Amyraldian features' in Rowland's sermons. However he relevantly quotes our friend Robert Jones, Rhoslan's amazing response to Rowland's equally-remarkable preaching of John 3: 16:

> Fervent and deep feeling was the last characteristic which I mark in Rowland. He never did anything by halves. Whether preaching or praying, whether in church or in the open air, he seems to have done all he did with heart and soul, and mind and strength. "He possessed as much animal spirits," says one witness, "as were sufficient for half-a. dozen men." This energy seems to have had an inspiring effect about it, and to have swept everything before it like a fire. One who went to hear him every month from Carnarvonshire, gives a striking account of his singular fervour when Rowland was preaching on John

3:16. He says, "He dwelt with such overwhelming, extraordinary thoughts on the love of God, and the vastness of his gift to man, that I was swallowed up in amazement. I did not know that my feet were on the ground; yea, I had no idea where I was, whether on earth or in heaven. But presently he cried out with a most powerful voice, 'Praised be God for keeping the Jews in ignorance respecting the greatness of the Person in their hands! Had they known who he was, they would never have presumed to touch him, much less to drive nails through his blessed hands and feet, and to put a crown of thorns on his holy head. For had they known, they would not have crucified the Lord of glory.'"[100]

All this surely confirms a summary provided by the authors of *The Calvinistic Methodist Fathers of Wales*:

The Methodist Fathers were never, at first, Hyper-Calvinists, ... The doctrine that was undoubtedly believed among them was that of the Articles of the Established Church, and in agreement with these they preached Jesus Christ as a sufficient Saviour for the whole world, inviting all to him. One need only read the journal of Howell Harris, the sermons of Daniel Rowland, and the hymns of William Williams, to see that they laid down no limits to the value of the Saviour's sacrifice. But just as one extreme always produces the opposite, many of the Calvinists, in the warmth of their zeal against the Wesleyans, claimed that there was no universal aspect to the call of the gospel; that the elect alone were to be called ...[101]

So Robert Jones, Rhoslan was right to compare Daniel Rowland and John Jones, Talsarn in the way he did. One is surely entitled to add that the two preachers, separated by a period of theological exaggeration and inevitable strife, shared the same theological emphases and compassionate concern. Hence what Owen Jones said of the hero from Talysarn also applies to the hero of Llangeitho:

His discourses brought the love of God, the death of Christ, heaven with all its bliss and glory within the reach of every man, and made every individual man responsible for the loss of them.[102]

God grant that in our respective spheres and callings we might in some measure do likewise! Amen!

Notes

1   Alan C. Clifford, *Atonement and Justification: English Evangelical Theology 1640–1790—An Evaluation* (Oxford: Clarendon Press, 1990).
2   See Owen Thomas, tr. John Aaron, *The Atonement Controversy in Welsh Theological Literature and debate, 1707–1841* (Edinburgh: The Banner of Truth Trust, 2002), 375. Hereinafter *Atonement Controversy*.
3   Owen Jones, *Some the Great Preachers of Wales* (London: Passmore & Alabaster, 1885), 474. Hereinafter *Great Preachers*.
4   Eifion Evans, *Daniel Rowland and the Great Evangelical Awakening in Wales* (Edinburgh: The Banner of Truth Trust, 1985). Hereinafter *Daniel Rowland*.
5   Iain H. Murray, *D. Martyn Lloyd-Jones: The Fight of Faith 1939–1981* (Edinburgh: The Banner of Truth Trust, 1990), 711.
6   *Atonement Controversy*, p. ix.
7   *Great Preachers*, 470.
8   Eryl Davies, *The Beddgelert Revival* (Bridgend: Bryntirion Press, 2004), 163.
9   Thus distinguished since there were numerous John Joneses in Caernarfonshire at that time!
10   *Great Preachers*, 528.
11   *Atonement* Controversy, p. xiv.
12   *Great Preachers*, 520–1.
13   See Elias Jones, John Williams, T. Charles Williams, *Cofiant a Phregethau Y Diweddar Barch. David Lloyd Jones, MA Llandinam* (Gwrecsam: Hughes A'i Fab, 1908); R. Hughes (ed), *Memoir and Sermons of the Late Rev. David Lloyd Jones, MA, Llandinam* (Wrexham: Hughes and Son, 1912).
14   Cited in *Great Preachers*, 462.
15   Ibid. 532.
16   See my review in *Evangelical Quarterly*, Vol. 77.2 (2005), 187–90.
17   *Atonement Controversy*, p. xxv.
18   For a discussion of competing theories of the atonement, see my *Atonement and Justification: English Evangelical Theology 1640–1790* (Oxford: The Clarendon Press, 1990/2002), 125ff. Hereinafter *Atonement and Justification*.
19   R. Tudur Jones, *John Elias—Prince Amongst Preachers* (Bridgend: The Evangelical Library of Wales, 1975), 28.
20   *Atonement Controversy*, p. xxvi.
21   Ibid. p. xxx.
22   Ibid. 323.

23 *Confession of Faith of the Calvinistic Methodists or the Presbyterians of Wales* (Caernarfon: D. O. Owen, 1900), 74.

24 *Atonement Controversy,* 323.

25 Ibid. 324.

26 'universality' was implied but not specifically mentioned. Dr J. Cynddylan Jones (1840–1930) was later to argue for this, in line with the emphasis evident in Calvin, Edward Williams, arguably Thomas Jones and John Jones, Talsarn (see Appendix 2, post script).

27 Ibid. 123.

28 Ibid. p. xxxii.

29 Ibid. p. xii.

30 Thomas Chalmers, *Institutes of Theology* (Edinburgh: Sutherland and Knox, 1849), ii. 403–6.

31 See William Hanna, *Memoirs of Thomas Chalmers, DD, LlD* (Edinburgh: Thomas Constable and Co., 1854), ii. 512.

32 Ibid. 150. This might well explain why Owen Thomas did not present Baxter's views in his historical survey. His whole case would have been reinforced had he known Baxter's agreement with Amyraut whom he did cite. Of a kind Dr Thomas would have approved, Baxter's views on the atonement are clearly evident in the *Call to the Unconverted.*

33 However, several of Baxter's works were translated into Welsh, including the famous *Call to the Unconverted;* see Eifion Evans, 'Richard Baxter's Influence in Wales' in *The National Library of Wales Journal,* XXXIII. 2, Winter 2003, 149ff.

34 See my *My Debt to the Doctor* (Norwich: Charenton Reformed Publishing, 2009), 51–2.

35 See *Atonement Controversy,* 379.

36 Ibid. 161.

37 Owen Thomas, tr. Pauline Edwards, *Cofiant Y Parchedig John Jones, Talsarn* (Wrexham: Hugues and Son, 1874), 85–6 (emphasis mine).

38 Edward Williams, *An Essay on the Equity of Divine Government, and the Sovereignty of Divine Grace* (London: J. Burditt, 1809), 106–111. Hereinafter, *Essay on Equity.*

39 Ibid. 106 (Calvin's Latin quotes given in English from modern editions). For more examples of Calvin's statements, see my *Calvinus—Authentic Calvinism, A Clarification* (Norwich: Charenton Reformed Publishing, 1995, 2nd. ed. 2007).

40 Edward Williams, *A Defence of Modern Calvinism* (London: James Black, 1812), 192.

41 Ibid. 373.

42 Ibid. 374.

43 Ibid.

44 See articles by Geoffrey Thomas, 'Edward Williams and the Rise of 'Modern Calvinism', *The Banner of Truth* (London: January, 1971, pp. 43–8; March, 1971, 29–35).

45 *Essay on Equity,* 374.

46 In the *Banner of Truth* special issue JOHN NEWTON (August/September, 2007), 16, Iain Murray cites Newton's 'dread of high Calvinism' (without realising that such was Owen's standpoint), also giving a footnote impression that there was

nothing amiss in Newton's sermon on John 1: 29! Yet in this sermon on the atonement, Newton rejects the commercial theory of the atonement, on which Owen's entire thesis rests (see *The Works of John Newton,* (1820; fac. Edinburgh: Banner of Truth Trust, 1985), iv. 188ff). He also refuses to reduce 'world' to 'the world of the elect' and he accepts the distinction between natural and moral inability. Murray is incorrect to side with A. A. Hodge that this distinction 'has no warrant in Scripture' ('Pink on the Sovereignty of God' in *The Banner of Truth* (January 2013), 9. On this issue, see J. C. Ryle in *Expository Thoughts on the Gospels,* St John, Vol. 2 (Edinburgh: The Banner of Truth Trust, 1987), 132. See also Calvin on John 8: 43, very probably part of the inspiration for Amyraut's teaching, also shared by Jonathan Edwards. See my 'The Case for Amyraldianism' in ed. Alan C. Clifford, *Christ for the World: Affirming Amyraldianism* (Norwich: Charenton Reformed Publishing, 2007), 15. Thus (as I have demonstrated in my *Atonement and Justification,* Oxford, 1990), Iain Murray's assessment of Newton's theology is simply deceptive and misleading to say the least. In short, between the polarised positions of Wesley and Whitefield, the earlier 'Anglican Calvinist' tradition [e.g. Davenant] re-emerged in the wake of the Methodist revival. While shunning Arminianism, John Newton (1725–1807) still shared Wesley's aversion for High Calvinism: 'That there is an election of grace, we are plainly taught; yet it is not said, 'that Jesus Christ came into the world to save 'the elect', but that he came to save 'sinners', to 'seek and save them that are lost' … And therefore the command to repent implies a warrant to believe in the name of Jesus, as taking away the sin of the world' (see *Atonement and Justification,* 80–1).

47 See W. T. Owen, *Edward Williams, DD—His Life, Thought and Influence* (Cardiff: University of Wales Press, 1963), 15. Hereinafter *Edward Williams.*

48 *An Essay on Equity,* 106.

49 R. W. Dale, cited in W. T. Owen, *Edward Williams, DD—His Life, Thought and Influence* (Cardiff: University of Wales Press, 1963), 149.

50 'Although R. W. Dale was to castigate that as "Calvinism in decay", it may well be that in some of its emphases it was a reversion to Calvin's Calvinism' (tutor's personal letter, 17 January 1983).

51 *Atonement Controversy,* 379.

52 Ibid. p. xxxii.

53 *Edward Williams,* 149.

54 Ibid. 136.

55 *Great Preachers,* 528.

56 *Atonement Controversy,* 324.

57 Ibid. 123.

58 See my Introduction to John Davenant, *Dissertation on the Death of Christ* (Weston Rhyn: Quinta Press, 2006), p. xiii; also Dr Owen Thomas's accurate depiction of Davenant's contribution at Dordt in *Atonement Controversy,* 124–5.

59 *Daniel Rowland,* 339.

60 *Atonement Controversy,* 342. John Newton's statement is: 'Calvinism should be diffused through our ministry as sugar is in tea; it should be tasted everywhere, though prominent nowhere'; see John H. Pratt (ed), *The Thought of the Evangelical Leaders* (Edinburgh: The Banner of Truth Trust, 1978), 281.

61 See n. 46.
62 See Edward Morgan, *John Elias: Life, Letters and Essays* (Edinburgh: The Banner of Truth Trust, 1973), 142.
63 John Morgan Jones & William Morgan, tr. John Aaron, *The Calvinistic Methodist Fathers of Wales* (Edinburgh: The Banner of Truth Trust, 2008), ii. 745. Hereinafter *Methodist Fathers*.
64 *Atonement Controversy*, 334.
65 *Great Preachers*, 487–9.
66 *Atonement Controversy*, 350–54.
67 Ibid. p. xxx.
68 Translated from Welsh by Noel Gibbard, this appears in *Christian Hymns* (Bridgend: Evangelical Movement of Wales, 1977), hymn 199. John Jones would have been happy to sing this hymn, and it can be sung to one of his tunes.
69 See Edward Morgan, *John Elias: Life, Letters and Essays* (Edinburgh: The Banner of Truth Trust, 1973), 141; *Methodist Fathers*, ii. 607–8, 628, 682.
70 See *Atonement Controversy*, 152ff.
71 Ibid., pp. xvi-xvii.
72 Ibid. 293–6.
73 Ibid. 296.
74 Ibid. 363.
75 *Great Preachers*, 424–6.
76 *Atonement Controversy*, 362.
77 *Daniel Rowland*, 130.
78 Ibid. 137.
79 Daniel Rowland, *Eight sermons upon practical subjects* (London, 1774), 47–72. Hereinafter *Eight Sermons*.
80 Ibid. 54.
81 Ibid.
82 *Daniel Rowland*, 134.
83 *Three Sermons upon practical subjects* (London, 1778), 15.
84 Ibid. 17.
85 Ibid. 27–8.
86 Ibid. 33–34.
87 Ibid. 31.
88 See ibid. 36, 62.
89 Ibid. 17 (emphasis mine).
90 *Eight Sermons*, 11.
91 Ibid. 44.
92 For a puritan precedent, see John Flavel's sermons on this text in *The Works of John Flavel* (London: The Banner of Truth Trust, 1968), iv. 1–268.
93 For a recent criticism, see Lee Gatiss, *For Us and For Our Salvation—'Limited Atonement' in the Bible, Doctrine, History and Ministry* (London: The Latimer Trust, 2012), 118. Hereinafter *For our Salvation*.
94 *Eight Sermons*, 45–6 (emphasis mine). Even in the second sermon *Free Grace indeed*, Rowland is happy to use biblical language without qualification. Christ is 'the Saviour of the world' (47) and 'greater is the Lord's mercy than the sins

of the whole world' (59). The fourth sermon, *The Superiority of the Lowly over the Proud*, concludes with 'Remember the prayer of the Saviour of the world, "Father forgive them for they know not what they do"' (130). In the sixth sermon, *Good News to the Gentiles*, we read that 'the atoning sacrifice admitted of neither increase nor diminution. It was always the same to all persons: and it prefigured that 'Lamb of God, which taketh away the sins of the world' John 1: 29' (161). In the seventh sermon, *Christ is all, and in all*, the preacher describes Christ as 'the Son of man, and the redeemer of a lost world' (196), adding that He was anointed by God 'for us men, and for our salvation' (196) and that 'the Lord Jesus, as mediator, [was] predestined by the "determinate council and foreknowledge of God" [Acts 2: 23] to the weighty business of redeeming and saving sinful man' (197). While Jesus was 'anointed that he might be the priest of his people' (207) and that He 'furthers the salvation of his chosen' (213), Rowland is at ease employing broader phraseology that Christ's 'work was to make atonement for sin, and to reconcile God to man ... So great is his tenderness, compassion, and long-suffering towards our fallen race' (208, 212).

95 See *For Our Salvation*, 114.
96 See my *Atonement and Justification*, 152ff.
97 See *For Our Salvation*, 11.
98 See *Eight Sermons*, 217.
99 See my *Atonement and Justification*, 81.
100 J. C. Ryle, *Christian Leaders of the Eighteenth Century* (Edinburgh: The Banner of Truth Trust, 1978), 214–5. Besides the *Great Preachers* version, 59–60, see a slightly differently-worded account in *Daniel Rowland*, 294.
101 *Methodist Fathers*, ii. 605.
102 *Great Preachers*, 486.

AN

ESSAY

ON THE

EQUITY OF DIVINE GOVERNMENT,

AND THE

SOVEREIGNTY OF DIVINE GRACE,

WHEREIN, PARTICULARLY, THE

LATITUDINARIAN HYPOTHESIS OF INDETERMINATE REDEMP-
TION, AND THE ANTINOMIAN NOTION OF THE DIVINE
DECREES BEING THE RULE OF MINISTERIAL CONDUCT,
ARE CAREFULLY EXAMINED.

BY EDWARD WILLIAMS, D. D.

Shall not the Judge of all the earth do right?—Gen. xviii. 25.

*And he doeth according to his will in the army of heaven, and among the
inhabitants of the earth.*—Dan. iv. 35.

*Why doth he yet find fault? for who hath resisted his will? Nay but, O man,
who art thou that repliest against God? Shall the thing formed say to him
that formed it, Why hast thou made me thus?*—Rom. ix. 19, 20.

*The secret things belong unto the Lord our God; but those things which are
revealed belong unto us, and to our children for ever.*—Deut. xxix. 29.

LONDON:

Published by J. Burditt, Paternoster Row; sold also by Maxwell and Wilson,
Skinner Street, Snow Hill; T. Crookes, Rotherham; and all other
Booksellers. 1809,

APPENDIX 4
THE GOSPEL ACCORDING TO
EDWARD WILLIAMS

BIO-OUTLINE:

B orn in Glanclwyd, North Wales in 1750, Edward Williams was brought to Christ through the Calvinistic Methodists. Eventually joining the Independents, he was educated at the Dissenting Academy at Abergavenny and later ordained at Ross-on-Wye in 1776. Moving to Oswestry, Williams engaged in training young men for the ministry. His talents and piety assured him of recognition. In 1789, he was honoured with a DD by Edinburgh University for his reply to the Baptist Abraham Booth's critique of infant baptism. He served for a while as Pastor at Carr's Lane Congregational Church, Birmingham (1792–95). From 1795 until his death in 1813, Williams was the Principal of the Rotherham Independent Academy. This was his longest and most influential post. A leading light in mission and evangelism, his views promoted the eventual formation of the Congregational Union. Although eclectic in his pursuit of Christian knowledge, Williams was a great admirer of Philip Doddridge and Jonathan Edwards, even producing editions of their works in 1802–5 and 1806 respectively. His early enthusiasm for John Owen's *Exposition of Hebrews* (an edition of which Williams published in 1790) evidently did not extend to the Puritan's 'limited atonement' treatise *The Death of Death*. Taking a broader biblical view, he also admired John Calvin and Richard Baxter. In his preaching and publications, Dr Williams did for Congregationalists and others what Andrew Fuller did among the Baptists in breaking the grip of Hyper-Calvinism on the churches. Despite much 'over-orthodox' criticism, his works on the *Equity of Divine Government* and *Modern Calvinism* greatly influenced the Calvinistic Methodist preacher John Jones, Talsarn (1796–1857). 'He couldn't bear anyone say anything derogatory about Doctor Williams' work. He would be particularly surprised to hear men of Calvinistic ideas doing that; and always judged that they had not read the writings themselves, or had done so prejudicially or else inappropriately by virtue of their mental disability to place fair judgement on such writings' (Owen Thomas, *Cofiant John Jones, Talsarn* (1874), 86). This much-neglected Nonconformist theologian, educator and pastor had a great influence on others throughout the United Kingdom, including John Angel James and the Scottish leaders Ralph Wardlaw and Thomas Chalmers. For further information, see W. T. Owen, *Edward Williams, D.D. His Life, Thought and Influence* (Cardiff: University of Wales Press, 1963).

AN EXTRACT FROM
AN ESSAY ON THE EQUITY OF DIVINE GOVERNMENT, AND THE SOVEREIGNTY OF DIVINE GRACE
(LONDON: J. BURDITT, 1809), 97–111
EDITED BY DR ALAN C. CLIFFORD

THE OBLIGATIONS OF MEN TO RECEIVE THE GOSPEL AND ALL THE BLESSINGS IT EXHIBITS

1. The Gospel of Christ finds all men sinners, condemned and perishing, helpless and hopeless; if therefore it addresses

them at all, it must address them as such. To suppose the reverse, is to suppose that there is some 'other way given among men whereby they may saved' beside the Gospel; and, that the rectoral design of God may be opposed with impunity. There is no previous condition required in us to qualify us for a share in the promise of mercy; since the evangelical promise is an absolute grant to the unworthy, the needy, and the ruined.[1] It denotes 'good tidings of great joy, which shall be to all people'; not to all good people exclusively. The Gospel is a salutary stream that issues from under the throne of God's high sovereignty, diffusing itself wider and wider, till at length it cover the whole earth as the 'waters do the sea'. Its progress, however, is directed with an awful mixture of sovereignty and equity. In that it flows to one part, and not to another, in any given time, how sovereign! In that it has no respect of persons, making no difference in its offers between external rank, or degrees of pretended merit, how equitable!

2. Yet we must say that its contents are peculiarly adapted to certain dispositions and circumstances. Are any made sensible of their spiritual sickness? How seasonable the information that Christ is a physician. Are any burdened and heavy laden? Jesus promises freedom from the toil. Are any poor in spirit? The riches of grace and heaven are opened for their use. Do they hunger and thirst after righteousness? With righteousness and glory they shall be filled. Do they mourn over their own sins and those of others, the dishonour done to God, and the consequent miseries of sinners? The Saviour declares that they shall be comforted. In short, the Gospel proposes to every soul of man, invaluable blessings suited to every state without exception. It brings righteousness near to 'the stout-hearted who are far from righteousness'. And yet the fact is, that none will receive it but such as are

convinced of their need of it. He who is made rich is first made poor. He who is satisfied is first made to hunger and thirst. He who enters in at the strait gate is first made to strive for an entrance. He who enjoys eternal rest and salvation, is first found a penitent, a believer, obedient and persevering.

3. Obligations result from the mere exhibition of blessings, as moral means held forth by the supreme Governor; and not only when blessings are actually possessed. Moral means are the grand medium whereby God governs His accountable creatures. His rectoral intention in giving them is, that we may be obedient and happy in the right use of them. To the benighted there is light; to the guilty, pardon; to the weak, strength; to enemies, reconciliation; to the sorrowful, comfort; to the needy, heavenly riches. If these things are proclaimed for our constant use, as they evidently are, we are under obligation to receive them according as they suit our case. And this obligation is augmented from express commands: to repent, that our sins may be blotted out; to awake from the sleep of sin, that Christ may give us light; to believe on the Lord Jesus Christ, that we may be saved; to run that we may obtain the heavenly prize. And we may add, that this obligation is heightened from the awful threatenings attending a refusal: those who refuse the invitation to the great supper, shall not taste of it; those who continue impenitent shall perish; those who persist in unbelief shall be damned; and those who obey not the Gospel shall be punished with everlasting destruction from the presence of the Lord and the glory of His power.

4. It appears to me, I own, not a little surprising, that any intelligent person, who believes the New Testament to be the expression of the Divine will, should scruple to own, that Jesus Christ and all His benefits are there proposed or offered to the acceptance of men as sinners. Is the Gospel

the primary instrument in conversion, or is it not? If it is, can it address men in any other character than as perishing sinners? And if they are addressed in that character, is it not their duty, are they not strictly obliged, while possessing such a character, to accept of the heavenly donation? The negative of this question is confronted by every principle of moral obligation. On the contrary, the rejection of Christ and His proffered salvation, ranks with crimes of highest aggravation and deepest guilt. He who rejects God's testimony, makes Him a liar. And this is the record; 'that God hath given to us eternal life; and this life is in His Son'. If Christ is preached at all to men, they under indissoluble obligations to believe on Him.

5. Corollary. That there might be a suitable, reasonable and consistent ground of believing in Christ for salvation, we must infer, that God's rectoral intention was, that Christ be a Mediator for every sinner whom the Gospel addresses. I am apprehensive that the chief reason why some have contended against the free offers of Christ and salvation to sinners have been a dread of the necessary consequence of that doctrine, which is expressed in the corollary. But is it a consequence to be dreaded by any lover of truth? Far from it. For it by no means militates against the honours of sovereign grace, or a decretive speciality in His mediation. The Scripture asserts 'that He died for all'; to answer Arminian objections advanced from such a passage, by saying that it means 'all the elect', 'some of all sorts', 'Gentiles as well as Jews', or the like, appears to me by no means fair and satisfactory.[2] But when we say, that the rectoral design of the death of Christ extends to all men without exception, in the same manner as the original and after promises, and innumerable blessings that perpetually flow from the Father of lights, are extended to them, and for their use, it at once does justice to the language

of Scripture, which is frequently universal, while it stands
perfectly consistent with every decretive designation of it.

6. The extent of the Gospel offer, or sovereign grant of
mercy; and that of the rectoral design of Christ's death, must
stand or fall together. If in the Gospel ministry reconciliation
is held forth to any who are not and will not be reconciled;
if God is, in Christ, making a proposal of reconciling the
world unto Himself not imputing their trespasses unto them;
it follows, that the death of Christ has the extent above-
mentioned in the plan of the Divine Government. If
reconciliation to God is proposed to the world of sinners,
as it certainly is in the ministry of the Gospel, there must be
a rational and true, not a fallacious and delusive, ground of
reconciliation. And can that be anything short of the death
of Christ? If the Gospel calls to its great supper, 'the poor
and the maimed, the halt and the blind'; if it invites many
who 'pray to be excused', and never come; the provision
must have been designed for them; as much designed as a
dinner is for one invited to it who sends a message that 'he
cannot come'.

7. The mediatorship, atonement, and merits of Christ, are
the foundation of all Gospel offers; and the rectoral designation
of them extends to all human characters on earth: but the
suretyship of Christ, the exertion of His power, and the
application of His grace, is the foundation of justification,
regeneration, sanctification, and perseverance; and the decretive
designation of them extends only to persons who eventually
love God and enjoy heaven; the chosen, the called, the faithful.
Every new-covenant blessing flows through the mediation
and merits of Christ; when therefore overtures of pardon
and reconciliation, righteousness and peace, are made to
sinners as such, and not merely to elect sinners, can the
consequence be avoided, that these blessings, purchased by

the death of Christ, are rectorally designed for them? Must not the provision be equally extensive with the overture? Is the proposal made, delusive or real? If the latter, must not the advantages proposed be the purchase of the mediator? Or is the overture made founded on the foreseen aversion of the sinner to the thing proposed, and the certainty of a refusal if left in the hand of His own counsel? And then the proposal would be hypothetical; thus: If you perform, what is certain you will not, you shall be saved. That is, if you believe a falsehood, that there is provision made for sinners as such, when , on the supposition, there is provision only for elect sinners, which election cannot be known as a qualification for believing, God is willing to bestow pardon! But is such a proposal worthy of the great Supreme, or better than delusive?—We conclude, therefore, that the rectoral design of the death of Christ (whatever higher speciality there is in it) extends to all the human race;[3] not merely to those who have been, or actually shall be, but also such as may be evangelised or discipled—that is, all the nations, past, present, and future; and with St John we may affirm, without either trembling for the cause of orthodoxy, or throwing dust in the eyes of its enemies by far-fetched criticisms: 'He is the propitiation for our sins, and not for ours only, but also for the sins of the whole world' (*1 Jn 2: 2*). And with St Paul: 'We thus judge, that if one died for all then were all dead; and' (we further judge) 'that he died for all', with the same rectoral intention by which He gives His promises and Himself to all, to the end that they may have the means of being obedient and happy; and with the higher and more specific end, 'that they who live' (as justified by sovereign grace, and made alive by virtue derived from Christ) 'should not henceforth live unto themselves, but unto Him who died for them and rose again' (*2 Cor 5: 14–15*). Thus, in a word,

Jesus Christ is, in the plan of DIVINE GOVERNMENT, the appointed and intended 'Saviour of all men, but, especially', with a decretive infallible speciality, 'of those that', through gracious influence, 'believe' (*1 Tim 4: 10*). 'There is one mediator between God and men, the man Christ Jesus, who gave Himself a ransom for all, to be testified in due time' (*1 Tim 2: 5–6*).

Notes (by Edward Williams)

1   The following words of the amiable Mr Hervey so fully expressing my ideas of the subject under consideration, I shall make no further apology for their insertion in this place: 'Nothing is required in order to our participation of Christ and His benefits, but only that we receive them. Receive them, as the freest of gifts, or as matter of mere grace, vouchsafed to the most unworthy. ... "I have prepared my dinner," says the King eternal. All things are ready (Matt 22: 4). Whatever is necessary for the justification, the holiness, the complete salvation of sinners, is provided in the merit and the grace of my Son. Let them come therefore, as to a nuptial banquet; ... *Theron and Aspasio, Works* (London, 1789), iii. 310–12.

2   'If those general expressions denote only the world of the elect, or of all believers, why is it not said in Scripture that God elected all and every man, the world, and the whole world? In that sense it is as true that God elected them all, as it is that Christ died for them all. Why then doth the Holy Spirit altogether forbear those general expressions in the matter of election, which it useth in the matter of redemption? Surely it imports thus much unto us, that redemption hath a larger sphere than election; and therefore the Scriptures contract election in words of speciality only, whilst they open and dilate redemption in emphatical generalities' (Edward Polhill, *On the Divine Will considered in its Eternal Decrees*, 296). ... 'How can those men receive grace in vain, for whom it was never procured? or neglect salvation, for whom it was never prepared? How can they fall short of eternal rest, for whom it was never purchased? or draw back from the kingdom of heaven which never approached unto them? How can there be life in Christ for those for whom he never died? and if not, which way doth their unbelief give God the lie?' (*Ibid.* 282). There are some things [continues Williams], even on the subject of redemption, in which I do not fully accord with this author; but where there "is an agreement in the substance and design of any doctrine" (to borrow the words of Dr Owen, in his recommendatory preface to the above Treatise) "as there is between my judgement and what is here solidly declared, it is our duty to bear with each other in things circumstantial, or different explanations of the same truth, when there is no incursion made upon the main principles we own."

3   That illustrious reformer and admirable writer, Calvin, has treated much of predestination and the doctrines of special grace; but though his works consist of nine volumes folio, I do not think that there is one sentence in them all that

militates against the above representation; and in many places he expresses himself in a manner that abundantly justifies it, particularly his comments on several passages of the New Testament. To instance only the following: 'The word 'many' does not mean a part of the world only, but the whole human race' (*Comm. Mark 14: 24*).—'Although Christ suffered for the sins of the world, and is offered by the goodness of God without distinction to all men, yet not all receive him' (*Comm. Rom 5: 18*).

The great Mr Charnock, who for depth of penetration and accuracy of judgement was equalled by few, expresses himself, in his *Discourse of the acceptableness of Christ's death*, thus: ... The blood of Christ is a stream, whereof all men may drink; an ocean, wherein all men may bathe. It wants not value to remove our sins, if we want not faith to embrace and plead it' (Charnock's *Works*, ii. 564 (London, 1699).

ADDITIONAL EDITORIAL NOTE: In *A Defence of Modern Calvinism* (London: James Black, 1812), (a response to an attempted refutation of Calvinism by the Bishop of Lincoln), Edward Williams appeals to Calvin against the bishop's assumption that all Calvinists teach the doctrine of limited atonement: 'His Lordship I hope will excuse me for asserting, in return, that this eminent reformer did not 'directly' oppose the doctrine of universal redemption, in the sense now explained, as far as I have been able to collect by a frequent search into his voluminous writings. He admitted a universal price of redemption; but he had reasons innumerable against the notion of an actual redemption of all men from sin and misery. He maintained that the remedy was universal, and that it was universally proposed to mankind, according to God's rectoral design; but not that it was the sovereign design of God by it to make mankind universally and indiscriminately submissive, and compliant with the terms on which the blessings resulting from it were to be enjoyed' (192).

Tonau Talysarn:

SEF

CASGLIAD O DONAU

Y

Parch. JOHN JONES, Talysarn,

GYDAG EMYNAU.

WEDI EU TREFNU A'U GOLYGU

GAN

D. EMLYN EVANS.

Y DDAU NODIANT YNNGHYD.

MACHYNLLETH:

Cyhoeddedig gan Mrs. Jones, Cambrian House.

GWRECSAM: HUGHES A'I FAB, ARGRAFFWYR.

Copyright, 1908.

John Jones's hymn tunes

APPENDIX 5
SONGS OF SALVATION

I

Besides composing several tunes, John Jones wrote a few hymns (or pennillion) during the final months of his life,[1] two of which are presented here. The first—to the best of my knowledge—has never appeared in any hymn book. The second has been published in Welsh hymn books in a severely abridged version. These hymns are coupled with the composer's tunes.

GWEDD WYNEB YR ARGLWYDD
(A Sight of the Lord's face)
(Numeri 6: 24–6; 2 Corinthiaid 4: 5–18)
(Tan-y-castell)

Y MAE gwedd dy wyneb grasol
I mi'n fywyd ac yn hedd;
Gwedd dy wyneb sydd yn symud
Ofnau uffern fawr a'r bedd;
Gwedd dy wyneb sy'n melysu
Dyfroedd Marah chwerwon iawn;
Gwedd dy wyneb sy'n diwallu
Fy anghenion oll yn llawn.

2 Gwedd dy wyneb di a'm gwared
O'm caethiwed mawr yn lân;
Gwedd dy wyneb di a'm harwain
Trwy'r anialwch maith ymlaen;
Gwedd dy wyneb sydd yn agor
Môr o rwystrau ger fy mron;
Gwedd dy wyneb di a'm ceidw
Yn ddihangol uwch y d"n.

3 Gwedd dy wyneb ddaw â'r manna
    Im' o'r nefoedd ar fy nhaith;
  Gwedd dy wyneb egyr ffynnon
    Loyw yn yr anial maith;
  Er archollion y seirph tanllyd
    Gwedd dy wyneb bywyd ddaw;
  Gwedd dy wyneb dry'r Iorddonen
    Yn ei hol er maint ei braw.

4 Gwedd dy wyneb sy'n marweiddio
    Pob rhyw lygredd ynwyf sydd;
  Gwedd dy wyneb a gynhyrfa
    Ynof gariad, gobaith, ffydd;
  Gwedd dy wyneb mewn gorthrymder
    A ddwg im' orfoledd pur;
  Gwedd dy wyneb a'm diddana
    Dan bob gofid, poen, a chur.

GOBAITH

(Hope)

(Rhufeiniaid 15: 13)

(Miriam)

GOBAITH mawr mae yr addewid
    Wedi ei osod o fy mlaen,
  Sydd yn cynnal f'enaid egwan
    Rhag im' lwfrhau yn lân—
  Gobaith wedi rhyfel caled
    Y caf fuddugoliaeth lawn,
  Gobaith boreu heb gymylau
    Ar ol noswaith dywyll iawn.

2 Gobaith ar ôl maith gystuddiau
    Gwelir fi heb boen na chlwy',
  Gobaith yn y ffwrnes danllyd
    Byddaf heb fy sorod mwy;
  Gobaith yn yr anial garw
    Y cyrhaeddaf Ganaan wlad,
  Wedi crwydro'n mhell o'm cartref
    Gobaith dod i dy fy Nhad.

3 Nid bob amser 'rwyf yn gweled
    Rhan i mi yn Nghanaan draw,
  Eto teithiaf tuag yno
    Er fod rhwystrau ar bob llaw;
  Gobaith y caf yno randir

Lawn, wrth goelbren mawr y nef,
Gyda'r llwythau etholedig
Yn ei bresennoldeb ef.

4 Pan caf olwg draw drwy'r cwmwl
Ar y nefol hyfryd wlad,
Cartref llawn dedwyddwch nefol—
Trigfan teulu mawr fy Nhad,
Gobaith yw mewn gorthrymderau
Ddwg orfoledd hyfryd, llawn—
Gobaith am ogoniant nefol
Wedi ei seilio ar ddwyfol Iawn!

II

*The following English hymns by the author can be sung to John
Jones's tunes.*

PRAYER FOR REVIVAL

(Psalm 85; Habakkuk. 3: 2)

(Llanllyfni)

O GOD, exalt your name,
Revive your prostrate cause;
The honours of your Son proclaim
And vindicate His laws;
Our lethargy we mourn,
The unresponsive heart,
We long to taste the liberty
Your Spirit can impart.

2 Reveal the sight of Him
For whom we feebly strive;
Our vision of your truth is dim,
We scarcely seem alive;
Our sins His heart have pained,
Our shame we cannot hide,
Are we the church, by blood redeemed,
For whom the Saviour died?

3 Lord, come with sovereign power,
Purge our hypocrisy,
Come in this late, this needy hour
And grant us sanctity;
Oh banish from our minds
Sin's least suggestive thought,

Fulfil the purpose of your wounds,
Implant what you have wrought.

4 Inspire our hearts to feel
The truth we have declared;
O God, the world has quenched our zeal,
By fear we are ensnared;
Free us from bondage, Lord,
Revive your work once more,
Then all the earth shall hear your word,
All shall your grace adore!

THE RICHES OF GOD'S GRACE

(Eph. 2: 1–10)

(Tan-y-castell)

GRACIOUS Saviour, King of glory,
My glad heart will sing Thy praise!
Thy rich grace and tender mercy
Cheers me all my earthly days;
In sin's darkened paths I wandered,
Stubbornly pursued my way,
But Thy hand to me extended
Was the dawning of new day.

2 Now my soul can sing of pardon,
Jesu's blood has washed away
All my guilt and condemnation,
Justice done, I've nought to pay!
Oh! Thy sufferings, dear Redeemer,
None can know nor comprehend;
My poor soul adores with wonder
Love, such love, which knows no end.

3 Lord and Master, now to serve Thee
Is my true, intense desire;
May Thy Spirit fill and mould me,
Purge my soul with holy fire!
Since thy blood was shed for cleansing,
I, by faith, am justified,
Listen to my earnest yearning
To be truly sanctified.

4 All my life with joy I'll serve Thee,
Till I see Thy blessed face!
Jesus, I will sing of mercy,
Humbly run the heavenly race;

In my weakness, guide and keep me,
Lest I falter in the way,
Bring me safely home to glory,
Thee to praise for endless day!

SPIRITUAL WORSHIP

(Philippians 3: 3)

(Beddgelert)

ALL-GLORIOUS, gracious God,
We worship You;
We praise You for Your word,
Truth ever new!
Your light shines on our minds,
Your love has filled our hearts,
Our mouths are full of praise
For saving grace.

2. Our Father and our friend,
Forever near;
Your mercy shall not end,
We need not fear;
Help us to trust Your love,
Always to look above;
O may we never rove,
Your heart to grieve.

3. Blest Saviour, Jesus, Lord,
We praise Your Name;
Through Your most precious blood
Salvation came.
Now pardon is received,
Because our souls are healed,
To You our lives we yield
To keep Your word.

4. Our Comforter Divine,
Most holy One;
O come within us shine,
Reveal the Son;
O keep us by Your power,
Help us from hour to hour,
To bless You and adore
For evermore!

WALKING WITH GOD

(Eccles. 12: 1)

(*Glasfryn*)

All your days, the LORD remember,
Learn His Word and love His Truth;
Troubled times, yes, without number,
Test our faith, in age and youth;
Yet, the LORD, His mercy showing,
Will not cease to care and lead,
All His promises ensuring
Help and peace in every need.

2. When perplexities disturb you,
Trust God's wisdom, love and power;
His sustaining grace is with you,
Look to Jesus, hour by hour;
Run the race, be true and faithful,
Do not wander from His way;
Through the darkness, ever prayerful,
You shall pass to endless day.

3. All your talents, gifts and graces,
All you have from Him above,
All that manifests His praises,
All employ, inspired by love;
Consecrate your heart to Jesus,
Dedicate your life to Him;
In this noble way He leads us
While we pray 'Your kingdom come'.

4. Let not sinful failure daunt you,
Ne'er forget, He saves by grace!
Jesu's love will never fail to
Lift you up from guilt's disgrace;
He will teach and guide with kindness,
He will lead you by His hand,
Then, despite your every weakness,
You shall reach the heavenly land.

JOY IN JESUS

(1 Peter 1: 8)

(*Trefriw*)

'Trefriw' possibly recalls John Jones's early years studying theology

in a class of other young men led by the (later) Revd Evan Evans (Geirionydd), then a member of the Calvinistic Methodist church at Trefriw (in the Vale of Conwy). This course of study established young John Jones in a proper understanding of the great foundation truths of the Christian Gospel. The simple melody and happy harmonies of 'Trefriw' suggest the joy of discovering the love of Christ, which fired his nation-wide evangelistic ministry. The subjoined words are not intended as a Welsh translation. Suggested by the tune, they offer an English interpretation of the Gospel joy which inspired 'the great orator from Talysarn'.

MY dear Redeemer and my God,
The Father's living, loving Word,
Saved by Your Grace, with joy I sing!
I worship You, my gracious King.

2 What truths You have displayed to me!
What depths in Scripture now I see,
What precious words I now may read;
What wondrous promises to plead!

3 My heart Your dying love has won,
My living Lord, Your reign within
Secures my happy liberty;
From guilt my burdened soul is free!

4 Your grace has now my heart subdued,
Your Spirit has my soul renewed,
With joy I see Your smiling face,
And sing the song, "Redeemed by Grace!"

5. Bless me with strength Your love to share,
May I to others Grace declare;
Your precious blood was shed for all!
So all with faith may on You call!

6. Your gracious reign, blest Prince of peace,
Begun, shall never, never cease,
For Calvary's love and light divine
Through all eternity will shine.

Notes

1   See Griffith Parry, Llanrwst (ed), *Pregethau Y Diweddar Barch. John Jones, Tal-y-Sarn* (Dinbych: Thomas Gee, 1869), 667–70.

PREGETH XLVIII.

Dyfroedd Iachawdwriaeth.[1]

Esa. lv. 1.

"O! deuwch i'r dyfroedd, bob un y mae syched arno; ïe, yr hwn nid oes arian ganddo; deuwch, prynwch, a bwytewch; ïe, deuwch, prynwch win a llaeth, heb arian, ac heb werth."

Yn yr adnod hon, y mae yr Arglwydd, fel Duw iachawdwriaeth, yn gwahodd ac yn galw pechaduriaid damniol, truenus, fel y cyfryw, i fwynhau iachawdwriaeth gyflawn a digonol trwy Iesu Grist. Er fod iachawdwriaeth gyflawn a digonol wedi ei threfnu gan Dduw i bechadur, nid ydyw hi yn eiddo i neb ond a ddêl i'w derbyn drwy ffydd i'r gwirionedd. Felly y mae eisieu galw a gwahodd pechaduriaid i'w derbyn.

O holl bethau rhyfedd y Beibl, un o'r pethau rhyfeddaf ydyw galwadau a gwahoddiadau Duw ar ol pechadur. Y mae y testyn yn alwad gyflawn o efengyl.

I. *Yr alwad.*

1. Gwelir yma daerineb yr alwad: "O! deuwch." 1af, Y mae Duw yn daer. Nid galw yn ddifater y mae—nid dangos y wledd ar y bwrdd yn unig; ond gwahodd yn daer. Nid am fod arno dy eisieu, ond o herwydd ei ras: "Megys pe byddai Duw yn deisyf" 2il, Y mae y cenhadon yn daer. Y mae golwg ar drueni y byd, golwg ar drefn achub, a chariad Crist yn eu cymmhell, yn peri nas gallant lai na bod yn daer. Os bach ydyw ein dawn, rhaid ein goddef; ein dyledswydd ydyw bod yn daer: "Yr ydym yn erfyn dros Grist, Cymmoder chwi â Duw."

2. Galwad ydyw hon sydd yn gofyn am ufudd-dod: "Deuwch." Yma gwelwn, 1af, Fod dyn fel pechadur yn mhell oddi wrth drefn Duw: yn mhell oddi wrth iawn syniad am dani, na gwneuthur gwir dderbyniad o honi—yn mhell oddi wrth ei

---

[1] Diau y darllenir y bregeth hon gyda dyddordeb neillduol, fel enghraifft o bregethau boreuaf y Parch. John Jones. Cyfansoddodd hi yn y flwyddyn 1823, pan ydoedd tua chwech ar hugain oed.

APPENDIX 6
JOHN JONES, TALSARN MSS

from the catalogue of the
National Library of Wales, Aberystwyth

19300E Bob Owen MSS

Articles, addresses, and notes by Bob Owen, including 'History of Plas Brondanw'; extracts from a Barmouth excise officer's account book, 1800–22; part of his diary for 1940; 'History of the Rhiwlas family'; list of Welsh schoolmasters before 1800; 'John Jones, Tal-y-sarn'; 'Ystyr Protestaniaeth '; 'The Parish of Ynyscynhaearn'; 'Crynwyr Sir Gaernarfon', etc., etc. 20fed gan.

Cymraeg & Saesneg.

NLW MS **15186A** Pregethau.
John Jones Talysarn.

NLW MS 437-A.
Note-Book of "http://isys.llgc.org.uk/isysquery/irlcf7/440/doc" \l "hit28"

John Jones "http://isys.llgc.org.uk/isysquery/irlcf7/440/doc" \l "hit30" , Talsarn. Williams MS 639. Paper. 122 x 100. 36 pp. Kept between two boards. Welsh. Heads and outlines of Sermons by the Rev. "http://isys.llgc.org.uk/isysquery/irlcf7/440/doc" \l "hit29"

John Jones "http://isys.llgc.org.uk/isysquery/irlcf7/440/doc"

\l "hit1" "http://isys.llgc.org.uk/isysquery/irlcf7/441/doc" , Talsarn.

12733C. (D. E. JENKINS 3.) BIOGRAPHY OF THE REVEREND JOHN JONES, TAL-Y-SARN. CO. CAERNARVON. A typescript copy (423 pp.) of a thesis entitled 'A Review and Revision of the Biography of John Jones, Talsarn, By Owen Thomas', submitted by D. E. Jenkins for the degree of M.A., of the University of Liverpool, 1924. English. XX cent.
(The biographical work which is analysed in this thesis is Owen Thomas: *Cofiant y Parchedig John Jones* [1796–1857], Talsarn, mewn Cysylltiad â Hanes Duwinyddiaeth a Phregethu Cymru (Wrexham [1874]).

12787E. (D. E. JENKINS 57.) THE REVEREND JOHN JONES, TAL-Y-SARN, AND HIS FAMILY. Typescript and printed material relating to the Reverend John Jones [1796- 1857, Calvinistic Methodist minister] of Tal-y-sarn [co. Caernarvon], and his family. The typescript items include two copies of the reminiscences (35 pp.) of Mrs. Fanny Jones [1829–1913], daughter of the Reverend John Jones, which, under the title 'Adgofion Mebyd yn Nhal y Sarn', had been published as a series of weekly articles in Y Dinesydd Cymreig, 15 Awst—7 Tachwedd 1917; two incomplete copies of a biographical essay (30 pp.) on Mrs. Fanny Jones (1805-[77]), wife of the Reverend John Jones, by 'Adgof Uwch Anghof', which likewise, under the title 'Bywyd, Cymeriad, a Dylanwad Mrs. Fanny Jones, Tal y Sarn', had been published as a series of weekly articles in the same paper, 14 Tachwedd 1917–13 Mawrth 1918; extracts from Hugh Hughes ('Tegai'): Cofiant John Jones, Talsarn [(Pwllheli, 1858)], typed on the dorse of printed copies of a circular letter in Welsh addressed by D. E. Jenkins from Denbigh to the officers of [Calvinistic Methodist] churches in the Vale of Clwyd, 1907, drawing their attention to recently published Welsh books on religious topics, and offering suggestions with regard to the formation of reading groups or societies for buying and studying these and other works of a similar nature; a copy of a letter from [the

Reverend] J[ohn] Jones from Talsarn, to William Roberts, Nefyn, 1855, announcing his inability to fulfill a preaching engagement owing to pressure of work at the quarry (see Y Goleuad, 7 Tachwedd 1934 t. 4); and notes of sermons preached by John Jones ?at Denbigh in 1846. The printed material consists of a copy of Y Pulpud, cyf. II, rhif I, containing notes of a sermon preached by John Jones in Liverpool, 16 May 1853; and cuttings from Y Darlunydd, Ionawr 1877, [Y Drysorfa, 1897], and [Baner ac Amserau Cymru], 26 Gorffennaf 1905, all containing reminiscences of, or biographical notes on, the said John Jones. Welsh. XIX-XX cent.

12788C. (D. E. JENKINS 58.) COPIES OF LETTERS FROM THE REVEREND JOHN JONES, TAL-Y-SARN, &c. Typewritten copies of letters from [the Reverend] John Jones [of Tal-y- sarn as in the preceding manuscript] from Dolgelley, London, and Talysarn, to his wife Fanny, 1838–54 (5), his son John in America, 1846–50 (5), his brothers Richiart and William, both in America, 1846–7 (5), his brother [-in-law] Thomas Edwart in America, 1847, 'Dafydd am Plant oll', 1856, and [ ] (possibly his son Thomas, see N.L.W. MS. 12733, p. 265), 1850; Ann Jones [daughter of the Reverend John Jones] to her brother [John] in America, 1847; and [the Reverend] David Jones [brother of the Reverend John Jones], Caernarfon, to his brother [Richard] in America, 1847, and an acquaintance, ?Richard Jones, 1842–53 (8). The originals of these letters are now letters Nos. 16–33 and 35–43 in the Tanycastell section of the J. Glyn Davies Collection of manuscripts and documents in the National Library of Wales. Included also is a holograph letter from George M[aitland] Ll[oyd] Davies from Maenan Hall Farm, near Llanrwst, to [D. E.] Jenkins, undated (information and suggestions relating to recipient's research work on the Reverend John Jones). Welsh; English. XX cent.

12789C. (D. E. JENKINS 59.) THE REVEREND JOHN JONES, TAL-Y-SARN. An incomplete, draft copy (typescript with manuscript emendations) of a thesis entitled 'A Review and Revision of the Biography of

John Jones, Talsarn, by Owen Thomas', submitted by D. E. Jenkins for the degree of M.A. of the University of Liverpool, 1924. For a copy of the thesis as finally submitted see N.L.W. MS. 12733 above.

5399E.   JOHN   JONES,   TALYSARN. Photostat facsimiles of the 'Preacher's Certificate', dated October 20, 1824, issued to John Jones, Talysarn, Caernarvonshire, Calvinistic Methodist preacher, and the pedigree (printed) of the family of Tanycastell, etc., of which he was a member. English; Welsh. XX cent.

CALVINISTIC METHODIST ARCHIVES
17789 Autograph sermons of the Rev. John Jones, Talysarn (1796–1857)

CALVINISTIC METHODIST ARCHIVES
13553–62 John Jones, Talysarn, Manuscripts

13553 A volume of sermons

13554–8 Note books containing sermons and a few unbound sermons

13559 Dyddiadur: neu Gydymaith i'r Almanac with entries by John Jones, Talysarn, 1828

13560 Y Dyddiadur Methodistaidd for the years 1852–6 with entries by John Jones, Talysarn

13561 A copy of [Cyfoeth i'r Cymru neu Dryssor y ffyddloniaid] by William Dyer, 1756, bearing the signatures of members of the family of John Jones, Talysarn

13562   Pedigree   of   John   Jones,   Talysarn Printed

CWRTMAWR
360B MS "http://isys.llgc.org.uk/isysquery/irld26/69/doc"

360 "http://isys.llgc.org.uk/isysquery/irld26/71/doc"

PREGETHAU JOHN JONES, TAL-SARN
XIXc A composite volume almost entirely in the hand of John
Jones (1796–1857), Calvinistic Methodist minister, of Tal-sarn, co.
Caernarvon, containing notes of sermons and ?addresses, and some
extracts from printed religious works, e.g. William Rees ('Gwilym
Hiraethog'): Traethawd ar Grefydd Naturiol a Datguddiedig ...
(Dinbych, 1841). One sermon is written partly on the dorse of a
statement of account due from John Jones to Richard Jones
[blacksmith], 1831. Welsh

THE HISTORY,

CONSTITUTION. RULES OF DISCIPLINE,

AND

CONFESSION ..
OF FAITH, ..

OF THE

.. CALVINISTIC
.. METHODISTS,

OR THE

PRESBYTERIANS OF WALES

ADOPTED AT THE ASSOCIATIONS OF ABERYSTWYTH AND
BALA, IN THE YEAR 1823.

TRANSLATED FROM THE WELSH.

ENTERED AT STATIONERS' HALL.

PUBLISHED FOR THE GENERAL ASSEMBLY BY D. O'BRIEN
OWEN, THE BOOKROOM, CARNARVON.

PRINTED BY R. E. JONES & BROS., CONWAY.

1900.

Calvinistic Methodist Confession

APPENDIX 7
METHODISM'S TWO VARIETIES[1]

INTRODUCTION

While Presbyterians, Congregationalists and Baptists are part of the story of Puritanism, Methodism was a phenomenon of the 18th century. A revival movement within the Church of England, it had a beneficial and far-reaching impact on the other branches of Protestant Dissent, itself joining the ranks of the Dissenters after John Wesley's death.

ORIGIN AND HISTORY

Probably no English Christian has been eulogised more than John Wesley (1703–91). Indeed, Bishop Ryle (writing in 1885) noted that 'If ever a good Protestant has been practically canonised, it has been John Wesley' (*Christian Leaders of the Last Century* (1885), p. 64). Famous Prime Ministers such as W. E. Gladstone and David Lloyd-George have acknowledged Wesley's importance for the social advances of this country. By no means least, Wesley's last letter (dated 24 February 1791) was an encouragement to William Wilberforce in his campaign against slavery. Stanley Baldwin said that historians of the 18th century 'who filled their pages with Napoleon and had nothing to say of John Wesley, now realise that they cannot explain 19th century England until they can explain Wesley' (J. Wesley Bready, *England Before and After Wesley* (1939), p. 181). Secular historians have endorsed the conclusions of scholars like J. Wesley Bready and Bernard Semmel (see

The Methodist Revolution (1974)), that the well-known Halévy thesis is substantially true, viz. that Methodism helped to improve and transform society in a non-revolutionary direction. In short, Methodism helped us avoid a French-style Revolution (1789).

While disagreeing with John Wesley on several issues, eminent Christians of other denominations have been generous in their praise of Wesley. The Calvinistic Baptist C. H. Spurgeon confessed to feeling 'quickened' in his spirit whenever he thought about the Wesley brothers, adding that 'The character of John Wesley stands beyond all imputation for self sacrifice, zeal, holiness and communion with God; he lived far above the level of common Christians, and was one of whom the world was not worthy' (*The Early Years* (1962), p. 173). The Anglican Ryle confessed 'Whether we like it or not, John Wesley was a mighty instrument in God's hand for good; and, next to George Whitefield [1714–1770], was the first and foremost evangelist of England a hundred years ago' (*Christian Leaders*, 105).

WESLEY'S 'HEART-WARMING'

However, John Wesley, the son of an Anglican clergyman and a graduate of Oxford University had a series of personal crises in his early years. In 1735, following ordination, he commenced his ill-fated career as a missionary to the new American colony of Georgia. His ministry was plagued by personal uncertainty, persistent criticism and a disastrous love affair. All contributed to a sense of frustration and failure. After his return to England in February, 1738, he met the Moravian Peter Böhler whose evangelical teachings he embraced after much discussion. Renouncing his legalistic 'works-righteousness' ideas (a feature of the original Oxford 'Holy Club', its members known by the nickname 'Methodist'), Wesley began to preach the doctrine of Justification by Faith alone. Then came his famous Aldersgate Street experience of May 24th, when his heart was 'strangely warmed': "I felt I did trust in Christ, Christ alone, for salvation: and an assurance was given me, that he had taken away my sins, even mine, and saved me from the law of sin and death" (*Journal*, 24 May 1738). This testimony remains one of the most frequently quoted conversions of Christian history.

Following their 'evangelical conversion' in May 1738, the Wesley brothers joined George Whitefield (similarly converted in 1735) in evangelistic endeavour. Methodism soon became a nationwide phenomenon as huge crowds gathered on village greens and at market places as well as other large open spaces in London, Bristol and Newcastle-upon-Tyne. The story of Wesley's ministry is best told by himself in his *Journal*, which has been described as 'the most amazing record of human exertion ever penned by man' (Augustine Birrell, KC in John Telford, *Life of John Wesley* (1886), p. xviii). Wesley's account reveals a rich tapestry of events and experiences woven into the geography and social fabric of eighteenth century Britain. It actually ends in Norfolk, with his account of preaching at East Dereham, Norwich and Diss. J. C. Ryle's summary of Wesley's activity helps explain something of his uniqueness: 'For fifty-three years—from 1738 to 1791—he held on his course, always busy, and always busy about one thing— attacking sin and ignorance everywhere, preaching repentance toward God and faith toward our Lord Jesus Christ everywhere—awakening open sinners, leading on enquirers, building up saints—never wearied, never swerving from the path he had marked out, and never doubting of success' (*Christian Leaders*, p. 78).

THE WESLEYS & OTHERS

The passing references to 'the Wesley *brothers*' and 'George Whitefield' serve to remind us that the Evangelical Revival was not the work of one man. Truly, it was—in the highest sense—the work of the Holy Spirit, albeit men were instrumental. However special John Wesley was, his brother Charles (1707–88) and their Oxford friend must not be ignored. It has been said that George Whitefield was Methodism's orator, John Wesley its organiser and Charles Wesley its poet. However well-known John's conversion testimony is, the hymns of brother Charles—'the sweet singer of Methodism'—are far better known than anything John ever wrote. 'Love divine, all loves excelling', 'O for a thousand tongues to sing', 'Jesu, lover of my soul', 'And can it be' and 'Hark, the herald angels sing' remain popular after more than 250 years. While Methodism was far from being a merely pietist movement with no practical social and philanthropic conscience, the dominant feature of Charles Wesley's hymns is the New Testament emphasis on assurance of salvation, the joy of sins forgiven and personal union with Christ. If the war-weary and battle-scared Nonconformists had almost lost their voice, the Methodists taught them again how to sing!

If the famous 'trio' is unlikely to be forgotten, we should also remember the likes of William Grimshaw, William Romaine, John Berridge, Henry Venn, Samuel Walker, James Hervey, Augustus Toplady and John Fletcher (as Ryle's *Christian Leaders* reminds us). Sadly, Ryle omits important Nonconformists from his *Christian Leaders*. Indeed, the Congregationalists Isaac Watts (1674–1748) and especially Philip Doddridge (1702–51) of Northampton (whose hymns helped the Dissenters to keep singing during the pre-Methodist era) should have been included alongside their Anglican brethren. Doddridge in particular was highly respected by the Wesleys and Whitefield. When the latter read Doddridge's sermon *Christ's Invitation to Thirsty Souls* (1729, pub. 1748), he was delighted, even acknowledging him as a 'Methodist'!

WESLEY—PROTESTANT EVANGELICAL

There is no doubt that Methodism—including the 19th century 'Primitive Methodist' movement (a protest against Wesleyan respectability)—revived and enriched the entire Protestant world. Until it too succumbed to the liberalism which infected every Christian body during the late 19th century and subsequently, it ensured that Christian faith, hope and love permeated national life. It remains a lasting legacy to the reality and power of the Grace of God in human history.

Reformed Christians honour 'the people called Methodists' for their zealous obedience to our Saviour's 'great commission' (see *Matt. 28: 18–20*). The early Methodists took the light and love of the Gospel into the dark corners of Great Britain. Whatever regrets Spurgeon, Ryle and others expressed about the Arminianism of the Wesleys (see below), there was a great deal of the original Reformation Anglican Protestant Evangelicalism in their theology and practice. Regarding the doctrine of Justification by Faith, John Wesley insisted that he followed John Calvin's teaching. Methodism was in many ways, the flowering of the Reformation after the weary (though mostly sadly necessary) battles of the previous century. It contributed its powerful energies to the infant missionary movement which went worldwide in the 19th century. Paedobaptist in sacramental conviction, the Methodist order of Societies, Circuits and Conference approximates closely to Reformed Presbyterian order.

WESLEY ANTI-CALVINIST?

John Wesley is well known for his opposition to the Calvinistic doctrine of election. In this respect, he and Whitefield were at odds. Wesley's doctrine of 'Christian Perfection' further disturbed the fellowship of the two men and their respective followers. Yet not entirely, since Whitefield requested that Wesley should preach his funeral sermon (which he did in 1770). It may be said with much justification that, Whitefield apart, Wesley over-reacted to a debased, antinomian ultra-Calvinism, of the kind too common in some Dissenting circles. Lack of evangelistic compassion and appetite for holiness were anathema to John Wesley.

As for evangelism, Wesley's so-called Arminian view of the Covenant of Grace—comprising the universal Gospel offer— was actually the same as Calvin's (see *Works*, 1841, x. 297). Writing sympathetically, even a Dutch Calvinist says 'it is possible that [Wesley] was confronted with a Calvinism that propagated a Covenant doctrine that identified the elect and the members of the Covenant as being one and the same' (C. van der Vaal, *The Covenantal Gospel*, 1990, 164). Indeed, this mistaken view was taught by many Puritans including Dr John Owen.

So let us ask: how opposed was John Wesley to Calvinism? At the 1745 Methodist Conference, it was admitted that 'the truth of the Gospel' lies 'very near' to Calvinism:

Wherein may we come to the very edge of Calvinism?

(1) In ascribing all good to the free grace of God.

(2) In denying all natural free will, and all power antecedent to grace, and

(3) In excluding all merit from man; even for what he has or does by the grace of God (*Works*, viii. 274).

In his 'free grace' view of universal atonement, Wesley was actually closer to Calvin than Whitefield was (who, contrary to the Thirty-Nine Articles, maintained 'limited atonement'). The sad division between the Wesleys and Whitefield might have been lessened had 'authentic Calvinist' Philip Doddridge lived longer. Agreeing with Calvin and Baxter, Doddridge was well placed to promote healing between 'Arminian' and 'Calvinistic' Methodists (including the Countess of Huntingdon).

Yet his efforts until his death in 1751 were by no means insignificant (see my *The Good Doctor,* 2002). Doddridge helped revise a new edition of Whitefield's *Journal,* and his *Family Expositor* (1738) was used by Wesley for his own *Notes on the New Testament* (1755).

AUTHENTIC CALVINISM

It is not commonly known that in Wales, Methodism was largely 'Calvinistic', due to the influence of Daniel Rowland, Llangeitho (1713–90), William Williams, Pantycelyn (1717–91) and others. David Lloyd-George was not quite correct when he said that Wales 'owed more to the movement of which Wesley was the inspirer and prophet and leader, than to any other movement in the whole of its history' (J. Wesley Bready, *England: Before and After Wesley,* 181). In Wales, Wesley's type of Methodist became known as 'Wesleyan' as distinct from the 'Methodistiaid Calfinaidd'. In fact, Whitefield was the Moderator at the first Calvinistic Methodist Association at Caerphilly in 1743.

Sadly, despite the moderating influence of Thomas Charles of Bala (1755–1814), Thomas Jones of Denbigh (1756–1820), Edward Williams of Rotherham (1750–1813) and John Jones, Talsarn (1796–1857), Welsh Calvinistic Methodism became more 'ultra' in the 1823 *Confession of Faith.* Against a background of yet more pronounced hypercalvinism, Dr Owen Thomas (1812–91) helped to redefine 'Calvinistic' Methodism in an 'authentic Calvinist' *alias* 'Amyraldian' manner (see Owen Thomas, tr. John Aaron, *The Atonement Controversy in Welsh Theological Literature and Debate, 1701–1841* (The Banner of Truth Trust: Edinburgh, 2002, 363). As a result, the Welsh Confession was significantly amended in 1874. If the lessons of this important work (so highly commended in the Welsh original by Dr D. Martyn Lloyd-Jones) were thoroughly learned, a union of minds and hearts would happily result to the glory of God and the welfare of souls.

WESLEY'S GOSPEL

We close with a typical specimen of John Wesley's fervent gospel preaching:

> [God] willeth not that any should perish, but that all should come to repentance; by repentance, to faith in a bleeding Lord; by faith, to spotless love, to the full image of God renewed in the heart, and producing all holiness of conversation. Can you doubt this, when you remember, the Judge of all is likewise the Saviour of all? Hath he not bought you with his own blood, that ye might not perish, but have everlasting life? O make proof of his mercy, rather than his justice; of his love, rather than the thunder of his power! He is not far from every one of us; and he is now come, not to condemn, but to save the world. He standeth in the midst! Sinner, doth he not now, even now, knock at the door of thy heart? O that thou mayest know, at least in this thy day, the things that belong unto thy peace! O that ye may now give yourselves to Him who gave himself for you, in humble faith, in holy, active, patient love! So shall ye rejoice with exceeding joy in his day, when he cometh in the clouds of heaven ('The Great Assize', *Works*, v. 173).

May all who read this enjoy the blessing proclaimed by John Wesley. Amen!

Notes

1   An amended extract from the author's book *Why Reformed? A Testimony to Authentic Christian Truth* (Norwich: Charenton Reformed publishing, 2009).

APPENDIX 8
A WINDOW ON WELSH CALVINISM[1]

Owen Thomas and D. Martyn Lloyd-Jones on the Atonement

The following review was first published in the
Evangelical Quarterly, Vol. 77.2 (2005), 187–90.
It is here presented with some additional material.

The Atonement Controversy in Welsh Theological Literature and Debate, 1701–1841
by Owen Thomas, tr. John Aaron
(The Banner of Truth Trust: Edinburgh, 2002. xl + 391 pp. hb.
£18.95. ISBN 0 85151 816 8)

This is a welcome yet highly intriguing book, doubly so in both respects. As a window-opener on a little-known controversy among the Welsh Calvinistic Methodists, locked away in the Welsh language for too long, it documents in English dress a fascinating era in the theology of the Principality. It is also welcome in providing additional source material for on-going scholarly debate over Calvinism in general and the extent of the atonement in particular. The publishers are to be congratulated for making John Aaron's translation of Owen Thomas' work available at a time when current discussion of these issues shows no signs of subsiding.

Before the elements of intrigue are considered, the work

may be summarised as follows. *The Atonement Controversy* started life as 'no less than a third' of a larger biography of an eminent Welsh preacher, John Jones of Talsarn (1796–1857). First published in 1874, the full work is considered to be 'the best biography ever written in Welsh. … No Welshman can consider himself to be cultured unless he has read it' (p. ix). The substantial section now published provided a comprehensive historical and theological background to the author's subject. Following his very illuminating introduction (pp. ix-xl), the translator has usefully edited this lengthy section thus: in Part 1, the author charts the debates between Calvinists and Arminians, 1707–1831 (1–107). Part 2 covers debates among the Calvinists of all denominations, 1811–41 (109–283). Part 3 focuses on internal debates among the Calvinistic Methodists (later known as the Presbyterian Church of Wales), 1814–41 (285–364). While the work includes detailed endnotes and two very helpful appendices, the omission of an index in a work of this kind is arguably a serious defect.

The author Owen Thomas (1812–91) was a part of the story he tells. Born in Holyhead, Anglesey, he was one of the first students of the Calvinistic Methodist Theological College at Bala. Completing his formal education at Edinburgh under Thomas Chalmers, Thomas absorbed much of the ethos of Scottish Presbyterianism. Early pastoral appointments in Pwllheli and Newtown led to more influential charges. Appointed to the denominational 'flagship' church in London (Jewin Crescent, Aldersgate Street) in 1851, he moved to Liverpool in 1865. Thomas became the most respected preacher in Wales. A highly erudite scholar as well as a powerful preacher, his scholarly output was honoured with a DD from Princeton University, USA in 1877 (pp. xi–xii).

This brings us to the first intriguing feature of this work.

In outlining Thomas' survey of the contending theological theories of the atonement (reformational, commercial and governmental, p. xvi), the translator alerts us to the 'weaknesses' of the author's own standpoint. His 'Word of Caution' is in effect a 'health warning' against the author's 'moderate Calvinism'! Lamenting Thomas' theological 'sympathies' (p. xxv), the translator tells us that Thomas 'was not as discerning a theologian as some of the previous generation. He was not acute enough to read the signs of his times nor sensitive enough to the consequences of acquiescing in a 'modification' of Calvinism' (p. xxvii). The 'consequences' in question were the looser theologies and evangelistic methods emanating from America (e. g. those of Charles G. Finney and D. L. Moody, etc.) which were beginning to make an impact in this country, not to mention the growth of late-19th century liberalism. Thomas is accused of 'wishful thinking' in his positive assessment of the 1859 revival and the associated 'trends of the day' (p. xxx). He is also accused of lacking 'objectivity in his arguments' in thinking that heroes such as John Elias and Henry Rees—both opponents of hypercalvinism—sympathised with the need to 'modify' the older Calvinism.

Confronted by this barrage of criticism, the reviewer found himself asking 'is all this negativity justified?' Is Owen Thomas guilty of so much? Are early biographers of William Wilberforce to be blamed for not foreseeing the American Civil War and the race riots? Mr Aaron's dubious analysis tends to deflect the reader from the heart of the problem being addressed by Owen Thomas. The author and many of his brethren were convinced that the scholastic 'Owenite' doctrine of limited atonement involved an 'unscriptural limitation' (323) which discouraged active and compassionate evangelism (*note:* unlike

Richard Baxter, John Owen never knew of anyone converted under his ministry).

Thomas and his friends were persuaded that Article 18 of the Calvinistic Methodist *Confession of Faith* (1823) was 'wise above what is written' (p. 323). Indeed, this article *Of Redemption* is more 'particular' than the *Westminster Confession of Faith* equivalent. These arguments had significant effect. In 1874, the year Thomas's book was published, the General Assembly of the denomination (Carmarthen, 1874; Portmadoc, 1875) modified the interpretation of the article with an appendix stressing the universal sufficiency of the atonement (324).

In short, the whole controversy concerned the true character of Calvinism. Despite the translator's criticisms, Owen Thomas had done his homework well. He was thoroughly aware that John Calvin and many other reformers both Continental and British did not teach the doctrine of limited atonement (123) and that the Canons of Dort maintain a universal dimension in the atonement (124). The first of these accurate and well-established observations is dismissed with a doubtful two-fold appeal to the highly debateable studies of Robert A. Peterson and Paul Helm (123, 126). In all this highly biased discussion, the translator fails to perceive the integrity and accuracy of the author's case. The former's reference to 'classical Reformed teaching' (p. xxxiii) is question begging. By blaming 'moderate Calvinism' as 'Calvinism in decay' (p. xxxii), Aaron is effectively saying that 'Calvin's Calvinism' is dangerous!

The simple fact is that Owen Thomas and his friends saw the need to 'moderate' the 'ultra-Calvinism' of the day in order to return to a Bible-based 'Authentic Calvinism'. One may say that they sought to rescue the denomination from 'Owenistic Methodism' and to be true to correctly-defined

'Calvinistic Methodism'. In this respect, contrary to the standpoint of both translator and publisher, the author produced one of the most praise-worthy and illuminating studies in historical theology ever written.

This brings us to the second intriguing feature of this very revealing study. Both translator and publisher (twice on the dust jacket) give a prominent profile to the highly-positive verdict on the book by the late Dr D. Martyn Lloyd-Jones. Insisting that the work was 'important to the whole question of a right preaching of Christ and the atonement', we are told that 'It would not be too much to say that [Dr Lloyd-Jones'] own gospel preaching was directly influenced by his knowledge of the pitfalls and dangers narrated by Owen Thomas' (pp. x–xi). The assumption throughout these remarks is that Dr Lloyd-Jones would have agreed with the translator's perspective on Thomas' evaluation of the controversies. Would he therefore endorse the criticisms of the translator? Probably not, to put it mildly. Two considerations justify such a verdict.

First, in 1933, the Presbyterian Church of Wales (for doubtless liberal reasons) adopted a looser attitude towards the *Confession of Faith*. Dr Lloyd-Jones showed little concern about this. In Volume 1 of his biography, Iain H. Murray makes no reference to this development or any thoughts Dr Lloyd-Jones might have had about it. The latter possibly welcomed the situation for thoroughly evangelistic reasons. Certainly, his *Evangelistic Sermons at Aberavon* (Banner of Truth Trust, 1983) reveal a very different emphasis from the ultra-orthodox Article 18 of the Welsh confession:

'But look at [Christ's] death for a moment and consider it as an expiation for the sin of the whole world. What are we told about it? Well, those sufferings were enough, according to John, for all. Listen! 'He is the propitiation for our sins; and not for ours only, but also for the sins of the whole world' (*1*

Jn. 2: 2). The whole world! ... The sins of the whole world
he had borne upon Himself ' (pp. 87–8).

'[If] ever you feel utterly helpless and hopeless, then turn
back to Him, the Christ of the cross, with His arms outstretched,
who still says: 'Look unto me and be saved, all ye ends of the
earth'. It is there that the whole of humanity is focused. He
is the representative of the whole of mankind. He died for all'
(p. 278).

Second, while the Westminster Chapel years—notably
the 1950s—seem to indicate a sympathy for the Banner
of Truth 'Owenite' view of the atonement, the depth of
Dr Lloyd-Jones' conviction on the issue is doubtful if
preaching content is anything to go by. Whatever he might
have said in private conversations or at conferences, limited
atonement never appeared in his sermons. During his
doctoral research, Dr R. T. Kendall had a number of
discussions with Dr Lloyd-Jones on John Calvin's position.
Conducting his own examination of the reformer's
commentaries, Dr Lloyd-Jones was obviously surprised to
discover how frequently universalist Calvin's statements
were. During a fortnight period, Dr Lloyd-Jones repeatedly
telephoned Dr Kendall and, in excited tones said, "I've
found another one!" During one discussion, he said to Dr
Kendall with regard to limited atonement, "I never preached
it, you know ... only once on Romans 5: 15 and I was in
great difficulty when I did so." Being present, Mrs Lloyd-
Jones then added, "I have never believed it and I never
will!" (for verification, see my biography of Philip Doddridge,
The Good Doctor, pp. 273–4).

These facts speak for themselves. One can only conclude
that Dr Lloyd-Jones preaching was indeed influenced by
Owen Thomas' monumental work, but not in the manner
assumed either by the translator or the publisher. While the

reviewer shares Mr Aaron's concerns over several theological developments in the post-Thomas era, he regrets that his enthusiasm for Thomas' book does not extend generally to his over-reactionary introduction.

Reflecting his background understanding of Calvin and Amyraut, Dr J. E. Hazlett Lynch is currently engaged on researching Dr Lloyd-Jones's views of the atonement. He succinctly revealed his grasp of the issues in an e-mail testimony:

> It was the Synod of Alençon that cleared Amyraut of the charges brought against him by the high orthodox scholastics, on the ground that were they to condemn Amyraut, they were smart enough to know that they would condemn Calvin also on precisely the same grounds. This was an unwitting admission on the part of Amyraut's critics that he, Amyraut, was closer to Calvin than they were. For many years, I would have used the name Amyraut as a theological swear-word. I did this in ignorance of the position held by the man. During this period, whilst having many of Calvin's commentaries, I left them on my bookshelf because they were not extreme or Calvinistic enough for me. When in later years I began to "think for myself," and saw that the Owenite commentators that I was using most frequently were forcing Scripture to say what complied with Owenite theology, I became increasingly dissatisfied with that exegesis. It was then (1990) that I rediscovered Calvin and was amazed at how faithful he was to Scripture and maintained the true biblical balance between the universalistic and the particularistic texts, something neither the Arminians nor the hyper-Calvinists were able or willing to do. Had the Reformed people in the sixteenth and seventeenth centuries maintained that balance, Arminius would never have made an issue of these matters, and the theological system called after his name would not have been necessary.[2]

SOME 'FRIENDS' OF OWEN THOMAS & JOHN JONES, TALSARN

It should be kept in mind that none of the following writers were Arminians. They all believed in predestination and the efficacious salvation of the elect. However, following the teaching of the Scriptures, none of them questioned a clear universal dimension to the atonement.

AUGUSTINE OF HIPPO

'For it is good for all men to hear [Christ's] voice and live, by passing to the life of godliness from the death of ungodliness. Of this death the Apostle Paul says, "Therefore all are dead, and He died for all, that they which live should not henceforth live unto themselves, but unto Him which died for them and rose again." (*2 Cor. 5: 14–15*). Thus all, without one exception, were dead in sins, whether original or voluntary sins, sins of ignorance, or sins committed against knowledge; and for all the dead there died the only one person who lived, that is, who had no sin whatever, in order that they who live by the remission of their sins should live, not to themselves, but to Him who died for all, for our sins, and rose again for our justification ...'3

JOHN WYCLIFFE

'Christ ... suffered bitter death upon a tree, and bought man again with his precious blood, and after that returned again to his Father, for the salvation of mankind. ... And thus Christ was without blemish, and was offered on the cross for the sin of all this world. ... Other lambs in a manner put away the sin of one country; but this Lamb properly put away the sin of all this world'.4

MARTIN LUTHER

'It is certain that you are a part of the world. Do not let your heart deceive you by saying: "The Lord died for Peter and Paul; He rendered satisfaction for them, not for me."

Therefore let every one who has sin be summoned here, for He has made the expiation for the sins of the whole world and bore the sins of the whole world'.[5]

JOHN CALVIN

'True it is that the effect of [Christ's] death comes not to the whole world. Nevertheless, forasmuch as it is not in us to discern between the righteous and the sinners that go to destruction, but that Jesus Christ has suffered his death and passion as well for them as for us, therefore it behoves us to labour to bring every man to salvation, that the grace of our Lord Jesus Christ may be available to them'[6]

'Paul makes grace common to all men, not because it in fact extends to all, but because it is offered to all. Although Christ suffered for the sins of the world, and is offered by the goodness of God without distinction to all men, yet not all receive him'.[7]

'God commends to us the salvation of all men without exception, even as Christ suffered for the sins of the whole world'.[8]

'Whereas it is said that the Son of God was crucified, we must not only think that the same was done for the redemption of the world: but also every of us must on his own behalf join himself to our Lord Jesus Christ, and conclude, It is for me that he hath suffered. ... But when we once know that the thing was done for the redemption of the whole world, pertaineth to every of us severally: it behoveth every of us to say also on his own behalf, The Son of God hath loved me so dearly, that he hath given himself to death for me'.[9]

'Christ is in a general view the Redeemer of the world, yet his death and passion are of no advantage to any but such as receive that which St Paul shows here. And so we see that when we once know the benefits brought to us by Christ, and which he daily offers us by his gospel, we must also be joined to him by faith'.[10]

'This is His wondrous love towards the human race, that He desires all men to be saved, and is prepared to bring even the perishing to safety ... It could be asked here, if God does not want any to perish, why do so many in fact perish? My reply is that no mention is made here of the secret decree of God by which the wicked are doomed to their own ruin, but only of His loving-kindness as it is made known to us in the Gospel. There God stretches out His hand to all alike, but He only grasps those (in such a way as to lead to Himself) whom He has chosen before the foundation of the world'.[11]

THE ANGLICAN REFORMERS

Archbishop *Thomas Cranmer* stated that Christ 'by His own oblation ... satisfied His Father for all men's sins and reconciled mankind unto His grace and favour'.[12] Bishop *John Hooper* affirmed that Christ died 'for the love of us poor and miserable sinners, whose place he occupied upon the cross, as a pledge, or one that represented the person of all the sinners that ever were, be now, or shall be unto the world's end'.[13] Bishop *Nicholas Ridley* declared that the sacrifice of Christ 'was, is, and shall be forever the propitiation for the sins of the whole world'.[14] Bishop *Hugh Latimer* preached that 'Christ shed as much blood for Judas, as he did for Peter: Peter believed it, and therefore he was saved; Judas would not believe, and therefore he was condemned'.[15] Even particularist *John Bradford* admitted that 'Christ's death is sufficient for all, but effectual for the elect only'.[16] The Elizabethan Anglicans were no different in their understanding. Bishop *John Jewel* wrote that, on the cross, Christ declared "It is finished" to signify 'that the price and ransom was now full paid for the sin of all mankind'.[17] Elsewhere, he made clear that 'The death of Christ is available for the redemption of all the world'.[18] *Richard Hooker* stated an identical view when he said that Christ's 'precious and propitiatory sacrifice' was 'offered for the sins of all the world' and that he 'hath thereby once reconciled us to God, purchased his general free pardon, and turned away divine indignation from mankind'.[19]

THE CANONS OF DORDRECHT

'The death of the Son of God is the only and most perfect sacrifice and satisfaction for sin; and is of infinite worth and value, abundantly sufficient to expiate the sins of the whole world. ... That, however, many who have been called by the gospel neither repent nor believe in Christ but perish in unbelief does not happen because of any defect or insufficiency in the sacrifice of Christ offered on the cross, but through their own fault. ... [This] was the most free counsel of God the Father, that the life-giving and saving efficacy of the most precious death of His Son should extend to all the elect'.[20]

WILLIAM TWISSE

'I am ready to profess ... that every one who hears the gospel, (without distinction between elect or reprobate) is bound to believe that Christ died for him, so far as to procure both the pardon of his sins and the salvation of his soul, in case he believes and repent'.[21]

JOHN DAVENANT

One of the English delegates at the Synod of Dort, he argued that 'The death of Christ is the universal cause of the salvation of mankind, and Christ himself is acknowledged to have died for all men sufficiently ... by reason of the Evangelical covenant confirmed with the whole human race through the merit of his death' ... This 'evangelical covenant' is the basis on which 'Christ ... sent his Apostles into all the world (*Mark 16: 15,16*). ... On which words of promise, the learned Calvin has rightly remarked, that 'this promise was added that it might allure the whole human race to the faith'.[22]

MOISE AMYRAUT

'Jesus Christ died for all men sufficiently, but for the elect only effectually: and that consequentially his intention was to die for all men in respect of the sufficiency of his satisfaction, but for the elect only in respect of its quickening and saving virtue and efficacy; which is to say, that Christ's will was that the sacrifice of his cross should be of an infinite price and value, and most abundantly sufficient to expiate the sins of the whole world; yet nevertheless the efficacy of his death appertains only unto the elect; ... for this was the most free counsel and gracious purpose both of God the Father, in giving his Son for the salvation of mankind, and of the Lord Jesus Christ, in suffering the pains of death, that the efficacy thereof should particularly belong unto all the elect, and to them only'.[23]

JEAN DAILLÉ

This reconciliation [2 Cor. 5: 19] may be ... considered two ways: first, in general, as made by Jesus Christ on the cross; and secondly, in particular, as applied to each of us by faith. In the first consideration, it is presented to all men as sufficient for their salvation, according to the doctrine of the apostle, that 'the grace of God that brings salvation has appeared to all men' (Tit. 2: 11); and that also of St John, that Jesus Christ 'is the propitiation for our sins: and not for ours only. but also for the sins of the whole world' (1 Jn. 2: 2). Under the second consideration it appertains only to the believer, according to that clause of the covenant which declares that the only-begotten Son was given to the world, 'that whosoever believeth in him should not perish, but have everlasting life' (Jn. 3: 16).[24]

EDMUND CALAMY

'I am far from universal redemption in the Arminian sense; but that that I hold is in the sense of our divines (e.g. Bishop Davenant) in the Synod of Dordt, that Christ did pay a price for all ... that Jesus Christ did not only die sufficiently for all, but God did intend, in giving Christ, and Christ in giving himself, did intend to put all men in a state of salvation in case they do believe'.[25]

RICHARD BAXTER

'When God saith so expressly that Christ died for all [2 Cor. 5: 14-15], and tasted death for every man [Heb. 2: 9], and is the ransom for all [1 Tim. 2: 6], and the propitiation for the sins of the whole world [1 Jn. 2: 2], it beseems every Christian rather to explain in what sense Christ died for all, than flatly to deny it' .[26]

PHILIP DODDRIDGE

'It is plain ... that there is a sense, in which Christ may be said to have died for all, i.e. as he has procured an offer of pardon to all, provided they sincerely embrace the Gospel. Cf. John 3: 16, 6: 50, 51, Romans 5: 18, 8: 32, 1 Corinthians 8: 11, 2 Corinthians 5: 14, 15, 19, 1 Timothy 2: 4, 6, Hebrews 2: 9, 1 John 2: 2'.[27]

JONATHAN EDWARDS

When asserting the 'particular' efficacious redemption of the elect, Edwards still grants that 'Christ in some sense may be said to die for all, and to redeem all visible Christians, yea, the whole world, by his death; ...'[28]

JOSEPH BELLAMY

'Because the door of mercy is thus opened to the whole world by the blood of Christ, therefore, in scripture, he is called, the Saviour of the WORLD (1 John 4: 14); the Lamb of God, which takes away the sin of the WORLD (John 1: 29); a propitiation for the sins of the WHOLE WORLD (1 John 2: 2);

that gave himself a ransom for ALL (*1 Timothy 2: 6*); and tasted death for EVERYMAN (*Hebrews 2: 9*)'.[29]

THOMAS BOSTON

When he published *The Marrow of Modern Divinity* (1726), he was clearly happy to endorse the words (of John Preston): 'Go and tell everyman without exception that here is good news for him, Christ is dead for him'.[30] In his own book *A View of the Covenant of Grace* (1734), Boston himself stated, '... the extent of the administration [of the covenant] is not founded on election, but on the sufficiency of Christ's obedience and death for the salvation of all'.[31]

THOMAS CHALMERS

'If Christ died only for the elect, and not for all', then ministers 'are puzzled to understand how they should proceed with the calls and invitations of the gospel. ... Now for the specific end of conversion, the available scripture is not that Christ laid down His life for the sheep, but that Christ is set forth a propitiation for the sins of the world. It is not because I know myself to be one of the sheep, or one of the elect, but because I know myself to be one of the world, that I take to myself the calls and promises of the New Testament'.[32]

J. C. RYLE

Commenting on John 1: 29, he wrote that 'Christ's death is profitable to none but to the elect who believe on His name. ... But ... I dare not say that no atonement has been made, in any sense, except for the elect. ... When I read that the wicked who are lost, "deny the Lord that bought them," (2 Pet. 2: 1) and that "God was in Christ, reconciling the world unto himself," (2 Cor. 5: 19), I dare not confine the intention of redemption to the saints alone. Christ is for every man'. Commenting on John 3: 16 and appealing to Bishop John Davenant, Calvin and others, he concludes: 'Those who confine God's love exclusively to the elect appear to me to take a narrow and contracted view of God's character and attributes. ... I have long come to the conclusion that men may be more systematic in their statements than the Bible, and may be led into grave error by idolatrous veneration of a system'.33

CHARLES HODGE

'There is a sense ... in which Christ did die for all men. His death had the effect of justifying the offer of salvation to everyman; and of course was designed to have that effect. He therefore died sufficiently for all'.34

ROBERT L. DABNEY

He criticised Scottish theologian William Cunningham for taking a narrow view of the atonement's design. Dabney also distanced himself from John Owen's particularism: 'I have already stated one ground for rejecting that interpretation of John 3: 16, which makes 'the world' which God so loved, the elect world. ... Christ's mission to make expiation for sin is a manifestation of unspeakable benevolence to the whole world'.35

JOHN MURRAY

For all his particularism, he still concedes that the 'Non-elect are said to have been sanctified in the blood of Christ, to have tasted the good word of God and the powers of the age to come, to have escaped the pollutions of the world through the knowledge of the Lord and Saviour, and to have known the way of righteousness (cf. *Heb. 6: 3, 5; 10: 29; 2 Pet. 2: 20, 21*). In this sense, therefore, we may say that Christ died for non-elect persons'.36

D. MARTYN LLOYD-JONES

'But look at [Christ's] death for a moment and consider it as an expiation for the sin of the whole world. What are we told about it? Well, those sufferings were enough, according to John, for all. Listen! 'He is the propitiation for our sins;

and not for ours only, but also for the sins of the whole world' (*1 Jn. 2: 2*).The whole world! ... The sins of the whole world he had borne upon Himself'.

'[If] ever you feel utterly helpless and hopeless, then turn back to Him, the Christ of the cross, with His arms outstretched, who still says:'Look unto me and be saved, all ye ends of the earth'. It is there that the whole of humanity is focused. He is the representative of the whole of mankind. He died for all'.[37]

Notes

1   This material—consisting chiefly of a book review—was previously published in pamphlet format.

2   J. E. Hazlett Lynch (e-mail, 14 Nov. 2006).

3   *The City of God, The Works of Aurelius Augustine*, ed. M. Dods (Edinburgh:T. & T. Clark, 1872), ii. 360.

4   *Writings of the Reverend and Learned John Wickliff, D. D.* (London:The Religious Tract Society, 1838), 89, 188.

5   Comment on 1 Jn. 2: 2, *The Catholic Epistles* in *Works of Martin Luther* (St Louis: 1963), xxx. 237.

6   J. Calvin, *Sermons on Job* (London: 1574; fac. Edinburgh: Banner of Truth Trust, 1993), 548.

7   J. Calvin, *Calvin's Commentaries*, D. W. Torrance, T. F. Torrance (eds.), 12 vols. (Oliver & Boyd/St Andrew Press, 1959-), *Comm. Rom. 5: 18*.

8   J. Calvin, *Calvin's Commentaries*, D. W. Torrance, T. F. Torrance (eds.), 12 vols. (Oliver & Boyd/St Andrew Press, 1959-), *Comm. Gal. 5: 12*.

9   J. Calvin, *Sermons on Galatians*, tr. A. Golding (London: 1574), 106–7; tr. K. Childress (Edinburgh: Banner of Truth Trust, 1997), 212–3.

10   J. Calvin, *Sermons on Ephesians*, tr. A. Golding (1577), rev., tr. S. M. Houghton, L. Rawlinson (Edinburgh: Banner of Truth Trust, 1973), 55.

11   J. Calvin, *Calvin's Commentaries*, D. W. Torrance, T. F. Torrance (eds.), 12 vols. (Oliver & Boyd/St Andrew Press, 1959-), *Comm. 2 Pet. 3: 9*.

12   *The Works of Thomas Cranmer* (Cambridge: Parker Society, 1844), i. 346.

13   *Later Writings of Bishop Hooper* (Cambridge: Parker Society, 1852), 31.

14   *The Works of Bishop Ridley* (Cambridge: Parker Society, 1841), 208.

15   *Sermons of Hugh Latimer* (Cambridge: Parker Society, 1844). ii. 521.

16   *Sermons of John Bradford* (Cambridge: Parker Society, 1848), i. 320.

17   *The Works of John Jewel* (Cambridge: Parker Society, 1848), iii. 66.

18   *Sermons or Homilies* (London: Prayer-Book and Homily Society, 1833), 310.

19   *The Works ... of Richard Hooker*, ed J. Keble (Oxford: OUP, 1836), iii. 71.

20   *The Second Canon*, see *The Creeds of the Evangelical Protestant Churches*, ed. H. B. Smith and P. Schaff (London: 1877), 586f; *Book of Praise: Anglo-Genevan Psalter* (Winnipeg: Premier Printing, 1998), 545ff.

21   *Works*, cited in J. Bellamy, *True Religion Delineated* (Edinburgh: M. Gray, 1788), 310.

22 *A Dissertation on the Death of Christ*, tr. J. Allport, *A Commentary on Colossians* (London: Hamilton, Adams; Birmingham: Beilby, Knott, 1832), ii. 401.

23 J. Quick, *Synodicon in Gallia Reformata* (London; 1692), 354.

24 Daillé, J., *Exposition of Philippians and Colossians* (Edinburgh: J. Nichol, 1863), 55.

25 A. F. Mitchell and J. Struthers (eds.), *Minutes of the Sessions of the Westminster Assembly of Divines* (London: 1874), 152.

26 Richard Baxter, *Universal Redemption of Mankind* (London: John Salisbury, 1694), 286. http://quintapress.macmate.me/PDF_Books/Universal_Redemption.pdf

27 *Lectures on Divinity, The Works of the Revd P. Doddridge, D. D.* (1702–51), ed. E. Williams and E. Parsons (Leeds: 1802–5), v. 214.

28 *The Freedom of the Will, The Works of Jonathan Edwards*, ed. E. Hickman (London: 1834; fac. Edinburgh: Banner of Truth Trust), i. 88.

29 J. Bellamy, *True Religion Delineated* (Edinburgh: M. Gray, 1788), 309.

30 J. Preston, *The Breast-plate of Faith and Love*, 5th ed. (London: 1634; fac. Edinburgh: Banner of Truth Trust, 1979), 8.

31 T. Boston, *A View of the Covenant of Grace* (Lewes: Focus Christian Ministries Trust, 1990), 151.

32 T. Chalmers, *Institutes of Theology* (Edinburgh: Sutherland and Knox, 1849), ii. 403–6.

33 J. C. Ryle, *Expository Thoughts on the Gospels* (London: W. Hunt, 1865), *St John*, i. 159.

34 C. Hodge, *Systematic Theology* (New York: 1873: fac. London: J. Clarke, 1960), ii. 560.

35 R. L. Dabney, *Systematic Theology* (St Louis: 1873; fac. Edinburgh: Banner of Truth Trust, 1985), 529, 535.

36 J. Murray, 'The Atonement and the Free Offer of the Gospel', *Collected Writings* (Edinburgh: Banner of Truth Trust, 1976), i. 68.

37 D. M. Lloyd-Jones, *Evangelistic Sermons at Aberavon* (Edinburgh: Banner of Truth Trust, 1983), 87, 278.

SELECT BIBLIOGRAPHY

ALUN, GLAN, *Pregethwr y Boble ... Y Parch. John Jones*, Tal-y-sarn (Wyddgrug, 1858)

AMBROSE, W., *Marwnad y Parch. John Jones, Tal-y-sarn* (Porth Madog, 1858)

BAXTER, RICHARD, *Making Light of Christ* (Norwich: Charenton Reformed Publishing, 2010)

CLIFFORD, ALAN C., *Atonement and Justification: English Evangelical Theology 1640–1790—An Evaluation* (Clarendon Press, Oxford, 1990)

_____, *Calvinus: Authentic Calvinism—A Clarification* (Norwich: Charenton Reformed Publishing, 1995)

_____, *The Good Doctor: Philip Doddridge of Northampton—A Tercentenary Tribute* (Norwich: Charenton Reformed Publishing, 2002)

_____, *Amyraut Affirmed* (Norwich: Charenton Reformed Publishing, 2004)

_____, 'Hymn for Revival', *The Treasury* (Caernarfon, Gwynedd: The Presbyterian Church of Wales, December 2011)

_____, 'The Footsteps of Faith, or Welsh Inspirational Touring', *The Treasury* (Caernarfon, Gwynedd: The Presbyterian Church of Wales, April–May 2012)

_____, 'Rejoice in the Lord! John Jones, Talsarn's Hymn Tunes', *The Treasury* (Caernarfon, Gwynedd: The Presbyterian Church of Wales, January 2013)

_____, *My Debt to the Doctor: An 110th Anniversary Tribute to Dr D. Martyn Lloyd-Jones* (Norwich: Charenton Reformed Publishing, 2009)

_____, *Calvin Celebrated: The Genevan Reformer & His Huguenot Sons* (Norwich: Charenton Reformed Publishing, 2009

DAVIES, ERYL, *The Beddgelert Revival* (Bridgend: Bryntirion Press, 2004)

DAVENANT, JOHN, *Dissertation on the Death of Christ*, with an Introduction by Dr Alan Clifford (Weston Rhyn, Oswestry, Shropshire: Quinta Press, 2006)

EVANS, D. EMLYN (ed), *Tonau Talysarn: Sef Casgliad o Donau y Parch. John Jones, Talysarn, Gydag Emynau* (Machynlleth a Gwrecsam: Hughes A'i Fab, 1908)

EVANS, EIFION, *The Welsh Revival of 1904* (Port Talbot: Evangelical Movement of Wales, 1969)

_____, *Daniel Rowland and the Great Evangelical Awakening in Wales* (Edinburgh: The Banner of Truth Trust, 1985)

_____, *Bread of Heaven: The Life and Work of William Williams, Pantycelyn* (Bridgend: Bryntirion Press, 2010)

_____, *When he is Come: The 1858–60 Revival in Wales* (Port Talbot: Evangelical Movement of Wales, 1959)

HUGHES, R. (ed), *Memoir and Sermons of the Late Rev. David Lloyd Jones, MA, Llandinam* (Wrexham: Hughes and Son, 1912)

JONES, ELIAS, WILLIAMS, JOHN, WILLIAMS, T. CHARLES, *Cofiant a Phregethau Y Diweddar Barch. David Lloyd Jones, MA Llandinam* (Gwrecsam: Hughes A'i Fab, 1908)

JONES, JOHN MORGAN & MORGAN, WILLIAM, TR. JOHN AARON, *The Calvinistic Methodist Fathers of Wales* (Edinburgh: The Banner of Truth Trust, 2008)

JONES, OWEN, *Some of the Great Preachers of Wales* (London: Passmore & Alabaster, 1885; New edition Stoke-on-Trent: Tentmaker Publications, 1995)

JONES, R. TUDUR, *Congregationalism in England* (London: Independent Press Ltd, 1962)

_____, *John Elias: Prince Amongst Preachers* (Bryntirion, Bridgend: Evangelical Library of Wales, 1974)

MORGAN, EDWARD, *John Elias, His Life and Letters* (Edinburgh: The Banner of Truth Trust, 1973)

OWAIN, O. LLEW, *Cofiant Mrs. Fanny Jones* (Machynlleth a Caernarfon, 1907)

OWEN, W. T., *Edward Williams, DD—His Life, Thought and Influence* (Cardiff: University of Wales Press, 1963)

PARRY, GRIFFITH, Llanrwst (ed), *Pregethau Y Diweddar Barch. John Jones, Tal-y-Sarn* (Dinbych: Thomas Gee, 1869)

PHILLIPS, THOMAS, *The Welsh Revival: Its Origin and Development* (1860 rep. Edinburgh: The Banner of Truth Trust, 1989)

REES, THOMAS, *History of Protestant Nonconformity in Wales* (London: John Snow, 1861)

ROBERTS, J., *The Calvinistic Methodism of Wales* (Caernarfon: The Calvinistic Methodist Book Agency, 1934?)

RYLE, J. C., *Christian Leaders of the Eighteenth Century* (Edinburgh: The Banner of Truth Trust, 1978)

The History, Constitution, Rules of Discipline and Confession of Faith of the Calvinistic Methodists or the Presbyterians of Wales ... Translated from the Welsh (Carnarvon: The General Assembly, 1900)

THOMAS, OWEN, *Cofiant Y Parchedig John Jones, Talsarn* (Wrexham: Hugues and Son, 1874)

THOMAS, OWEN, TR. JOHN AARON, *The Atonement Controversy in Welsh Theological Literature and debate, 1707–1841* (Edinburgh: The Banner of Truth Trust, 2002)

WILLIAMS, EDWARD, *An Essay on the Equity of Divine Government, and the Sovereignty of Divine Grace* (London: J. Burditt, 1809)

_____, *A Defence of Modern Calvinism* (London: James Black, 1812)

_____, *The Works of the Rev. Edward Williams, DD*, Vols I–IV (London: James Nisbet and Co., 1862), available at: http://quintapress.macmate.me/PDF_Books/EdwardWilliams/Williams_Works

WILLIAMS, WILLIAM (SWANSEA), *Welsh Calvinistic Methodism* (London: The Presbyterian Church of England, 2nd edit., 1884)

THE AUTHOR

Born and educated in Hampshire, Alan Clifford pursued a career in mechanical and electrical engineering at the Royal Aircraft Establishment and the Institute of Aviation Medicine at Farnborough. Converted within Anglicanism in his teens, a change of religious conviction led eventually in a Nonconformist direction. He worshipped for three years at Westminster Chapel, London during the latter years of the ministry of Dr D. Martyn Lloyd-Jones. Graduating in Philosophy in the University of Wales in 1969, he was ordained at Primrose Hill Congregational Church, Northampton. Pastorates on Tyneside and in Norfolk facilitated further part-time academic study in philosophy and theology (MLitt, 1978; PhD, 1984). Dr Clifford's doctoral tutor in the University of Wales was Dr R. Tudur Jones of Coleg Bala-Bangor. His thesis 'Atonement and Justification' was published by Oxford University Press in 1990 and reprinted in 2002.

Post-doctoral study turned the author's interests in a Huguenot direction. This led to a 'reformation' of several views. Somewhat disillusioned with 'independency', personal contact with several evangelical friends within the Presbyterian Church of Wales led to an application for pastoral service within that denomination. This was approved by the General Assembly in 1988. Invitations to minister in Wales only came after resigning his Norfolk Baptist pastorate on theological grounds in 1994. These were declined because of pastoral commitment to the congregation of newly-formed Norwich Reformed Church. Since 1994, Dr Clifford has organised regular conferences for the Amyraldian Association, a platform for disseminating what he regards as 'authentic Calvinism'. Reflecting this theological perspective, he has also published several books on theological and historical subjects. Maintaining an interest in 'the Welsh connection', he has latterly had articles on the Calvinistic Methodists published in *The Treasury*, the English-language magazine of the Presbyterian Church of Wales.

Dr Clifford is married to Marian whom he met at Bangor in 1966. They have four grown-up children—three sons and a daughter—and three granddaughters and a grandson. Besides theological and historical reading, he enjoys trains, planes, photography and music, his favourite composers being Buxtehude and Hummel.

Lightning Source UK Ltd.
Milton Keynes UK
UKOW03f1532090514

231391UK00001B/17/P